USING MATHEMATICS
IN ECONOMICS

USING MATHEMATICS IN ECONOMICS

R. W. QUINCEY, B.Sc., M.Sc., A.F.I.M.A.
Senior Lecturer in Mathematics and Operational Research,
Sheffield Polytechnic

F. NEAL, B.Sc.(Econ.), M.A.
Principal Lecturer in Economics, Sheffield Polytechnic

LONDON   BUTTERWORTHS

THE BUTTERWORTH GROUP

ENGLAND
Butterworth & Co. (Publishers) Ltd
London: 88 Kingsway, WC2B 6AB

AUSTRALIA
Butterworths Pty Ltd
Sydney: 586 Pacific Highway, NSW 2067
Melbourne: 343 Little Collins Street, 3000
Brisbane: 240 Queen Street, 4000

CANADA
Butterworth & Co. (Canada) Ltd
Toronto: 14 Curity Avenue, 374

NEW ZEALAND
Butterworths of New Zealand Ltd
Wellington: 26–28 Waring Taylor Street, 1

SOUTH AFRICA
Butterworth & Co. (South Africa) (Pty) Ltd
Durban: 152–154 Gale Street

First published in 1973

ISBN 0 408 70531 0 Standard
       0 408 70532 9 Limp

Text set in 10/12 pt IBM Press Roman, printed by photolithography
and bound in Great Britain at The Pitman Press, Bath

PREFACE

Graphical methods of presenting economic theory have traditionally predominated in textbooks and the journals and, indeed, are still the most popular teaching aid for students of economics. The reason for this is easy to understand: given that economic theory is concerned with the assumed relationships between variables and the logically deduced implications of such relationships, graphical methods of analysis give a visual appreciation of the main features of the system under examination, particularly the idea of equilibrium. However, these methods are subject to serious limitations, such as that imposed by the two-dimensional surface of a page, which enables the relationship between only three variables, at most, to be examined. However, if we use mathematical methods other than graphs, a fuller understanding of economic theory is possible, the relationship between economic variables often being made much clearer. Both graphical methods and verbal explanations are obviously valuable but, where theoretical relationships are complex and precision is needed, mathematical methods have distinct advantages. Particularly attractive is the generality that mathematics gives to analysis.

Over the last decade, the presentation of elementary economic theory using algebra and calculus has become increasingly common, with many of the more important textbooks containing mathematical footnotes to develop points raised in the text. We are now reaching the stage where the mathematics is leaving the footnotes and becoming incorporated in the text and, related to this trend but separate from it, has been the development of mathematical economics (which is not the same as using mathematics in economics). Thus mathematical methods are now firmly established and are necessary to the student — not only as a vehicle for obtaining a better understanding of economic theory but to give access to much important work appearing in the journals. For those who may later wish to construct theories, the application of mathematics to a problem is often essential for examining the full implications of the theory. The mathematics used by economists is

Preface

also of use in management sciences and operational research disciplines where they overlap with economics.

This book is for all those undertaking an economics principles course at first-year and second-year undergraduate level, and assumes a knowledge of mathematics to GCE Ordinary level. It will also be useful to those students who are taking an Advanced level course in mathematics combined with an Advanced level course in economics. The aim is not to teach economics or mathematical economics, but to introduce the reader to those aspects of mathematics which can be applied to the economic theory presented in introductory principles courses. The mathematics in each chapter is therefore followed by examples of how it can be used to look at familiar theory in a different and useful way. The economic concepts included are those which the student would come across in the introductory textbooks available, and we assume that the methodology of economics has been covered in the reader's economics course. We have concentrated on the immediate application of the mathematical methods to familiar economic concepts and theories because we believe that non-mathematicians are impatient to see some immediate benefits from what is, for most economists, a long haul. It will soon become evident that facility with mathematics is not only necessary for a good economist but greatly expands the student's ability to explore fully the logical consistency of theoretical systems.

We should like to thank Mr Ron Shone of the Department of Economics, the University of Sheffield, for many constructive comments made during long conversations concerning the teaching of mathematics to economics and business studies students. Additionally, we are grateful to our colleagues at Sheffield Polytechnic and to the students on the BA (Business Studies) course, who have all cheerfully put up with our enthusiasm for the introduction of quantitative methods in their courses. We would also like to thank Mrs Janet Quincey for her painstaking reading of the mathematics. The deficiencies in the book are entirely our responsibility.

R. W. Q.
F. N.
Sheffield

CONTENTS

Chapter 1

BASIC FOUNDATIONS

ECONOMIC RELATIONSHIPS

Economic theory is characterised by statements of assumed relationships between economic quantities. Thus we state that in a competitive market the quantity demanded is related to price, or that the total cost of producing a commodity is related to the quantity produced. Further, we specify the nature of the relationships, asserting in demand theory, for example, that, as price decreases, the quantity demanded increases. Similarly, in the theory of production, because of what we assume about diminishing returns to a variable factor, we state that marginal cost will fall as output increases but eventually will rise.

These relationships, embodying economic hypotheses, are usually presented in the diagrammatic or graphical form common to practically every economics textbook in existence. They could be, and often are, presented in algebraic form. The advantages of an algebraic presentation are that more complex relationships can be handled than is possible with graphical methods and, more importantly, the logic of elementary theory can be explored more fully. However, even the apparently simple methods of presenting economic theory are based on relatively sophisticated mathematical concepts, and we must therefore start with a formal treatment of these ideas, beginning with mappings and functional relationships, together with some of the basic principles of algebra.

MAPPINGS

Suppose we have two collections (or sets) of objects. These could be, for example, a set of employees of a company together with a set of job names, such as machine operative, managing director, clerk, canteen worker, secretary, and accountant. If we associate with each employee the job that he does, then this association is called a *mapping* from the first set to the second. A simple diagrammatic version of this could be as in Figure 1.1.

1

The mapping 'associate with each member of set X his job out of set Y' could be denoted by a letter such as f. We could then say that 'f maps X into Y' and denote it by

$$f : X \rightarrow Y$$

This notation can also be used to represent the individual association. For example, f maps B into 'clerk' can be written as

$$f : B \rightarrow \text{clerk}$$

and f maps A into 'secretary' as

$$f : A \rightarrow \text{secretary}$$

Extending this notation, we sometimes denote

$$f : B \rightarrow \text{clerk}$$

by

$$\text{clerk} = f(B)$$

This means that 'clerk' is the result when the mapping f acts on B. Similarly,

$$\text{secretary} = f(A)$$

and also managing director = f(C), secretary = f(D), and machine operative = f(E).

Figure 1.1 illustrates the rules concerning the definition of a mapping. A rule f associating the members, or elements, of one set with

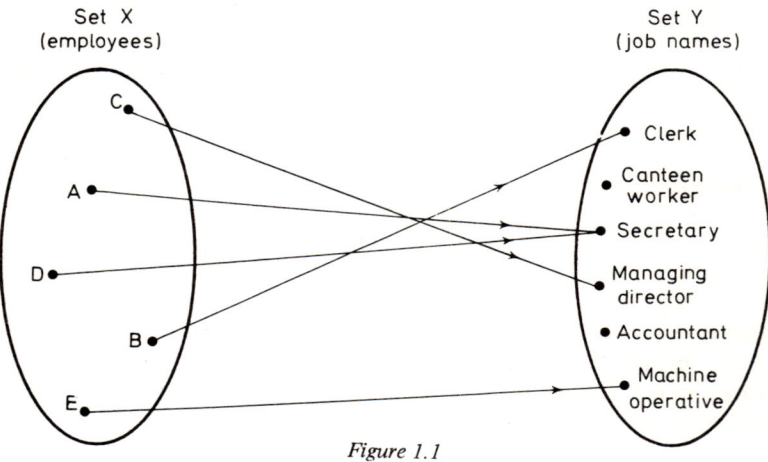

Figure 1.1

the members (elements) of another is a mapping if, and only if: (a) it is possible to associate every element of the first set X with some element of the second set Y; and (b) each element of the first set X is associated with only one element of the second set Y.

Notes

(1) It is *not* necessary for all the elements of the second set Y to be used (although all the elements of the first set X must be used). For example, it does not matter that there is no-one in set X who is a canteen worker or an accountant.

(2) Although one element of X cannot be associated with two elements of Y, it is quite permissible for one element of Y to have two (or even more) elements of X associated with it. For example, there is nothing wrong with having two elements of X who are secretaries.

FUNCTIONS

A mapping between two sets of numbers is called a *function*. For example, consider the function shown diagrammatically in Figure 1.2. The rule f associating each element of X with an element of Y is clearly: 'associate the element of X with its square (i.e. the number formed when it is multiplied by itself) in Y'. Then

$$f : -3 \to 9, \quad f : -2 \to 4, \quad f : -1 \to 1, \quad f : 0 \to 0,$$
$$f : \ 1 \to 1, \quad f : \ 2 \to 4, \quad f : \ 3 \to 9$$

or these could be written as

$$f(-3) = 9, \quad f(-2) = 4, \quad f(-1) = 1, \quad f(0) = 0,$$
$$f(1) = 1, \quad f(2) = 4, \quad f(3) = 9$$

Again, it should be stressed that it does not matter that all the elements of Y have not been used or that two elements of X map into the same element of Y [for example, $f(-2) = 4$, $f(2) = 4$]. However, it is important that every element of X has been used and that each element of X maps into only one element of Y.

If x is used to represent any one of the elements of X (i.e. x could be $-3, -2, -1, 0, 1, 2$, or 3), then the element of Y. that x maps into would be x^2, i.e.

$$f : x \rightarrow x^2$$

or
$$f(x) = x^2$$

If we continue the notation and let y represent the element of Y that x maps into, then

$$f : x \rightarrow y$$

or
$$y = f(x)$$

where in this case
$$y = x^2$$

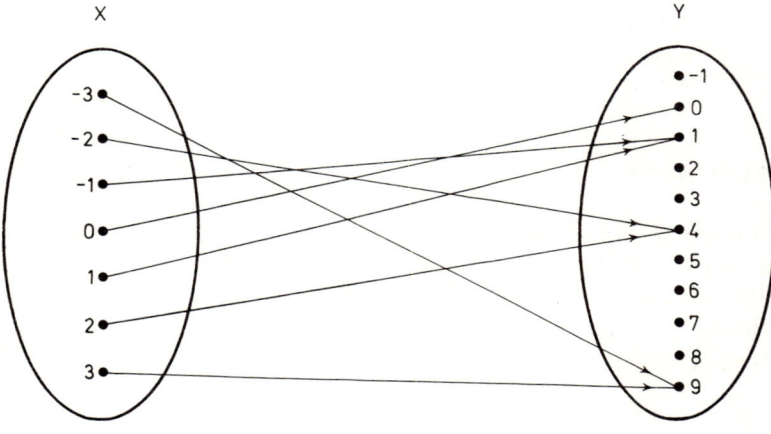

Figure 1.2

We now have the main notations used to represent functions:

$$y = f(x)$$

is called the *implicit form* and is usually used when we know that there is some relationship between x and y (i.e. between set X and set Y) but do not know or are not interested in what it is; and

$$y = x^2$$

[or $f(x) = x^2$, which is equivalent] is called the *explicit form* and is used when we know, and need, the exact relationship between the two sets.

Notes

(1) The reader should not be scared of the notation $y = f(x)$. It is a very simple concept and just means that there is some relationship between the values of y and the values of x. It gives no indication of what this relationship is. The expression $y = f(x)$ is read as 'y is a function of x' or, shorter, 'y is f of x'.

(2) There is no real significance in the choice of the letter f. If there were two relationships between y and x, one of them could be denoted by f and the other by some other letter, g say; then the first relationship would be written

$$y = f(x)$$

and the second $\qquad y = g(x)$

(3) The terms x and y are called *variables*. The variable x is known as the *independent variable* because it can take any value we like to give it (from some understood set X), and y is the *dependent variable* because its value is determined by the value given to x. In economic theory, this notation is used frequently. One of the most familiar relationships is that of the demand for a commodity and its price. If we are speaking of a monopolist who chooses to fix his output, we argue that

$$p = f(\bar{q}_s)$$

where p is the price and $\bar{q}_s$ is the quantity supplied to the market. In this case p is assumed to be dependent on quantity supplied. In the case of a competitive industry it is assumed that output sold is a function of price and so we write

$$\bar{q}_d = g(p)$$

i.e. the quantity demanded $\bar{q}_d$ is the dependent variable whilst price is the independent variable.

FUNCTIONS OF INFINITE SETS AND GRAPHS

Figure 1.2 gives an example of a function of *finite* sets, i.e. the number of elements in the sets can be counted. However, sets do not have to be finite to have functions defined on them: consider, for example, that described in Figure 1.3. Here the sets X and Y each represent all the whole numbers (integers), both positive and negative, and the number of elements in each is *infinite*. It can be seen that

$$f(-3) = -1, \quad f(-2) = 0, \quad f(-1) = 1, \quad f(0) = 2, \text{ etc.}$$

The function is obviously

$$f : x \rightarrow 2 + x$$

or
$$f(x) = 2 + x$$

or
$$y = 2 + x$$

The method of illustrating functions as used in Figures 1.2 and 1.3 is reaching the limits of usefulness when sets having infinite numbers of elements have to be indicated by lines of dashes (Figure 1.3). For some

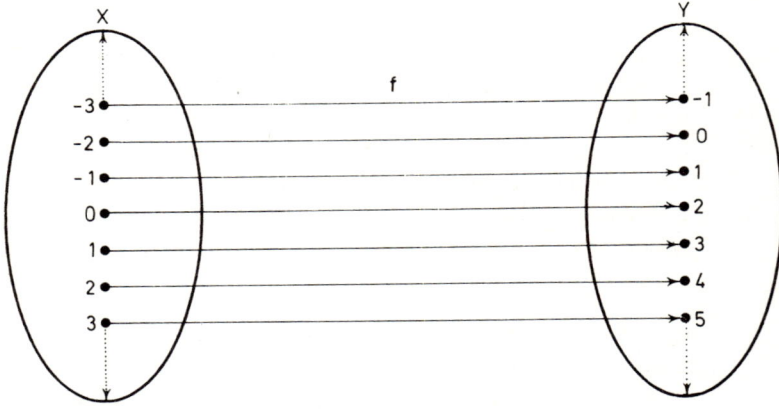

Figure 1.3

other infinite sets this method becomes totally unsatisfactory. Consider, for example, the same function as in Figure 1.3 but this time operating on the set of all real numbers (this is the set of all whole numbers, together with all the decimal numbers). The problem here is that, between any two real numbers, there is an infinite number of others: for example, between 1 and 2 there are 1.1, 1.003, 1.000 000 5, 1.234 567, 1.999 999 9, etc.

A way of representing a function for any real value of *x* is by using a *graph* (Figure 1.4). Here the sets X and Y are represented by points on two lines (called axes) drawn perpendicular to one another. A scale for the axis representing the X set (the x axis) is determined by fixing the distance between two integer elements of the X set (0 and 1, for example) and then marking off consecutive integers this same distance apart along the axis. A similar procedure is carried out on the y axis (although the fixed distance between two integers need not be the same as on the x axis). A pair of values of x and y can then be denoted by a point. For example, for the function $y = 2 + x$, $x = 1$ corresponds with $y = 3$, $x = -2$ corresponds with $y = 0$, and $x = -3.4$ corresponds with $y = -1.4$. These three points are indicated by A, B, and C in Figure 1.4.

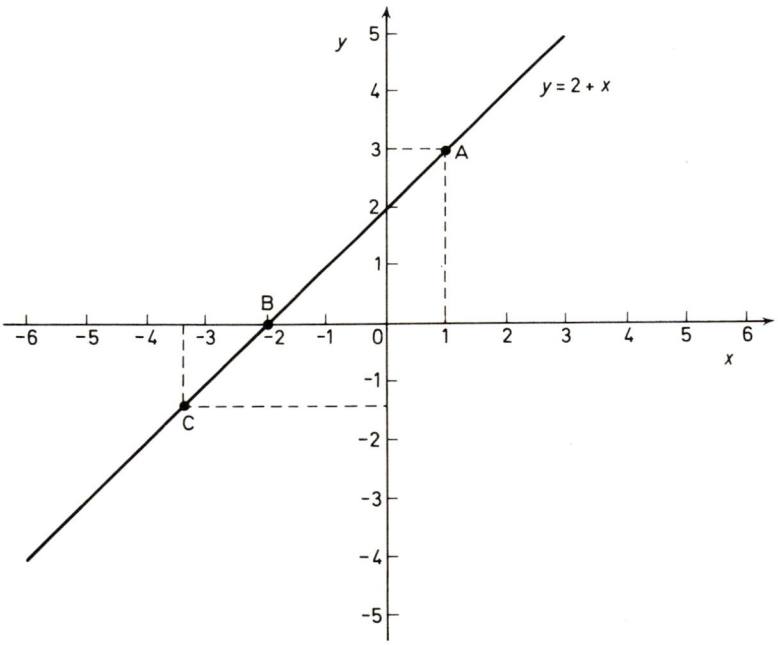

Figure 1.4

If other corresponding pairs of values in this example were marked on the graph, they would all be found to lie on a *straight line*. Straight lines are studied in greater detail on pages 10–13.

Not all functions produce graphs that are straight lines, however. If we consider the function $y = x^2$ again but this time letting the set X be the set of all real numbers, it can be seen that the points lie on a *curve*, as shown in Figure 1.5. For some functions it is not even possible to draw a curve, but these will not be dealt with in this book.

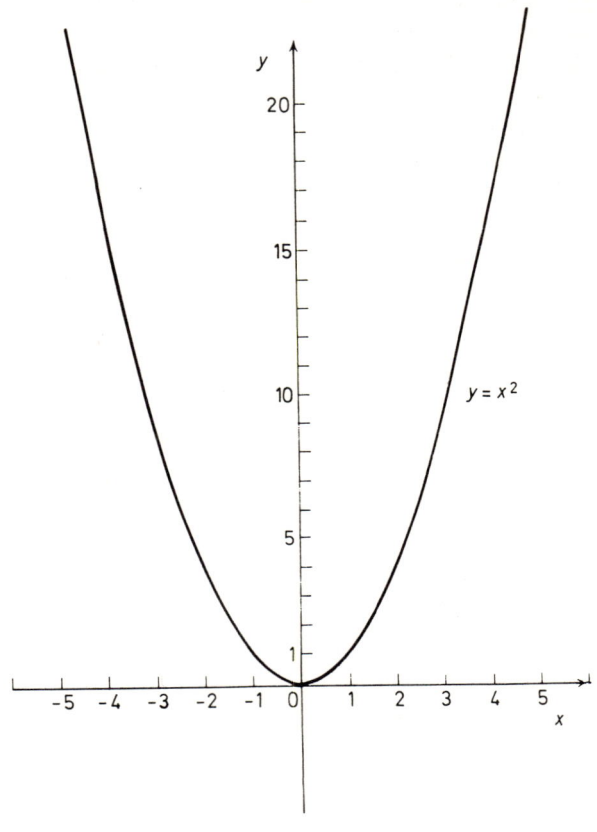

$$y = x^2$$

Figure 1.5

CONTINUOUS FUNCTIONS

We shall assume that the functions met in economic theory are normally continuous. Continuity is a very sophisticated concept in pure mathematics, but for our purposes we shall define a continuous function as a function whose graph contains no gaps or jumps. Figure 1.6 shows

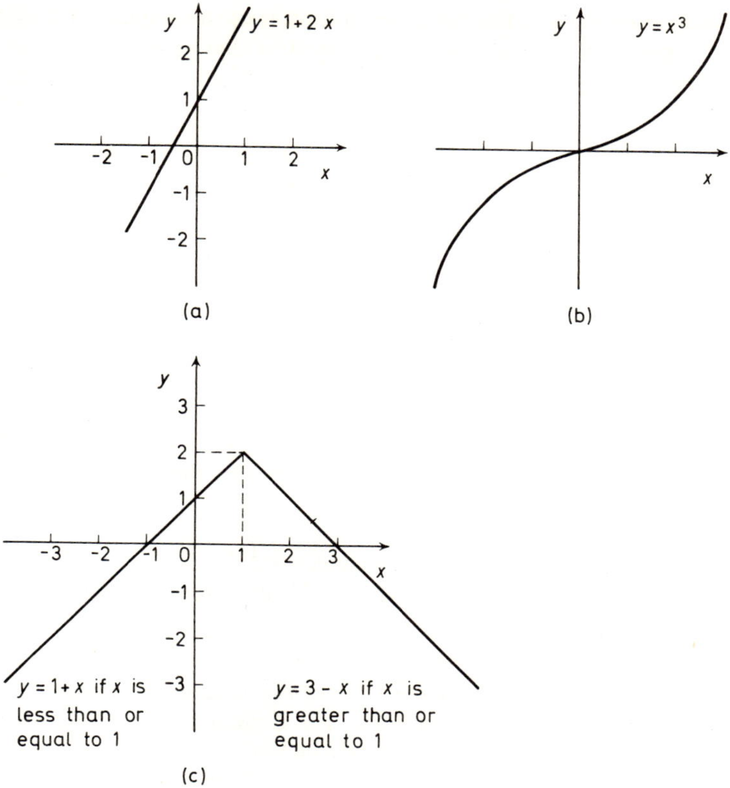

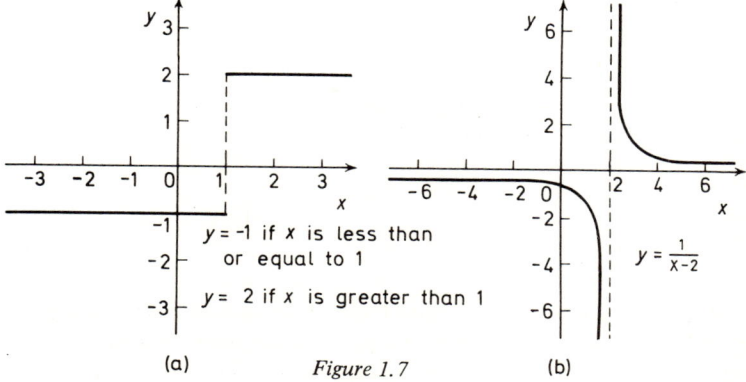

Figure 1.6

Figure 1.7

some examples of continuous functions, whereas the graphs in Figure 1.7 are examples of discontinuous functions. Note that in Figure 1.7a the discontinuity occurs at $x = 1$, and in Figure 1.7b it occurs at $x = 2$. In each of the examples in Figure 1.7 the function is continuous except at one particular value of x.

STRAIGHT LINES

The graph of any function of the form

$$y = a + bx \tag{1.1}$$

over a set of real numbers, and where a and b are constants, is a straight line. Such a function is said to be *linear*. Note that the example

$$y = 2 + x$$

plotted in Figure 1.4 is of this form, with $a = 2$ and $b = 1$. In economic theory the relationship between variables is often assumed to be linear.

The positions of only two points need be known in order to determine the equation of the one straight line which passes through these points. This is because the equation of the line is completely determined by the values of the two constants a and b. Consider, for example, two points P ($x = 1$ and $y = 4$) [which could be written just as $(1, 4)$] and Q [$x = 2$ and $y = 3$, or $(2, 3)$]. Since the point P specifies that $y = 4$ when $x = 1$, these values can be substituted into equation 1.1 to give

$$4 = a + b(1)$$

or
$$4 = a + b \tag{1.2}$$

Similarly (from the point Q) $y = 3$ when $x = 2$, so

$$3 = a + b(2)$$

or
$$3 = a + 2b \tag{1.3}$$

Therefore we have formed a pair of simultaneous equations for a and b, the values of which can now be uniquely determined. This means that *only one straight line passes through the two given points* P *and* Q.

To find the equation of this line, equations 1.2 and 1.3 must be solved. Subtracting equation 1.2 from equation 1.3 gives

$$-1 = b$$

or $$b = -1$$

Substituting $b = -1$ into equation 1.2 then gives

$$4 = a + (-1)$$
$$= a - 1$$

∴ $$4 + 1 = a$$
∴ $$a = 5$$

Therefore the equation of the straight line through P and Q is

$$y = 5 + (-1)x$$

or $$y = 5 - x$$

The fact that only one straight line passes through two given points can be used in plotting the graph of a linear function: we need only plot any two points satisfying the given equation, and draw a straight line through them, to produce the graph of the given linear function.

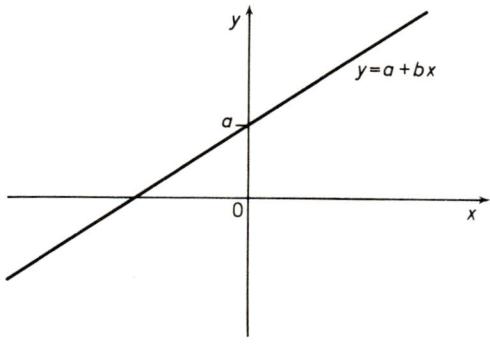

Figure 1.8

The only other thing we need for the moment note about a linear function is the significance of the value of a. Consider the general equation of a straight line

$$y = a + bx$$

Substituting the value $x = 0$ in this general equation gives

$$y = a + b(0)$$
$$= a + 0$$
$$= a$$

i.e. when $x = 0, y = a$. Therefore the line crosses the y axis at $y = a$ (the distance a being called the intercept on the y axis). This is shown in Figure 1.8.

There is a special significance attached to the value of b, but consideration of this is left mainly until Chapter 2. The only point to make here is that, if we plot the linear function

$$y = 5 - x$$

then we obtain the graph shown in Figure 1.9. It can be seen that this slopes in the opposite way to the graph of the equation

$$y = 2 + x$$

plotted in Figure 1.4. This difference in slope is because b is positive (equal to +1) in the equation $y = 2 + x$ but b is negative (equal to −1)

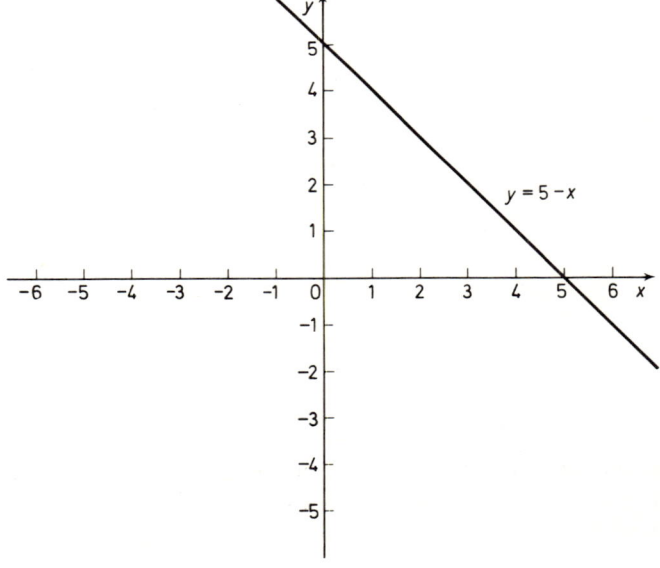

Figure 1.9

in the equation $y = 5 - x$. In general then: when b is positive, the straight line slopes upwards to the right

but when b is negative, the straight line slopes downwards to the right

INDICES

Before we move on to apply the concepts of variables and functions to economic analysis, it would be useful to look at some of the basic principles of algebra.

The reader will probably be familiar already with the idea of indices. On page 4, for instance, x^2 was used to denote $x \times x$. In general, any number a multiplied by itself n times is written as a^n:

$$\overbrace{a \times a \times \ldots \times a}^{n} = a^n$$

The notation a^n is read as 'a to the power n'.

Rule 1

The first important rule concerning indices is

$$a^m \times a^n = a^{m+n} \qquad (1.4)$$

This is very easy to show, for

$$a^m \times a^n = (\overbrace{a \times a \times \ldots \times a}^{m}) \times (\overbrace{a \times a \times \ldots \times a}^{n})$$

$$= \overbrace{a \times a \times \ldots \times a \times a \times a \times \ldots \times a}^{m+n}$$

$$\therefore \qquad a^m \times a^n = a^{m+n}$$

A particular example would be

$$2^2 \times 2^3 = (2 \times 2) \times (2 \times 2 \times 2) = (2 \times 2 \times 2 \times 2 \times 2) = 2^5$$

i.e. $4 \times 8 = 32$.

The general result is simple to use, for instance

$$3^5 \times 3^4 = 3^9, \quad 10^4 \times 10^7 = 10^{11}, \quad x^3 \times x^{10} = x^{13}$$

Rule 2

The second important rule is

$$(a^m)^n = a^{mn} \tag{1.5}$$

Consider first a particular example:

$$(2^2)^3 = (2 \times 2)^3 = (2 \times 2) \times (2 \times 2) \times (2 \times 2) = 2^6 = 2^{2 \times 3}$$

This is, of course, the same as $(4)^3 = 4 \times 4 \times 4 = 64$.

The general result is again quite simple to demonstrate:

$$(a^m)^n = \left(\overbrace{a \times a \times \ldots \times a}^{m} \right)^n$$

$$= \overbrace{(\overbrace{a \times a \times \ldots \times a}^{m}) \times (\overbrace{a \times a \times \ldots \times a}^{m}) \times \ldots \times (\overbrace{a \times a \times \ldots \times a}^{m})}^{n}$$

$$\therefore \ (a^m)^n = a^{mn}$$

EXTENSION OF INDEX NOTATION

In performing mathematical operations, certain extensions of the index notation are extremely useful. One of these is that

$$a = a^1 \tag{1.6}$$

It can be seen that

$$a^n \times a = \overbrace{(a \times a \times \ldots \times a)}^{n} \times a$$

$$= a^{n+1}$$

For example, $a^3 \times a = (a \times a \times a) \times a = a^4$. Let us write a as a^x and determine what value x must take. Since $a = a^x$,

$$a^n \times a = a^n \times a^x$$

$$= a^{n+x}$$

from equation 1.4. But we already have

$$a^n \times a = a^{n+1}$$

$$\therefore \quad a^{n+x} = a^{n+1}$$

$$\therefore \quad n + x = n + 1$$

$$\therefore \quad x = n + 1 - n$$

$$\therefore \quad x = 1$$

$$\therefore \quad a = a^1$$

Another useful extension of the index notation is that

$$1 = a^0 \tag{1.7}$$

It is clear that

$$a^n \times 1 = a^n$$

Let us write 1 as a^x and determine what value x must take. Using equation 1.4 again,

$$a^n \times 1 = a^n \times a^x$$

$$= a^{n+x}$$

But

$$a^n \times 1 = a^n$$

$$\therefore \quad a^{n+x} = a^n$$

$$\therefore \quad n + x = n$$

$$\therefore \quad x = n - n$$

$$\therefore \quad x = 0$$

$$\therefore \quad 1 = a^0$$

So far we have considered only powers that are positive integers. Powers that are negative are interpreted in the following way:

$$\frac{1}{a^n} = a^{-n} \tag{1.8}$$

Consider first the relationship

$$a^n \times \frac{1}{a^n} = \frac{a^n}{a^n}$$

$$= 1$$

$$= a^0$$

from equation 1.7. Let us write

$$\frac{1}{a^n} = a^x$$

and determine what value x must take. Then, from equation 1.4,

$$a^n \times \frac{1}{a^n} = a^n \times a^x$$

$$= a^{n+x}$$

But

$$a^n \times \frac{1}{a^n} = a^0$$

∴

$$n + x = 0$$

∴

$$x = -n$$

∴

$$\frac{1}{a^n} = a^{-n}$$

A result which follows from equation 1.8 is

$$\frac{a^m}{a^n} = a^{m-n} \tag{1.9}$$

This can be shown easily since

$$\frac{a^m}{a^n} = a^m \times \frac{1}{a^n}$$

Therefore, from equations 1.8 and 1.4,

$$\frac{a^m}{a^n} = a^m \times a^{-n}$$

$$= a^{m+(-n)}$$

∴

$$\frac{a^m}{a^n} = a^{m-n}$$

This result is also very easy to use, for example

$$\frac{6^8}{6^3} = 6^{8-3} = 6^5$$

$$\frac{11^5}{11^8} = 11^{5-8} = 11^{-3} = \frac{1}{11^3}$$

and

$$\frac{Z^{10}}{Z^4} = Z^{10-4} = Z^6$$

Finally, we shall consider powers that are not integers, for example

$$\sqrt{a} = a^{1/2}$$

The symbol $\sqrt{a}$ (the square root of a) denotes a number that, when multiplied by itself, produces a, i.e.

$$\sqrt{a} \times \sqrt{a} = a$$
$$= a^1$$

from equation 1.6. Let us write $\sqrt{a}$ as a^x and determine what value x must take. Then from equation 1.4,

$$\sqrt{a} \times \sqrt{a} = a^x \times a^x$$
$$= a^{x+x}$$
$$= a^{2x}$$

But $\sqrt{a} \times \sqrt{a} = a^1$

$\therefore$ $a^{2x} = a^1$

$\therefore$ $2x = 1$

$\therefore$ $x = \frac{1}{2}$

$\therefore$ $\sqrt{a} = a^{1/2}$

In the same way $\sqrt[3]{a}$ (the cube root of a) can be written as $a^{1/3}$ since

$$a^{1/3} \times a^{1/3} \times a^{1/3} = (a^{1/3})^3$$
$$= a^1$$
$$= a$$

A particular example would be

$$32^{1/5} = 2$$

since $2 \times 2 \times 2 \times 2 \times 2 = 32$.

We can now attach meaning to any power that is a whole number or fraction, whether positive or negative.

Example 1

From equations 1.5 and 1.10

$$a^{5/2} = (a^{1/2})^5$$
$$= (\sqrt{a})^5$$

Alternatively,

$$a^{5/2} = (a^5)^{1/2}$$
$$= \sqrt{(a^5)}$$

Note that the forms $(\sqrt{a})^5$ and $\sqrt{(a^5)}$ are identical.

Example 2

From equation 1.5

$$125^{2/3} = (125^{1/3})^2$$
$$= (5)^2$$
$$= 25$$

Therefore $125^{2/3} = 25$.

Example 3

From equation 1.8

$$a^{-4/3} = \frac{1}{a^{4/3}}$$

and from equation 1.5

$$\frac{1}{a^{4/3}} = \frac{1}{(a^{1/3})^4}$$

$$\therefore \qquad a^{-4/3} = \frac{1}{(\sqrt[3]{a})^4}$$

EQUALITIES, IDENTITIES, AND INEQUALITIES

The representations $y = 2 + x$ and $y = x^2$, considered already, are examples of *equations* or *equalities*. The main feature of an equality is that it is valid for only certain pairs of values of the variables x and y. For example, $y = 2 + x$ is valid for $x = 1$ and $y = 3$ or for $x = 108$ and $y = 110$, but is not valid for $x = 4$ and $y = 7$ or for $x = 23$ and $y = 68$.

In this particular example we have already seen that the pairs of values of x and y for which $y = 2 + x$ all lie on a straight line. The equation is not valid for points not on the straight line.

The manipulation of equalities should be well known:

(1) A constant may be added to or subtracted from each side of the equality, i.e. if

$$y = f(x)$$

then $\qquad y + a = f(x) + a$

for any constant a. For example, if

$$y = x + 2$$

then $\qquad y + (-2) = x + 2 + (-2)$

or $\qquad y - 2 = x$

(2) Each side of the equality may be multiplied by a non-zero constant, i.e. if

$$y = f(x)$$

then $\qquad ay = af(x)$

for any constant a not equal to zero. For example, if

$$y = x + 2$$

then $\qquad 2y = 2(x + 2)$

or $\qquad 2y = 2x + 4$

(3) Each side of the equality may be raised to some power, i.e. if

$$y = f(x)$$

then $\qquad y^n = [f(x)]^n$

where n is any positive or negative integer or fraction. For example, if

$$y = x + 2$$

then $\qquad y^2 = (x + 2)^2$

or $\qquad y^2 = x^2 + 4x + 4$

There is also a mathematical form (written with the sign ≡) called an *identity*. The main feature of this is that it is valid for *all* values of the variables. Examples of identities are $x + 1 \equiv x + 1$, $(x + y)^2 \equiv x^2 + 2xy + y^2$, and $x^2 - y^2 \equiv (x + y)(x - y)$. These are always true, whatever values are given to x and y. An indentity can generally be reduced to the form $0 \equiv 0$.

The manipulation of identities is just the same as that of equalities, namely:

(1) A constant may be added to or subtracted from each side of the identity, i.e. if

$$f \equiv g$$

then
$$f + a \equiv g + a$$

for any constant a. For example, since

$$x^2 - y^2 \equiv (x + y)(x - y)$$

then
$$x^2 - y^2 + 3 \equiv (x + y)(x - y) + 3$$

(2) Each side of the identity may be multiplied by a non-zero constant, i.e. if

$$f \equiv g$$

then
$$af \equiv ag$$

for any constant a not equal to zero. For example, since

$$x^2 - y^2 \equiv (x + y)(x - y)$$

then
$$(-1)(x^2 - y^2) \equiv (-1)(x + y)(x - y)$$

or
$$y^2 - x^2 \equiv -(x + y)(x - y)$$

(3) Each side of the identity may be raised to some power, i.e. if

$$f \equiv g$$

then
$$f^n \equiv g^n$$

where n is any positive or negative integer or fraction. For example, since

$$x^2 - y^2 \equiv (x + y)(x - y)$$

then
$$(x^2 - y^2)^2 \equiv [(x + y)(x - y)]^2$$

or
$$x^4 - 2x^2y^2 + y^4 \equiv (x + y)^2(x - y)^2$$

Consider again the equality $y = x + 2$, which could also be written as $y - x = 2$. Sometimes circumstances require that $y - x$ is not to equal 2 but is always to be less than 2. This requirement is written as

$$y - x < 2$$

and is an example of an *inequality*. If $y - x$ could be less than 2 or equal to 2, we would write $y - x \leqslant 2$. If $y - x$ must always be greater than 2, we would write $y - x > 2$; and if $y - x$ could be greater than 2 or equal to 2, we would write $y - x \geqslant 2$. All these are examples of inequalities.

There are slight differences between the manipulation of inequalities and that of equalities or identities:

(1) A constant may be added to or subtracted from each side of the inequality, i.e. if

$$f < g$$

then
$$f + a < g + a$$

for any constant a. For example,

$$5 < 9$$

$\therefore$
$$5 + 3 < 9 + 3$$

i.e.
$$8 < 12$$

(2a) Each side of the inequality may be multiplied by a non-zero *positive* constant, i.e. if

$$f < g$$

then
$$af < ag$$

where a is a positive constant not equal to zero (i.e. $a > 0$). For example,

$$5 < 9$$

$\therefore$
$$4 \times 5 < 4 \times 9$$

i.e.
$$20 < 36$$

(2b) If each side of the inequality is multiplied by a non-zero *negative* constant, then the direction of the inequality is reversed ($<$ becomes $>$ and $\leqslant$ becomes $\geqslant$ and vice versa), i.e. if

$$f < g$$

then
$$af > ag$$

where *a* is a negative constant not equal to zero (i.e. $a < 0$). For example,

$$5 < 9$$

∴ $-2 \times 5 > -2 \times 9$

i.e. $-10 > -18$

Similarly, $-3 < 2$

∴ $-4 \times (-3) > -4 \times 2$

i.e. $12 > -8$

(3a) Each side of the inequality may be raised to a *positive* power, i.e. if

$$f < g$$

then $f^n < g^n$

where *n* is any positive integer or fraction (i.e. $n > 0$). For example,

$$5 < 9$$

∴ $5^2 < 9^2$

i.e. $25 < 81$

(3b) If each side of the inequality is raised to a *negative* power, then the direction of the inequality is reversed, i.e. if

$$f < g$$

then $f^n > g^n$

where *n* is any negative integer or fraction (i.e. $n < 0$). For example,

$$5 < 9$$

∴ $5^{-1} > 9^{-1}$

i.e. $\dfrac{1}{5} > \dfrac{1}{9}$

DIMENSIONS IN ECONOMICS

Now that we have discussed the concepts of functions, identities, and equalities, we can begin to examine their significance in terms of

economic analysis. First, however, it would be useful to investigate
the dimensions and units used in economics.

All students of economics are familiar with graphs that show the
assumed relationships between such economic magnitudes as price and
quantity of a commodity demanded per time period; price and quantity
supplied; cost and quantity produced; and consumption expenditure
and disposable income. It is important to be clear about the units in
which such magnitudes are expressed, but in many presentations it is
convenient to omit the *actual* units and just to stipulate the *kind* of
units used. Consider, for example, the demand and supply diagram in
Figure 1.10. This shows that the price at which demand and supply are
equal (i.e. the equilibrium price) is p_0 whilst the quantity demanded
and supplied is q_0. Notice that the vertical axis is not labelled pounds
or dollars, simply price. Similarly, the horizontal axis is not labelled
tons or number of cars, simply quantity (which implies some physical
unit). The basic dimensions of economic analysis are physical units
(commodity units), time units, and money units. Time is treated
separately from other physical units because of its importance in
economic analysis.

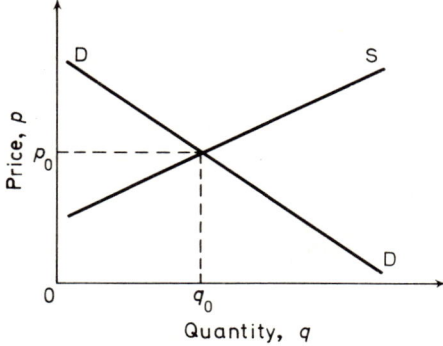

Figure 1.10

To help clarify various points concerning the dimensions of variables,
we shall use the following symbols:

M to represent money units,
Q to represent commodity units,
and   T to represent time units.

When we speak of price, we are referring to a money unit over a commodity unit. For example, the price of butter can be stated as 60p per pound, and that of cigarettes as 27p for twenty. Thus

$$\text{Dimensions of price} = \frac{M}{Q}$$

Similarly, when speaking of quantity demanded or supplied at a price, we are referring to a commodity unit over a time unit — such as 1000 items supplied per hour, or so many tons of a material demanded per week. Thus

$$\text{Dimensions of quantity demanded or supplied} = \frac{Q}{T}$$

Similarly, we speak of a man's pay as being so much per hour, per day, etc., and here we are referring to a money unit over a time unit. Thus

$$\text{Dimensions of wages} = \frac{M}{T}$$

Not all of the magnitudes relevant to economists have a dimension. For example, the marginal propensity to consume is defined as the change in consumption expenditure over the change in income. However, consumption expenditure is the output bought by consumers per time period, multiplied by price. Thus the dimensions of output bought by consumers per time period are Q/T, and the dimensions of price are M/Q as shown above. Similarly, income is a money flow per time period, i.e. its dimensions are M/T. Therefore the marginal propensity to consume has the dimensions

$$\frac{(Q/T) \times (M/Q)}{M/T} = \frac{M/T}{M/T} = 1$$

Thus the marginal propensity to consume is dimensionless.

Similarly, price elasticity of demand is defined as

$$- \frac{\text{The proportionate change in quantity demanded}}{\text{The proportionate change in price}}$$

The resulting value of elasticity is a number, not a commodity unit or a money unit.

The problems raised by dimensions are important, but to cover these fully would be beyond the intended scope of this book. It is sufficient for the moment to point out that units must be handled carefully and that the following obvious but important rule applies: *if two magnitudes are to be added or subtracted, they must have the same units, which will also be the units of the resulting magnitude* (for example, tons cannot be added to gallons).

EXOGENOUS AND ENDOGENOUS VARIABLES

We have already introduced the term 'variable' and the idea of dependent and independent variables (see page 5). However, in economic theory the terms endogenous and exogenous variables are also used. The distinction is necessary in the construction of economic models.

Take, for example, the simple model of demand and supply in a competitive market, as shown in Figure 1.10. The curve D represents the demand function, i.e. the relationship between quantity demanded $\overline{q}_d$ and price p. In a competitive market, quantity demanded is considered to be a function of price, and so we can write

$$\overline{q}_d = f(p)$$

Similarly, S represents the supply function and, if $\overline{q}_s$ is the quantity supplied at any price p, we can write

$$\overline{q}_s = g(p)$$

Thus, in this example, the endogenous variables, i.e. those explained within the model, are quantity demanded, quantity supplied, and price. However, we know that the demand for a commodity is affected by a number of other things, such as income per head, consumers' tastes, and prices of substitutes: all of these are exogenous variables, i.e. variables outside the model. Similarly, the quantity supplied could be affected by changes in the exogenous variables, for example a lowering of costs due to technological progress or an increase in costs resulting from a rise in factor prices. It is important to understand that in the simple demand and supply model we are assuming that *all the exogenous variables are held constant.* In addition, we are assuming that a change in any of the exogenous variables will affect price, quantity demanded, and quantity supplied, but that a change in price, quantity demanded, and quantity supplied will not affect these variables outside of the model and assumed constant. These assumptions can be illustrated by considering the case shown in Figure 1.11.

The demand curve D_1 represents the initial demand conditions and shows the relationship between quantity demanded and price [$\bar{q}_d = f(p)$], other variables affecting demand assumed constant. Similarly, the supply curve S represents the initial supply conditions [$\bar{q}_s = g(p)$], other variables than price affecting supply assumed constant. Suppose that income per head increases, with the result that, over a large range of prices, more is demanded. The new demand curve D_2 represents the new demand conditions. The original equilibrium price was p_1 with the quantity q_1 demanded and supplied, and the new equilibrium price is p_2 and the new quantity demanded and supplied is q_2. Thus a shift in the value of an exogenous variable (income per head) has caused a change in the values of the endogenous variables p, $\bar{q}_s$, and $\bar{q}_d$. However, we assume that changes in the market price and quantities demanded and supplied do not influence the exogenous variables.

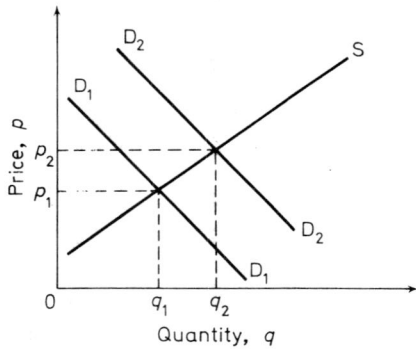

Figure 1.11

Which variables should be treated as exogenous depends on which features of a problem one is interested in. Price theory has been so dominant in traditional economic theory that price has always been singled out as the variable whose movements are of interest. In practical work one has to be careful: for example, if there were a small country whose staple commercial crop was wool, then changes in the price and quantities of wool marketed could affect income per head and so income would not be exogenous to this model.

DEMAND AND SUPPLY

Let us now examine in more detail various aspects of demand and supply. The familiar diagram shown in Figure 1.10 represents a theory of price determination in a competitive market. The endogenous variables in this model are the quantity demanded, the quantity supplied, and the market price. The line DD is the demand curve and shows what quantities consumers plan to purchase at any particular price in the feasible range of prices. Similarly, the supply curve S shows the quantities that firms in the industry plan to sell at any price in the feasible range. Thus, when we speak of demand and supply functions, we mean the *intention* of buyers and sellers to purchase or sell according to the price. It is important to realise that, in this sense, demand and supply will be equal only at the equilibrium price. Indeed, the term 'equilibrium' means, in this context, that there is no reason why buyers and sellers should alter the quantity they purchase or sell because, at the equilibrium price, the quantity consumers wish to purchase is the same as the quantity that firms wish to supply.

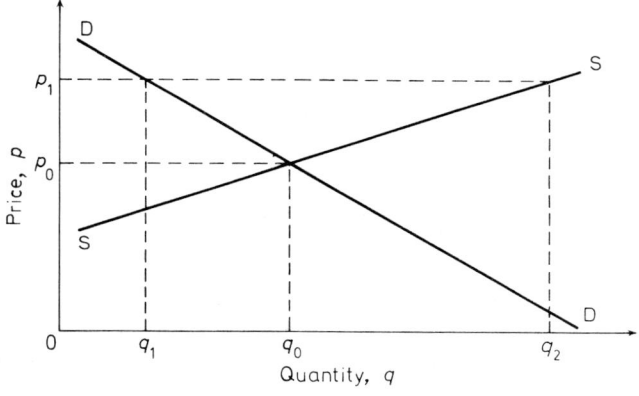

Figure 1.12

In Figure 1.12, p_0 is the equilibrium price and it can be seen that, at any other price, demand and supply are not equal. If the price were p_1, then the quantity demanded would be q_1 whereas the quantity firms wished to sell (i.e. which they put on the market) would be q_2. Thus there would be an excess supply $q_2 - q_1$ at the price p_1. It is assumed that price will then fall until it reaches p_0, for *only* at p_0 are demand and supply equal. However, the quantity bought at the price p_1 is q_1 and this must equal the quantity sold. Obviously, at any price, the quantity sold must be the same as the quantity bought. We now have a distinction between what is bought and sold, and what is demanded and supplied. The distinction is important because the fact that demand and supply are not equal at any price other than p_0 gives rise to 'market forces' adjusting to the inequality and moving towards an equality of demand and supply. The necessary identity of quantities bought and sold at any price tells us nothing about what determines the quantity demanded and supplied and so does not help us to understand what determines the market price or movements in price. Such explanations and predictions are contained in the theory, subsumed in the demand and supply curves in Figure 1.12.

The model contained in Figures 1.10 and 1.12 can be stated algebraically. Let

$\bar{q}_d$ = the quantity demanded,
$\bar{q}_s$ = the quantity supplied,
and p = the market price.

Then it is possible to write

$$\bar{q}_d = f(p) \tag{1.11}$$

$$\bar{q}_s = g(p) \tag{1.12}$$

and $$\bar{q}_d = \bar{q}_s \tag{1.13}$$

Equations 1.11 and 1.12 state that the quantity demanded and the quantity supplied are each a function of p. From economic theory it is known that $\bar{q}_d$ is a decreasing function of price and $\bar{q}_s$ is an increasing function of price (see Chapter 2). Equation 1.13 is an equilibrium condition in that, when the quantity demanded equals the quantity supplied, the *plans* of buyers and sellers coincide. This might be clearer if we use numerical examples of demand and supply functions to show that only one price and quantity will satisfy both the demand and supply functions.

As an example, suppose that the demand and supply functions are

$$\bar{q}_d = f(p) = \frac{p - 10}{-0.8} \tag{1.11a}$$

and $$\bar{q}_s = g(p) = \frac{p - 3}{0.6} \tag{1.12a}$$

Let the equilibrium quantity of the commodity be q_0, so that equation 1.13 becomes

$$\bar{q}_d = \bar{q}_s = q_0 \qquad (1.13a)$$

Then, in equilibrium, the quantity q_0 demanded and supplied is related to the equilibrium price p_0 by the equations

$$q_0 = \frac{p_0 - 10}{-0.8} \qquad (1.14)$$

and

$$q_0 = \frac{p_0 - 3}{0.6} \qquad (1.15)$$

We must therefore solve equations 1.14 and 1.15 for q_0 and p_0. From these two equations

$$\frac{p_0 - 10}{-0.8} = \frac{p_0 - 3}{0.6}$$

$\therefore \qquad 0.6(p_0 - 10) = -0.8(p_0 - 3)$

$\therefore \qquad 0.6p_0 - 6 = -0.8p_0 + 2.4$

$\therefore \qquad 0.6p_0 + 0.8p_0 = 2.4 + 6$

$\therefore \qquad 1.4p_0 = 8.4$

$\therefore \qquad p_0 = \frac{8.4}{1.4}$

or $\qquad p_0 = 6$

Thus in equilibrium the market price is $p_0 = 6$. To find the equilibrium quantity, the value $p_0 = 6$ can be substituted into equation 1.14. Then

$$q_0 = \frac{6 - 10}{-0.8}$$

$$= \frac{-4}{-0.8}$$

$$= 5$$

Thus, with the given demand and supply functions, $\bar{q}_d = \bar{q}_s = 5$ when $p = p_0 = 6$. This means that at $p = 6$ the quantity demanded and supplied is the same as the quantity bought and sold, but at any other price this is not so. It is the *inequality* of $\bar{q}_d$ and $\bar{q}_s$ that brings about the workings of 'market forces'.

It must be remembered that the simple micro-model in the above example (and contained in the demand and supply diagrams) rests on a complex theory containing hypotheses about the behaviour of consumers and firms, technical assumptions, etc. For instance, the supply function is based on the 'law' of variable proportions and on assumptions about profit-maximising firms, stock-holding on the part of firms, and the speed with which information is transmitted throughout the market and the consequent speed of adjustments by buyers and sellers. Similarly, the demand function rests on hypotheses about consumer behaviour, rationality, etc. It is these hypotheses and assumptions that constitute the 'theory' represented by the demand and supply models.

Now suppose

q_d = the quantity bought,

and q_s = the quantity sold.

Then, no matter what the price is,

$$q_d \equiv q_s$$

At the equilibrium price, the quantity bought and sold equals the quantity demanded and supplied, and so

$$q_d = \bar{q}_d$$

and $q_s = \bar{q}_s$

i.e. planned purchases at the market price equal actual purchases, and planned sales equal actual sales. In equilibrium, therefore, we can simply speak of the equality of demand and supply and mean the quantities bought and sold. At any price other than the equilibrium price, demand and supply do not mean the quantities bought and sold.

NATIONAL INCOME DETERMINATION – IDENTITIES, EQUALITIES, AND THEORIES

Many students and teachers have struggled with the question of reconciling the statement that 'saving and investment are always equal' with the apparently contradictory argument that 'saving will equal investment only when income is in equilibrium'. This confusion arises because the distinction between, and the use of, identities and equalities is not made clear in many textbooks on economic theory. We shall consider the case of equilibrium levels of income as usually presented to first-year students. This means that we are considering a simple model, with a goods and services sector, no government expenditure or taxation, and no foreign trade.

It is usual to denote the various concepts in the following way:

Y = the value of current income received by factors of production,
C = the value of current expenditure on goods and services by households (consumption),
S = current saving by households (personal saving),
I = current expenditure by business units (investment),
O = the value of current output,

and E = the value of current expenditure.

The national accounting definitions can also be set out:

(1) The value of current income is the same as the total of current consumption expenditure by households plus current personal saving, i.e.

$$Y \equiv C + S \qquad (1.16)$$

(2) The value of current output is the same as the value of current consumption expenditure by households plus current expenditure by business units, i.e.

$$O \equiv C + I \qquad (1.17)$$

(3) The value of current output is the same as the value of current income, which is the same as the value of current expenditure by households and business units, i.e.

$$O \equiv Y \equiv E \qquad (1.18)$$

Thus output, income, and expenditure are three different names for the same thing — the flow of goods and services that are generated over a time period.

(4) Identity 1.16 can be rearranged to give

$$Y - C \equiv S \qquad (1.19)$$

Thus current saving is defined as the value of current income minus current consumption expenditure.

(5) Similarly, by rearranging identity 1.17, we obtain

$$O - C \equiv I \qquad (1.20)$$

Thus the value of current output minus the value of current consumption expenditure by households is, by definition, the value of current investment.

By identity 1.20 above we have defined investment to be the value of current output *not sold to household units*. Thus output not sold as consumption includes output bought by firms (for example, machinery and plant for use in the productive process), and changes in stocks of finished output. Such stock changes may be the result of firms deliberately increasing or running down stockpiles, or they may be unintended investment by firms who have not sold the output they expected. However, by definition, investment is $O - C$, and since $Y \equiv O$ we can substitute O for Y in identity 1.19 to obtain

$$O - C \equiv S$$

But identity 1.20 states that

$$O - C \equiv I$$

Therefore, by definition,

$$S \equiv I \qquad (1.21)$$

This necessary identity of saving with investment follows from our definitions and holds for *any* value of Y and C.

The above definitions of income, output, etc., are necessary as a preliminary to constructing a theory. Obviously, we must define our terms, but the definitions can give no information about the relationships between Y, C, S, I, O, and E; they cannot explain why income might change, why it settles at a particular level, what the effect on income would be of a change in investment, and so on.

Consider again the identities $O \equiv C + I$ and $O \equiv Y \equiv E$. It is obvious from these that

$$Y \equiv C + I$$

But we do not know the relationship between Y, C, and I from this identity, and there is nothing to indicate what determines any particular income level. To know this we need a *theory* of income determination, and this involves moving from *definitions* to *hypotheses* about the behaviour of consumers and businessmen. It is beyond the scope of this book to deal with macro-economic theory as such, but the following issues discussed are those that students of economics necessarily come across.

The simple theory of income determination most familiar to first-year students is often presented diagrammatically as in Figure 1.13. The

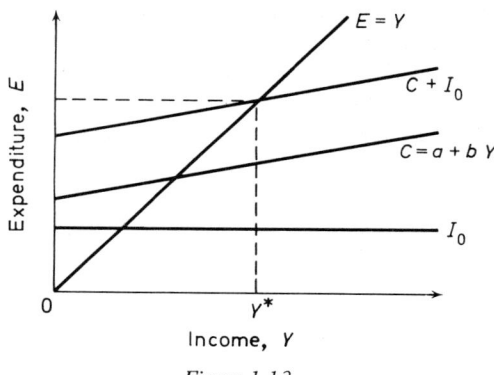

Figure 1.13

diagram includes a hypothesis about consumption: that what consumers *plan* to spend is a linear function of their income, and this is shown by the line $C = a + bY$ (the slope b of this line is the marginal propensity to consume). Thus we have moved from a definition ($C \equiv Y - S$) to a hypothesised relationship between Y and C. This is the subtle move from accounting definitions to a theory of income determination. Also, as part of the same process, we are hypothesising that businessmen *plan* to invest an amount I_0. This means again that we have moved from a definition of actual investment ($I \equiv O - C$) to an assumption about behaviour. The line $C + I_0$ therefore represents *planned* aggregate expenditure. Furthermore, the line $E = Y$ represents the equilibrium values of income and expenditure in that it locates all the points at which expenditure equals income. Now it is clear that aggregate expenditure ($C + I_0$) can exceed income because households and firms can finance expenditure by using savings and loans. When $C + I_0$ is greater than income, income will rise, and conversely, if $C + I_0$ is less than income, then income will fall. When $Y = C + I_0$, we thus have an equilibrium condition, and in Figure 1.13 this occurs at an income level Y^*. In this simple model, the equilibrium conditions are often presented in terms of withdrawals from the circular flow of income (i.e. saving) equalling injections into the flow (i.e. investment by firms). The dynamics of the *process* of achieving equilibrium involves introducing time explicitly into the model, but as this is not usually part of a first-year principles course we shall concentrate on establishing equilibrium conditions.

Once the hypotheses have been stated, we can analyse causes of movements in income levels and can determine equilibrium levels of Y. At the income level Y^* in Figure 1.13, aggregate expenditure equals income. More particularly, since this is an equilibrium level of Y, the amount I_0 that business units plan to invest must equal actual investment. This simple model can be expressed algebraically in the following way:

$$Y \equiv C + I \tag{1.22}$$

$$C = a + bY \quad (0 < b < 1) \tag{1.23}$$

and $$I = I_0 \tag{1.24}$$

Identity 1.22 is an accounting identity and is true for *all* values of Y and C (each pair of values of Y and C determining a value of I). Equation 1.23 is a hypothesis about the relationship between C and Y (i.e. it is the way we shall *assume* C and Y behave), and equation 1.24 fixes the level of planned investment at I_0. In simple terms, we are asking the question: Suppose the relationship between C and Y is assumed to be $C = a + bY$ and suppose the level of intended investment is held constant at I_0, then what will the equilibrium level of income Y^* be?

To try to answer this question, first put $I = I_0$ into identity 1.22. Then

$$Y = C + I_0$$

This now gives a specific relationship between Y and C. It is no longer true for all values of Y and C and is an equation and not an identity. In fact it is true only for the pairs of values of Y and C giving points along the line $Y = C + I_0$ as shown in Figure 1.13. (As an illustration of this, if we suppose $I_0 = £100$, then $Y = C + I_0$ holds for $C = £200$ and $Y = £300$ but it does not hold for $C = £200$ and $Y = £350$; however, $Y \equiv C + I$ is valid for $C = £200$ and $Y = £350$, for this *defines*

I to be £150.) The equilibrium level of income Y^* will occur when

$$Y^* = C^* + I_0 \qquad (1.25)$$

where C^* denotes the equilibrium level of consumption. Secondly, we have assumed that $C = a + bY$, and therefore in equilibrium

$$C^* = a + bY^* \qquad (1.26)$$

Substitution of C^* from equation 1.26 into equation 1.25 gives

$$Y^* = a + bY^* + I_0$$

$$\therefore \qquad Y^* - bY^* = a + I_0$$

$$\therefore \qquad Y^*(1 - b) = a + I_0$$

$$\therefore \qquad Y^* = \frac{a + I_0}{1 - b} \qquad (1.27)$$

Thus the equilibrium level of income Y^* is as given by equation 1.27. Here we have the endogenous variable Y^* in terms of constants and the exogenous variable I_0, and it can be seen that changes in I_0 will *cause* changes in Y^*.

To find the equilibrium level of consumption C^*, equation 1.27 can be substituted into equation 1.26 to give

$$C^* = a + b\left(\frac{a + I_0}{1 - b}\right)$$

$$= a + \frac{ab + bI_0}{1 - b}$$

$$= \frac{a - ab + ab + bI_0}{1 - b}$$

$$\therefore \qquad C^* = \frac{a + bI_0}{1 - b} \qquad (1.28)$$

We have now found the equilibrium levels of C and Y compatible with planned investment I_0. These are at the intersections of the aggregate planned expenditure line and the $E = Y$ line in Figure 1.13.

The student will be familiar with the idea of equilibrium occurring where injections (planned investment) equal withdrawals (planned saving) from the stream of income. To finish this section, let us consider the relationship between saving and investment in the above theory of income determination. By definition $S \equiv I$, but in addition we have now hypothesised behaviour concerning consumption and investment. In equation 1.23 we assumed that what consumers plan to spend is a linear function of their income, and so we have implicitly said something about their intended saving because, by definition,

$$Y - C \equiv S$$

Our hypothesis about consumption can now be put into the above identity, giving

$$Y - (a + bY) = S \qquad (1.29)$$

Notice the equality sign and not the identity sign is used because we are now dealing with a hypothesis. From equation 1.29

$$Y - a - bY = S$$

$$\therefore \qquad S = -a + Y - bY$$

$$= -a + Y(1 - b)$$

We have now obtained saving as a linear function of income. We speak of *planned* saving because it is derived from our hypothesis about planned consumption. In equilibrium, therefore,

$$S^* = -a + Y^*(1 - b) \qquad (1.30)$$

where Y^* is the equilibrium income and S^* is the equilibrium level of S. But from equation 1.27

$$Y^* = \frac{a + I_0}{1 - b}$$

Substituting this into equation 1.30 gives

$$S^* = -a + \left(\frac{a + I_0}{1 - b}\right)(1 - b)$$

$$= -a + a + I_0$$

or $\qquad S^* = I_0$

Therefore, in equilibrium, planned saving equals planned investment (injections equal withdrawals). At any value of Y other than Y^* this is not true. Remember we started by stating that, whilst Y and C ($C = a + bY$) could take on any pair of values [and therefore so could $S = -a + Y(1 - b)$], only one pair of values of Y and C is compatible with a given level of planned investment.

To conclude, *only* in equilibrium are planned investment and planned saving equal. At *any* level of income $S \equiv I$, but in definitions such as this we are *not* looking at saving and investment as hypotheses. This change in the meaning of the terms that necessarily occurs when we

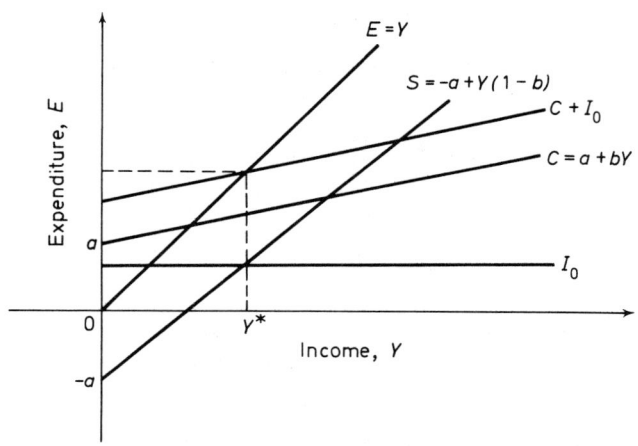

Figure 1.14

move from definitions to a theory caused a major controversy among economists that lasted many years. Everything said above is contained explicitly and implicitly in Figure 1.14, which should be a familiar diagram to students.

Example

Suppose we have the system given by the equations

$$Y = C + I_0 \qquad (1.31)$$

$$C = 10 + 0.8Y \qquad (1.32)$$

and $\qquad I = I_0 = 100 \qquad (1.33)$

Equation 1.31 states that, in equilibrium, aggregate expenditure equals income. We know from equations 1.27, 1.28, and 1.30 that the equilibrium values of Y, C, and S are given by the equations

$$Y* = \frac{a + I_0}{1 - b}$$

$$C* = \frac{a + bI_0}{1 - b}$$

and
$$S* = -a + Y*(1 - b)$$

Numerical values can be obtained by substitution. From equations 1.32 and 1.33, $a = 10$, $b = 0.8$, and $I_0 = 100$, so

$$Y* = \frac{10 + 100}{1 - 0.8} = 550$$

$$C* = \frac{10 + 0.8(100)}{1 - 0.8} = 450$$

and
$$S* = -10 + 550(1 - 0.8) = 100$$

We have shown that, in equilibrium, planned saving equals planned investment, and in our example have found that

$$S* = I_0 = 100$$

If Y had any other value, then $S* \neq I_0$. Consider the case of $Y = 1000$, for example. Then

$$C = 10 + 0.8(1000)$$

$$= 810$$

But we are given that $I_0 = 100$, so

$$C + I_0 = 810 + 100$$

$$= 910$$

But we have assumed $Y = 1000$ (not $Y = 910$). Thus, at an income of $Y = 1000$, Y is *not* equal to $C + I_0$, and if we check the level of planned saving at $Y = 1000$ we obtain

$$S = -a + Y(1 - b)$$

$$= -10 + 1000(1 - 0.8)$$

$$= 190$$

$$\therefore \qquad S \neq I_0$$

Thus only at $Y = 550$ will $S* = I_0$, a necessary and sufficient condition for equilibrium.

Chapter 2

DIFFERENTIATION

SLOPES OF STRAIGHT LINES

Suppose we consider the relationship between consumption expenditure and disposable income as embodied in the consumption function of the simple Keynesian model of income determination. The specific form of the function is usually given as

$$C = a + bY$$

where C = consumption expenditure,

        Y = disposable national income, and

        a and b are constants.

Thus we are discussing a function that can be shown graphically as a straight line (see, for example, the line representing the consumption function f_1 in Figure 2.1). We can see from this graph that, as income increases, consumption expenditure increases.

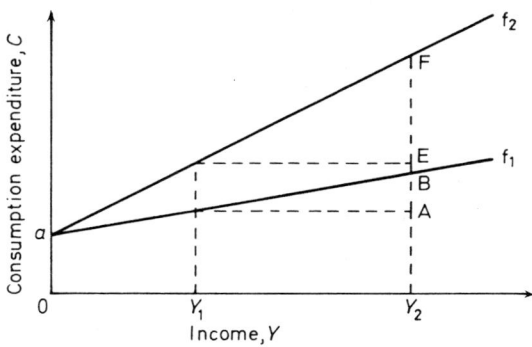

Figure 2.1

Consider, next, another consumption function f_2 drawn on the same axes as f_1. Both these consumption functions have the same fixed level of consumption expenditure a for zero income (this is sometimes

39

referred to as the autonomous consumption expenditure because it is not related to income). On the other hand, is there any difference between the two functions? A person knowing no mathematics and being faced with this question would probably say that f_2 has a steeper slope than f_1, and he would be correct. More formally, he means that, if if we consider the same increase in income for both functions, consumption expenditure rises more in the case of f_2 than in the case of f_1. To show this more clearly, let us take a basic income level Y_1 and then suppose income increases to Y_2. The corresponding increases in consumption expenditure can be read from the graph. For f_1 the increase in consumption expenditure is represented by the length of the line AB, whilst for f_2 it is represented by the length of the line EF. It is easily seen that EF is longer than AB, and so consumption expenditure for f_2 has increased more than for f_1.

Let us now consider this same situation more mathematically. We have already seen that the equation of a straight line is given in general terms by

$$y = a + bx$$

In the economic example above, C (consumption expenditure) is being plotted against Y (income), instead of y against x. Since both f_1 and f_2 pass through the same point a on the consumption expenditure axis, the equation of f_1 may be written as

$$C = a + b_1 Y$$

and of f_2 as

$$C = a + b_2 Y$$

where a, b_1, and b_2 are constants. The only difference between the two equations is in the terms b_1 and b_2, and it can be shown that these represent the slopes of the lines.

Consider, first, an increase in income from Y_1 to Y_2. For f_1

$$\text{when } Y = Y_1, \quad C = a + b_1 Y_1$$

and

$$\text{when } Y = Y_2, \quad C = a + b_1 Y_2$$

Then

The change in C = (value of C when $Y = Y_2$) − (value of C when $Y = Y_1$)

$$= (a + b_1 Y_2) - (a + b_1 Y_1)$$
$$= a + b_1 Y_2 - a - b_1 Y_1$$
$$= b_1 Y_2 - b_1 Y_1$$
$$= b_1 (Y_2 - Y_1)$$

Similarly, we can carry out this operation for f_2:

$$\text{when } Y = Y_1, \quad C = a + b_2 Y_1$$

and $$\text{when } Y = Y_2, \quad C = a + b_2 Y_2$$

Then

$$
\begin{aligned}
\text{The change in } C &= (a + b_2 Y_2) - (a + b_2 Y_1) \\
&= a + b_2 Y_2 - a - b_2 Y_1 \\
&= b_2 Y_2 - b_2 Y_1 \\
&= b_2 (Y_2 - Y_1)
\end{aligned}
$$

Now, referring back to Figure 2.1, the change in C for f_1 is given by

$$\text{AB} = b_1 (Y_2 - Y_1)$$

and the change in C for f_2 is given by

$$\text{EF} = b_2 (Y_2 - Y_1)$$

But we have seen from the graphs that

$$\text{EF} > \text{AB}$$

$$\therefore \qquad b_2 (Y_2 - Y_1) > b_1 (Y_2 - Y_1)$$

$$\therefore \qquad b_2 (Y_2 - Y_1) - b_1 (Y_2 - Y_1) > 0$$

$$\therefore \qquad (b_2 - b_1)(Y_2 - Y_1) > 0$$

Then, since $Y_2 - Y_1 > 0$, we must have $b_2 - b_1 > 0$ if the above inequality is to be true. But $b_2 - b_1 > 0$ only if $b_2 > b_1$. Thus we have shown that, the steeper the slope of the straight line, the greater the value of the term b in the equation $C = a + bY$.

To save writing 'the change in C' every time it is needed, we can abbreviate this to ΔC (pronounced 'delta C'). Thus for f_1

$$\Delta C = b_1 (Y_2 - Y_1)$$

and for f_2 $$\Delta C = b_2 (Y_2 - Y_1)$$

Similarly, we can write 'the change in Y' as ΔY (delta Y). For both f_1 and f_2

$$\Delta Y = Y_2 - Y_1$$

Using this notation we can therefore write, for f_1

$$\Delta C = b_1(\Delta Y) \tag{2.1}$$

and for f_2 $$\Delta C = b_2(\Delta Y) \tag{2.2}$$

Let us now examine the rate at which C changes as Y changes, which is another way of considering the slope of the consumption function. This rate of change is given by the ratio

$$\frac{\text{The change in } C \text{ due to a given change in } Y}{\text{The given change in } Y}$$

which in our new notation can be written as $\Delta C/\Delta Y$. Therefore for f_1, from equation 2.1,

$$\frac{\Delta C}{\Delta Y} = \frac{b_1(\Delta Y)}{\Delta Y} = b_1$$

and for f_2, from equation 2.2,

$$\frac{\Delta C}{\Delta Y} = \frac{b_2(\Delta Y)}{\Delta Y} = b_2$$

It is important to notice that for f_1 and f_2 the ratio $\Delta C/\Delta Y$ will equal b_1 and b_2 respectively, no matter what values are given to Y_1, Y_2, and ΔY (providing Y_2 is not equal to Y_1, in which case we would be trying to divide by zero). Thus the constants b_1 and b_2 are the slopes of the functions f_1 and f_2 respectively.

In mathematics, the terms b_1 and b_2 are often called the *gradients* of the linear functions f_1 and f_2: here we have shown that the gradient of a straight line is the same at every point along the line and that, the greater the gradient of the line, the greater the value of b. As a matter of interest, in the model of income determination, b represents the marginal propensity to consume (the rate of change of consumption expenditure given a change in income, which in simple linear models is therefore constant over all income levels).

GRADIENTS OF CURVES

Unfortunately, not all of the functions we shall meet can be represented by straight lines. We shall therefore see what can be established about the rate of change of consumption expenditure with respect to income when the graph of C against Y is a curve. In Figure 2.2 let the initial income level again be Y_1 and suppose it is increased to Y_2. Since we are not assuming an equation for C, suppose that, when income equals Y_1, consumption expenditure equals C_1 and, when income equals Y_2, consumption expenditure equals C_2. In Figure 2.2, we are also

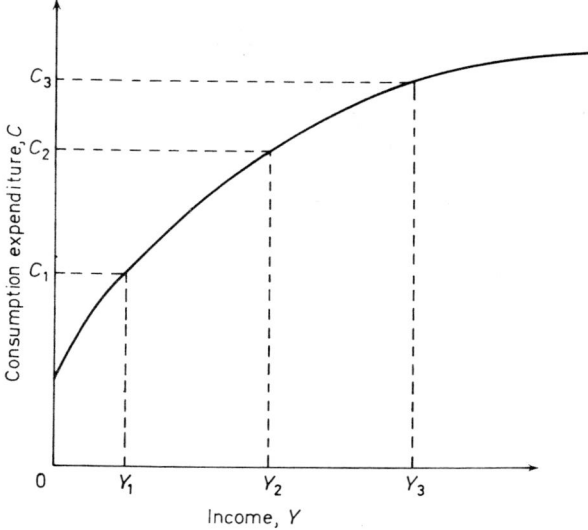

Figure 2.2

assuming a second increase in income from Y_2 to Y_3 that is equal to the increase in income from Y_1 to Y_2. But note carefully that the corresponding increase in consumption (from C_2 to C_3) is less than the increase from C_1 to C_2, i.e.

$$C_3 - C_2 < C_2 - C_1$$

Thus we can see that the rate at which C changes as Y changes is not the same for all parts of this curve. This leads to a general proposition that, with certain exceptions which do not concern us at present, a curve has different gradients at different points so, *whenever we talk about the gradient of a curve, it is essential to indicate the point at which this gradient is taken.*

The rest of this section is concerned with finding the gradient of the curve for the particular value Y_1 in Figure 2.2. This curve is repeated in Figure 2.3 for convenience.

In the case of a straight line we found that the gradient, represented by $\Delta C/\Delta Y$, was constant for all values of ΔY. However, in the curve shown in Figure 2.3 this is no longer true for, if ΔY is doubled [i.e.

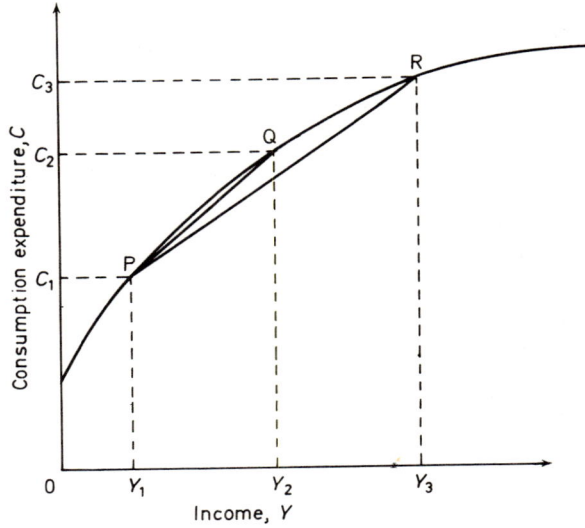

Figure 2.3

income is increased to a new value Y_3 such that $Y_3 - Y_1 = 2(Y_2 - Y_1)$], then ΔC does *not* double [i.e. $C_3 - C_1 \neq 2(C_2 - C_1)$]. The reason for this changing value of $\Delta C/\Delta Y$ is easy to see from Figure 2.3. Here, the ratio

$$\frac{C_2 - C_1}{Y_2 - Y_1}$$

represents the gradient of the *straight line* PQ. Similarly, the ratio

$$\frac{C_3 - C_1}{Y_3 - Y_1}$$

represents the gradient of the *straight line* PR. Obviously then, when we refer to the ratio $\Delta C/\Delta Y$ between the income levels Y_1 and Y_2, we are acting as though the curve between P and Q were a straight line; and similarly, between Y_1 and Y_3, as though the curve between P and R were a straight line. But as can be seen from Figure 2.3, the straight lines PQ and PR have different gradients and neither of them represents the curve as it actually is.

However, it can also be seen that the straight line PQ is closer to the curve between P and Q than is the straight line PR to the curve between P and R; and ΔY between P and Q is less than ΔY between P and R. Therefore, if we wish to find the gradient of the curve exactly at P, we should continue to make ΔY as small as possible and find the value of $\Delta C/\Delta Y$ for this small value of ΔY. In principle, the smallest value of ΔY would of course be zero, but we cannot divide by zero. To overcome this problem we calculate the value of $\Delta C/\Delta Y$ when ΔY *tends to zero* (written $\Delta Y \to 0$). This means we calculate the ratio $\Delta C/\Delta Y$ as ΔY gets smaller and smaller, and *approaches zero.* To indicate that we have performed this operation of letting ΔY tend to zero, we denote the gradient by dC/dY. Thus we have defined

$$\frac{dC}{dY} = \underset{\Delta Y \to 0}{\text{Limit}} \frac{\Delta C}{\Delta Y} \tag{2.3}$$

The process of determining dC/dY is called *differentiation*, and the result is known as the *derivative*. In our particular example, the derivative at P is the rate of change of consumption expenditure with respect to income *at the income level* Y_1.

Let us consider this limiting process graphically by examining Figure 2.4. The points P and P_n corresponding to the income levels Y_1

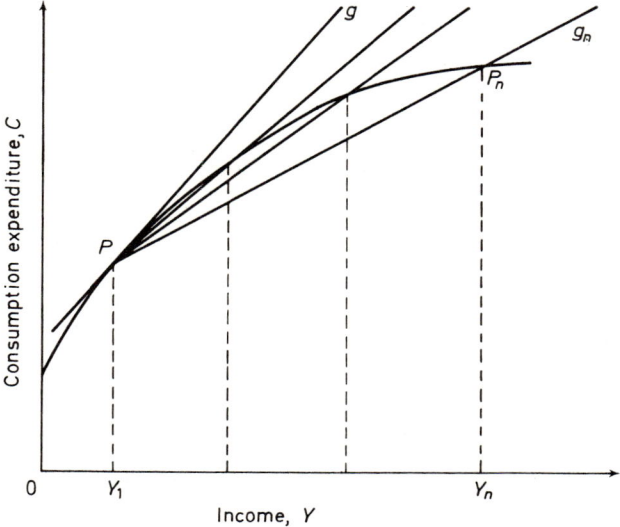

Figure 2.4

and Y_n are shown on the consumption curve. The straight line joining P and P_n has been drawn in and its gradient denoted by g_n. Thus for $\Delta Y = Y_n - Y_1$, the ratio $\Delta C/\Delta Y = g_n$. Now suppose the point Y_n approached nearer and nearer to Y_1, then ΔY would become smaller and smaller, eventually approaching zero. The line g would then appear not to cut the consumption curve but just to touch it at P. The gradient of the curve for the income level Y_1 can therefore be defined as the gradient of the straight line that just touches the curve at P. Such a line is called a *tangent*.

INCREASING AND DECREASING FUNCTIONS

A consumption function is an example of an *increasing function* since *C increases* when *Y* increases; *C* is said to be an increasing function of *Y* (see Figure 2.5a). The gradient at Y_1 on the consumption function shown is given by

$$\frac{dC}{dY} = \underset{\Delta Y \to 0}{\text{Limit}} \frac{\Delta C}{\Delta Y} = \underset{Y_2 \to Y_1}{\text{Limit}} \left(\frac{C_2 - C_1}{Y_2 - Y_1} \right)$$

and this will be positive because C_2 is greater than C_1 and Y_2 is greater than Y_1. It can be seen that, in general, the gradient of an increasing function is positive.

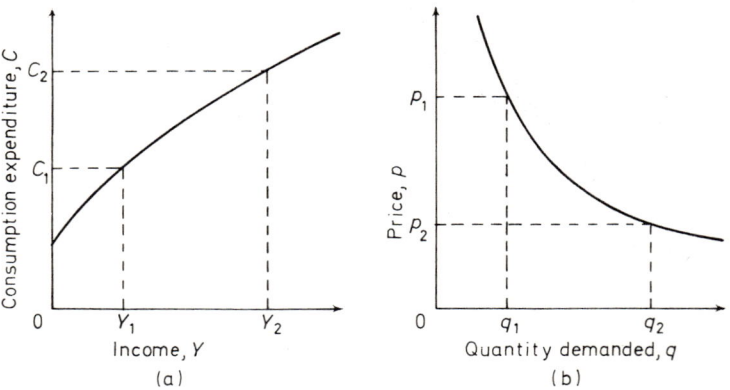

Figure 2.5

A demand function is an example of a *decreasing function* since price p *decreases* when the quantity demanded q increases; p is said to be a decreasing function of q (see Figure 2.5b). The gradient at q_1 on the demand function shown is given by

$$\frac{dp}{dq} = \underset{\Delta q \to 0}{\text{Limit}} \frac{\Delta p}{\Delta q} = \underset{q_2 \to q_1}{\text{Limit}} \left(\frac{p_2 - p_1}{q_2 - q_1} \right)$$

This result will be negative because, although q_2 is greater than q_1, p_2 is less than p_1. Again it can be seen that, in general, the gradient of a decreasing function is negative.

CALCULATING DERIVATIVES

Let us leave economic relationships for the moment and simply consider functional relationships in general. If we consider the function $y = f(x)$, we are stating that, as x changes, y changes. The derivative will give the rate at which y changes for a particular value of x, but we still have the problem of how to calculate dy/dx if given a specific functional form.

Example 1

Consider the function

$$y = x^2$$

Then the following method shows how dy/dx is derived.

Let x increase from x_1 to x_2 and let the resulting change in y be from y_1 to y_2. Thus

$$y_1 = x_1^2$$

and

$$y_2 = x_2^2$$

Then

$$\Delta x = x_2 - x_1$$

i.e.

$$x_2 = x_1 + \Delta x$$

and

$$\Delta y = y_2 - y_1$$

Hence
$$\frac{\Delta y}{\Delta x} = \frac{y_2 - y_1}{\Delta x}$$

$$= \frac{x_2^2 - x_1^2}{\Delta x}$$

$$= \frac{(x_1 + \Delta x)^2 - x_1^2}{\Delta x}$$

$$= \frac{x_1^2 + 2x_1(\Delta x) + (\Delta x)^2 - x_1^2}{\Delta x}$$

$$= \frac{2x_1(\Delta x) + (\Delta x)^2}{\Delta x}$$

$$= \frac{\Delta x(2x_1 + \Delta x)}{\Delta x}$$

Therefore, cancelling Δx,

$$\frac{\Delta y}{\Delta x} = 2x_1 + \Delta x$$

Then
$$\underset{\Delta x \to 0}{\text{Limit}} \frac{\Delta y}{\Delta x} = \underset{\Delta x \to 0}{\text{Limit}} (2x_1 + \Delta x) = 2x_1$$

Hence at x_1
$$\frac{dy}{dx} = 2x_1$$

We can therefore deduce that, if $y = x^2$, then for any value of x

$$\frac{dy}{dx} = 2x$$

Suppose, for example, that $x = 2$. Then

$$\frac{dy}{dx} = 2 \times 2 = 4$$

or, if $x = -5$,

$$\frac{dy}{dx} = 2(-5) = -10$$

Example 2

Let us now consider a different functional form, namely

$$y = \frac{1}{x} \tag{2.4}$$

and let x increase to $x + \Delta x$. Then the value of y becomes $1/(x + \Delta x)$ and

$$\frac{\Delta y}{\Delta x} = \frac{\dfrac{1}{x + \Delta x} - \dfrac{1}{x}}{\Delta x} = \left(\frac{1}{x + \Delta x} - \frac{1}{x} \right) \frac{1}{\Delta x}$$

Therefore, putting the terms in brackets over the common denominator $x(x + \Delta x)$,

$$\frac{\Delta y}{\Delta x} = \left[\frac{x - (x + \Delta x)}{x(x + \Delta x)} \right] \frac{1}{\Delta x}$$

$$= \frac{x - x - \Delta x}{x(x + \Delta x)(\Delta x)}$$

$$= \frac{-\Delta x}{x(x + \Delta x)(\Delta x)}$$

$$= \frac{-1}{x(x + \Delta x)}$$

$$= \frac{-1}{x^2 + x(\Delta x)}$$

Then

$$\underset{\Delta x \to 0}{\text{Limit}} \frac{\Delta y}{\Delta x} = \underset{\Delta x \to 0}{\text{Limit}} \left[\frac{-1}{x^2 - x(\Delta x)} \right] = -\frac{1}{x^2}$$

Hence

$$\frac{dy}{dx} = -\frac{1}{x^2} \qquad (2.5)$$

As an example, suppose $x = 4$. Then

$$\frac{dy}{dx} = -\frac{1}{4^2} = -\frac{1}{16}$$

or, if $x = 10$,

$$\frac{dy}{dx} = -\frac{1}{10^2} = -\frac{1}{100}$$

We could have written equation 2.4 as

$$y = x^{-1}$$

and equation 2.5 could similarly have been written as

$$\frac{dy}{dx} = -x^{-2}$$

Example 3

To find a general result we shall consider the function

$$y = x^n \qquad (2.6)$$

where n is a positive or negative whole number or fraction. This proof is unavoidably difficult but is included for completeness: any reader finding it too hard should move straight to the result (equation 2.7).

Let x increase to $x + \Delta x$, and therefore

$$\Delta y = (x + \Delta x)^n - x^n$$

It can be shown that, if we first write $(x + \Delta x)^n$ as

$$x^n \left(1 + \frac{\Delta x}{x}\right)^n$$

then

$$(x + \Delta x)^n = x^n \left[1 + \frac{n(\Delta x)}{x} + \frac{n(n-1)(\Delta x)^2}{2} \frac{1}{x^2} + \frac{n(n-1)(n-2)}{2 \times 3} \frac{(\Delta x)^3}{x^3} + \ldots \right]$$

This result is known as the *binomial expansion*. For example, if $n = 2$, the expansion becomes

$$(x + \Delta x)^2 = x^2 \left[1 + \frac{2(\Delta x)}{x} + \frac{2 \times 1}{2} \frac{(\Delta x)^2}{x^2}\right] = x^2 + 2x(\Delta x) + (\Delta x)^2$$

a result that should be well known.

Therefore, applying this binomial expansion, we obtain

$$\frac{\Delta y}{\Delta x} = \frac{(x + \Delta x)^n - x^n}{\Delta x}$$

$$= \frac{x^n \left[1 + \frac{n(\Delta x)}{x} + \frac{n(n-1)}{2} \frac{(\Delta x)^2}{x^2} + \frac{n(n-1)(n-2)}{2 \times 3} \frac{(\Delta x)^3}{x^3} + \ldots \right] - x^n}{\Delta x}$$

and multiplying all the terms inside the square brackets by x^n gives

$$\frac{\Delta y}{\Delta x} = \frac{\begin{array}{l}[x^n + n(\Delta x)x^{n-1} + [n(n-1)/2] (\Delta x)^2 x^{n-2} \\ \qquad + [n(n-1)(n-2)/2 \times 3] (\Delta x)^3 x^{n-3} + \ldots] - x^n\end{array}}{\Delta x}$$

$$= \frac{\begin{array}{l}n(\Delta x)x^{n-1} + [n(n-1)/2] (\Delta x)^2 x^{n-2} \\ \qquad + [n(n-1)(n-2)/2 \times 3] (\Delta x)^3 x^{n-3} + \ldots\end{array}}{\Delta x}$$

by subtracting the terms x^n. Taking out the common factor Δx from the terms on the top, and then cancelling Δx, gives

$$\frac{\Delta y}{\Delta x} = \frac{\Delta x [nx^{n-1} + [n(n-1)/2](\Delta x)x^{n-2} + [n(n-1)(n-2)/2 \times 3](\Delta x)^2 x^{n-3} + \ldots]}{\Delta x}$$

$$= nx^{n-1} + \frac{n(n-1)}{2}(\Delta x)x^{n-2} + \frac{n(n-1)(n-2)}{2 \times 3}(\Delta x)^2 x^{n-3}$$

$$+ \text{ terms containing some power of } \Delta x$$

Note now that every term except the first still contains a Δx. Therefore

$$\underset{\Delta x \to 0}{\text{Limit}} \frac{\Delta y}{\Delta x} = nx^{n-1} + 0 + 0 + \ldots$$

Hence

$$\frac{dy}{dx} = nx^{n-1} \tag{2.7}$$

This is the general result for differentiating a function of the form $y = x^n$.

Note that, if we put $n = 2$, we have the function $y = x^2$ and the derivative $dy/dx = 2x^1 = 2x$; similarly, if we put $n = -1$, then $y = x^{-1}$ and $dy/dx = -x^{-2}$. These are the results obtained in examples 1 and 2 above.

Example 4

The function $y = \sqrt{x}$ can be rewritten (see equation 1.10) as $y = x^{1/2}$ (i.e. $n = \frac{1}{2}$). Therefore, applying the general result obtained in equation 2.7, we get

$$\frac{dy}{dx} = \frac{1}{2}x^{(1/2)-1} = \frac{1}{2}x^{-1/2}$$

Hence

$$\frac{dy}{dx} = \frac{1}{2}\frac{1}{x^{1/2}} = \frac{1}{2\sqrt{x}}$$

Example 5

The function $y = x$ can be rewritten (see equation 1.6) as $y = x^1$ (i.e. $n = 1$). Applying equation 2.7 again,

$$\frac{dy}{dx} = 1x^{1-1} = x^0$$

But, from equation 1.7,

$$x^0 = 1$$

$\therefore$
$$\frac{dy}{dx} = 1$$

Example 6

The function $y = 1$ can be rewritten as $y = x^0$ (i.e. $n = 0$). Then from equation 2.7

$$\frac{dy}{dx} = 0x^{0-1} = 0$$

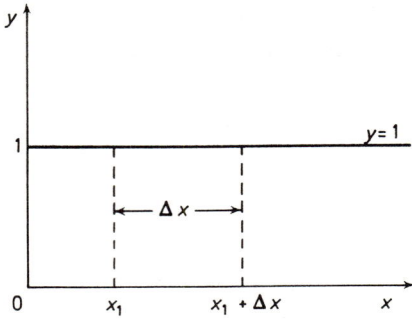

Figure 2.6

An alternative method of finding this last derivative is by considering Figure 2.6. It can be seen that

$$\text{when } x = x_1, \qquad y = 1$$

and
$$\text{when } x = x_1 + \Delta x, \ y = 1$$

Therefore
$$\frac{\Delta y}{\Delta x} = \frac{1-1}{\Delta x} = \frac{0}{\Delta x} = 0$$

Hence $\Delta y/\Delta x = 0$ for any value of Δx, and

$$\underset{\Delta x \to 0}{\text{Limit}} \frac{\Delta y}{\Delta x} = 0$$

∴
$$\frac{dy}{dx} = 0$$

NOTATION

For the function $y = f(x)$ we can denote the derivative by either

$$\frac{dy}{dx} \quad \text{or} \quad f'(x)$$

The latter notation is particularly useful for denoting the derivative for a specific value of x, say $x = a$. The derivative could be written as either

$$\left.\frac{dy}{dx}\right|_{x=a} \quad \text{or} \quad f'(a)$$

For example, if

$$f(x) = x^3$$

then the derivative of $f(x)$ is given by

$$f'(x) = 3x^2$$

If we required the value of this derivative at $x = 2$, we could write

$$f'(2) = 3(2^2) = 3 \times 4$$

i.e.
$$f'(2) = 12$$

Suppose now that $y = f(x)$ and let x increase to $x + \Delta x$. Then the new value of y will be $f(x + \Delta x)$ and

$$\frac{\Delta y}{\Delta x} = \frac{f(x + \Delta x) - f(x)}{\Delta x}$$

∴
$$\frac{dy}{dx} = \underset{\Delta x \to 0}{\text{Limit}}\left[\frac{f(x + \Delta x) - f(x)}{\Delta x}\right]$$

or
$$f'(x) = \underset{\Delta x \to 0}{\text{Limit}}\left[\frac{f(x + \Delta x) - f(x)}{\Delta x}\right]$$

DERIVATIVE OF A FUNCTION MULTIPLIED BY A CONSTANT

Suppose $y = cf(x)$ where c is a constant, and let x increase to $x + \Delta x$. Then the new value of y will be $cf(x + \Delta x)$ and

$$\frac{\Delta y}{\Delta x} = \frac{cf(x + \Delta x) - cf(x)}{\Delta x}$$

$$= c \left[\frac{f(x + \Delta x) - f(x)}{\Delta x} \right]$$

$\therefore$

$$\underset{\Delta x \to 0}{\text{Limit}} \frac{\Delta y}{\Delta x} = \underset{\Delta x \to 0}{\text{Limit}} \left\{ c \left[\frac{f(x + \Delta x) - f(x)}{\Delta x} \right] \right\}$$

$$= c \left\{ \underset{\Delta x \to 0}{\text{Limit}} \left[\frac{f(x + \Delta x) - f(x)}{\Delta x} \right] \right\}$$

$$= cf'(x)$$

Hence

$$\frac{dy}{dx} = cf'(x)$$

For example, if

$$y = 6x^4$$

then

$$\frac{dy}{dx} = 6(4x^3) = 24x^3$$

As another example, consider the function $y = c$, where c is any constant. This can be rewritten as

$$y = cf(x)$$

where $f(x) = 1$. But if $f(x) = 1$, we have already shown that $f'(x) = 0$. Therefore

$$\frac{dy}{dx} = c(0) = 0$$

Thus the derivative of any constant is zero.

DERIVATIVES OF SUMS OF FUNCTIONS

Suppose $y = f(x) + g(x)$ and let x increase to $x + \Delta x$. Then the new value of y will be $f(x + \Delta x) + g(x + \Delta x)$. Then

$$\frac{\Delta y}{\Delta x} = \frac{f(x + \Delta x) + g(x + \Delta x) - [f(x) + g(x)]}{\Delta x}$$

$$= \frac{f(x + \Delta x) + g(x + \Delta x) - f(x) - g(x)}{\Delta x}$$

$$= \frac{f(x + \Delta x) - f(x)}{\Delta x} + \frac{g(x + \Delta x) - g(x)}{\Delta x}$$

$$\therefore \ \underset{\Delta x \to 0}{\text{Limit}} \frac{\Delta y}{\Delta x} = \underset{\Delta x \to 0}{\text{Limit}} \left[\frac{f(x + \Delta x) - f(x)}{\Delta x} \right] + \underset{\Delta x \to 0}{\text{Limit}} \left[\frac{g(x + \Delta x) - g(x)}{\Delta x} \right]$$

or $\quad \dfrac{dy}{dx} = f'(x) + g'(x)$

This result can be extended to sums of any number of functions. For example, if

$$y = x^3 + 12x^2 - 6x + 2 + x^{-1} - 2x^{-2}$$

then $\quad \dfrac{dy}{dx} = 3x^2 + 12(2x) - 6(1) + 0 + (-1x^{-2}) - 2(-2x^{-3})$

$$= 3x^2 + 24x - 6 - x^{-2} + 4x^{-3}$$

THE APPLICATION OF THE DERIVATIVE IN ECONOMIC ANALYSIS

Without taking our study of calculus any further, we can apply the concept of a derivative to much of the analysis that appears in an elementary economics course. To do this, we must accept the assumption of such analysis that the functions dealt with are continuous. As a start, let us examine some of the features of demand curves that appear in most economics textbooks and use the derivative to explore the concept of price elasticity of demand and the related topics of total and marginal revenue. The reason for doing this is not only to show an alternative to the usual geometrical methods of analysis but also to provide a basis for more-sophisticated uses of calculus in areas in which geometrical methods are not only clumsy but, in some instances, unusable.

THE DEMAND CURVE

One of the most important functional relationships in economic theory is embodied in the concept of the demand curve. Many factors influence the demand for a commodity, such as income per head, tastes of consumers, and prices of substitutes. In price theory our attention is concentrated on the relationship between the price p and the quantity q demanded per time period, while other factors are assumed to be held constant (income per head, tastes, etc., are treated as exogenous variables). The usual diagrammatic presentation of the demand curve is of the type shown in Figure 2.7.

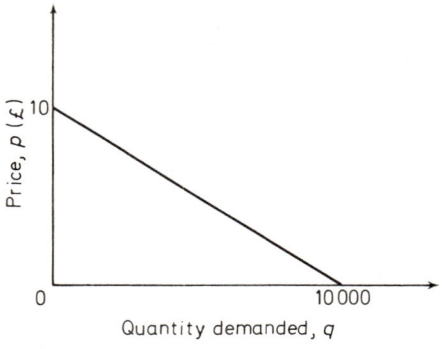

Figure 2.7

The equation for a linear demand curve could be written as

$$p = a - bq \tag{2.8}$$

i.e. $p = f(q)$, or as

$$q = \frac{p-a}{-b} \tag{2.9}$$

i.e. $q = g(p)$; in both equations, p and q are variables and a and b are constants. Algebraically equations 2.8 and 2.9 are two ways of expressing the same relationship, but mathematically and economically they imply two different relationships. For example, if we state that

$$p = f(q)$$

we are implying that q is the independent variable and that, if q changes, p changes. This is true in the case of a monopolist who, faced with a downward-sloping demand curve, adjusts the quantity supplied (which in turn affects the quantity demanded) in order to maximise profits. However, in the case of a perfectly competitive industry, the quantity demanded increases if the price falls and contracts if the price rises; therefore p is the independent variable and we write

$$q = g(p)$$

Thus, if we speak of quantity demanded responding to changes in price, we are referring to a perfectly competitive market or to a monopolist adjusting price whereas, if we speak of price changing with respect to changes in quantity supplied, we are referring to a monopolist (or oligopolist) adjusting output.

Here, explicit reference must be made to a point that is a cause of some confusion when dealing with economic theory. It is *implicit* in demand and supply models that the output put on the market by firms is sold. Thus in a competitive market where, at the prevailing price, there is excess supply, firms reduce prices and current output. As price falls, demand expands and supply (current output) contracts. In the case of the monopolist referred to above, the firm puts an amount of output on the market and the prevailing demand conditions determine the price. Hence $p = f(q)$, and q means in this context the amount put on the market, which, it is assumed, will be demanded if the firm allows the demand conditions to determine the price. We are still using q to mean the quantity demanded, that is, the amount that consumers plan to buy at any particular price.

The situation is further confused because, even when economists are referring to the demand curve facing a perfectly competitive industry, so that $q = g(p)$, they draw a demand curve as in Figure 2.7 in which quantity q demanded per time period (the dependent variable) is on the horizontal axis whilst price p (the independent variable) is on the vertical axis; this is the reverse of the mathematical convention of putting the independent variable on the horizontal axis.

Consider now the particular demand curve shown in Figure 2.7. This can be represented by equation 2.8:

$$p = a - bq$$

It can be seen that, for this demand curve, the quantity of the commodity demanded is zero when the price is £10. Therefore substituting the values $q = 0$ when $p = 10$ into equation 2.8 gives

$$10 = a - b(0)$$

∴ $$a = 10 \qquad\qquad (2.10)$$

Thus, as we established in Chapter 1, a corresponds to the intercept on the vertical axis.

It can also be seen from Figure 2.7 that, when the price of the commodity is reduced, the quantity demanded increases. The rate at which demand will increase as price is reduced is determined by the value of $-b$, the slope of the demand curve. If we use the 'delta' notation introduced earlier in this chapter, then we can say that the slope is equal to the change in price (Δp) divided by the resulting change in quantity demanded (Δq), i.e.

$$-b = \frac{\Delta p}{\Delta q}$$

For a linear demand function the slope is of course constant (see page 42). Note that b itself is a positive number: the minus sign in front of it indicates that quantity demanded is a decreasing function of price.

THE RESPONSIVENESS OF DEMAND TO PRICE CHANGES

A demand curve such as that in Figure 2.7 may be the demand curve for the product of an individual firm or for the output of a number of firms. For the moment let us suppose it is the demand curve for the product of an individual firm, for example a monopolist. If the firm cuts the price of the product, it will receive less per unit sold but it will sell more. Conversely, if it raises the price, it will receive more per unit sold but it will sell fewer units. Both in economic theory and in applied studies of markets we are often interested in the sensitivity of demand to price changes, and consequently we must examine some of the problems that arise in measuring such responses. It will be useful if we use the demand curve shown in Figure 2.7, putting in the values of a and b so that we can use numerical examples to demonstrate the points we wish to emphasise. For a monopolist adjusting output, we assume the demand curve has the general form given by equation 2.8:

$$p = a - bq$$

We know from equation 2.10 that $a = 10$ and, from Figure 2.7, that $p = 0$ when $q = 10\ 000$. The value of b can therefore easily be obtained by substitution into equation 2.8:

$$p = 10 - bq$$

∴ $$0 = 10 - b(10\ 000)$$

∴ $$10\ 000b = 10$$

∴ $$b = \frac{10}{10\ 000}$$

$$= 0.001$$

Thus $$p = 10 - 0.001q \qquad (2.11)$$

We now have some quantitative information about the relationship between price and quantity demanded per time period. If the price were £8, for example, then the quantity demanded can be found by substituting $p = 8$ into equation 2.11, as follows:

$$8 = 10 - 0.001q$$

∴ $$0.001q = 10 - 8$$

∴ $$q = \frac{2}{0.001}$$

∴ $$q = 2000 \qquad (2.12)$$

Similarly, if the price were put up to £9, then the quantity demanded could be found by substituting $p = 9$ into equation 2.11:

$$9 = 10 - 0.001q$$

∴ $$q = \frac{10 - 9}{0.001}$$

or $$q = 1000$$

Thus the quantity demanded per time period has declined from 2000 units to 1000 units. Therefore, given the demand conditions represented by Figure 2.7, raising the price from £8 to £9 would cause a contraction in demand of 1000 units per time period. We could describe this situation by saying that the sensitivity of demand to a change in price from £8 to £9 is 1000 units/£ (i.e. in terms of quantity units per money unit). However, such a method of measuring the response of demand to price changes would make it difficult to compare demand conditions in different markets. For example, if we wished to compare the sensitivity of demand to price changes in the markets for potatoes and petrol in the United Kingdom, we would have two quantity units. Similarly, if we wished to compare the responsiveness of demand to price changes of milk in the Argentine and Britain, we would have two quantity units and two currency units. If the responsiveness in Britain were quoted in gallons per pound and that in the Argentine in litres per dollar, we could not easily compare the two cases: what could one make of the statement that the responsiveness of demand to price changes was 2 pints/£ in Britain and 0.3 litres/$ in the Argentine? Because of this difficulty economists use a measurement that is independent of any units and this is called an *elasticity*. Note that elasticity is dimensionless (see page 24).

PRICE ELASTICITY OF DEMAND

There are various kinds of elasticities, depending on the relationships under examination. We shall examine further the relationship between price changes and the response in terms of quantity demanded. This response is termed *price elasticity of demand* and can be denoted by the Greek letter η (eta). Price elasticity of demand is defined as

$$\eta = -\frac{dq}{dp}\left(\frac{p}{q}\right) \tag{2.13}$$

where dq/dp is the derivative of quantity demanded with respect to price, p is the price at which the elasticity is being measured, and q is the quantity demanded at that price.

Note that the demand function represented by equation 2.11 gives p in terms of q, i.e.

$$p = 10 - 0.001q$$

If we differentiate this with respect to q, we shall obtain dp/dq, but for our definition of elasticity we need dq/dp. Therefore it is useful to rearrange equation 2.11 as follows:

$$0.001q = 10 - p$$

$$\therefore \quad q = \frac{10}{0.001} - \frac{p}{0.001}$$

$$\therefore \quad \frac{dq}{dp} = \frac{-1}{0.001} \qquad (2.14)$$

Now suppose we wish to find the price elasticity of demand when the price is £8. Then, from equation 2.13,

$$\eta = -\left(\frac{-1}{0.001}\right)\left(\frac{8}{q}\right) \qquad (2.15)$$

Also, from equation 2.12 above, we have already shown that, when the price is £8, the quantity demanded is 2000. Therefore we can substitute $q = 2000$ into equation 2.15 to give

$$\eta = -\left(\frac{-1}{0.001}\right)\left(\frac{8}{2000}\right) = \frac{8}{2} = 4$$

Hence the price elasticity of demand when the price is £8 is 4. The significance of 4 as a measure of elasticity we shall consider later, but for the moment we shall examine closer the formula for η.

The general statement of the relationship between the price of a commodity and the quantity demanded is that $p = f(q)$, and a further assertion of economic theory is that demand curves slope downwards to the right (with price on the vertical axis and quantity demanded on the horizontal). This means that price is a decreasing function of output and, in the case of a linear demand curve, the slope of the function is constant and negative. Consequently, dq/dp is constant no matter what the value of p, and in addition it is negative. However, the minus sign in front of dq/dp cancels out the negative with the result that η is positive. For instance, in the above example

$$\frac{dq}{dp} = \frac{-1}{0.001}$$

but the value of η is positive.

Again in the case of the linear demand curve that is common in elementary theory, each price has a unique value of η associated with it. The definition of η contains two terms: dq/dp (which is constant for a

linear function), and p/q. Obviously p and q will change as η is
measured at different prices, and so the value of η will be different for
each price (we shall come to the example of a constant-elasticity curve
later). Furthermore, not only will η vary depending on the price, but its
value will range from $\eta = 0$ at $p = 0$ to $\eta = \infty$ (infinity) at $p = a$ (where a
is the intercept on the price axis). Using the demand curve $p = 10 - 0.001q$,
we can easily demonstrate this proposition. First, let us calculate the
value of η at $p = 0$. It is obvious from Figure 2.7 that, when $p = 0$,
$q = 10\,000$. Therefore substituting for p, q, and $\mathrm{d}q/\mathrm{d}p$ in equation 2.13
gives

$$\eta = -\left(\frac{-1}{0.001}\right)\left(\frac{0}{10\,000}\right) = 0$$

Notice that η must be zero in this case as the second term has a zero
in the numerator. Consider now the value of η when the price is £10.
From Figure 2.7 it is again obvious that, when $p = 10$, $q = 0$, so
substituting into equation 2.13 gives

$$\eta = -\left(\frac{-1}{0.001}\right)\left(\frac{10}{0}\right)$$

The usual convention in mathematics is that division by zero gives
infinity. Therefore, at $p = 10$, $\eta = \infty$. The price £10 here is the intercept
of the demand curve on the price axis, and we can see that, in general,
$\eta = \infty$ at $p = a$ where a is the intercept on the price axis. It can also be
seen that, as the price increases from $p = 0$ to $p = a$, the value of η also
increases.

CONSTANT-ELASTICITY CURVE

The definition of price elasticity of demand given above can be used to
calculate η for both linear and non-linear demand curves, and is sometimes referred to as point elasticity of demand to emphasise that
elasticity is being measured at a particular price. One constant-elasticity
curve referred to in many textbooks is the non-linear demand function
which has the property that, no matter what change in price takes place,
the total amount spent on the commodity (i.e. total revenue, which is
equal to pq) is constant. This results in a value of $\eta = 1$ at all prices
($\eta = 1$ is known as unit elasticity). Graphically such a function appears

as a rectangular hyperbola, and the area representing total revenue is the same no matter what the price is. In Figure 2.8, for example, the area of the rectangle OP_1SQ_1 is equal to the area of the rectangle OP_2TQ_2, representing a constant total revenue.

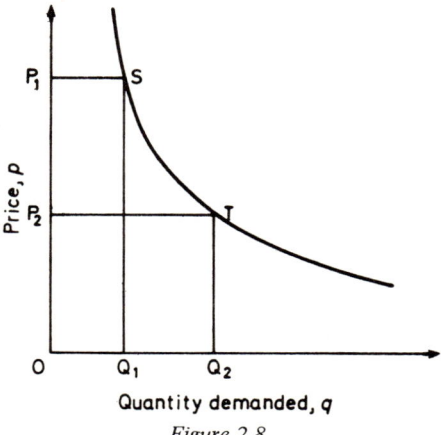

Figure 2.8

Consider now the following demand function in which total revenue always equals 6000, i.e.

$$pq = 6000$$

$$\therefore \quad q = \frac{6000}{p}$$

$$= 6000p^{-1}$$

$$\therefore \quad \frac{dq}{dp} = -6000p^{-2}$$

$$= \frac{-6000}{p^2}$$

Substituting this value into equation 2.13 gives

$$\eta = -\frac{dq}{dp}\left(\frac{p}{q}\right)$$

$$= \frac{6000}{p^2}\left(\frac{p}{q}\right)$$

$$= \frac{6000}{pq}$$

But $pq = 6000$ and therefore

$$\eta = \frac{6000}{6000} = 1$$

Thus $\eta = 1$ at any price p.

PRICE ELASTICITY OF DEMAND AND TOTAL REVENUE

If a firm is considering cutting the price of its product, it would like to know if its total sales revenue will rise or fall. Equally, if it is considering a price increase, it would like the same information. Assuming that quantity demanded is a decreasing function of price, then a price reduction would result in less revenue being received per unit sold but more would be sold. The increase in the firm's sales might be such that its total revenue was increased: this situation could be described by stating that the proportionate increase in demand exceeded the proportionate change in price. Conversely, it might happen that a price reduction is accompanied by an increase in the number of units sold that is insufficient to make up the loss of revenue per unit, with the result that total revenue falls: in such a case the proportionate change in price is greater than the proportionate change in quantity demanded. Lastly, a reduction in price per unit may be accompanied by an increase in demand that just offsets the loss of revenue per unit and so total revenue is unchanged. The above possible effects on total revenue can also be considered with respect to a price increase.

The relationship between total revenue and price elasticity of demand now becomes clear. We have defined price elasticity of demand as

$$\eta = -\frac{dq}{dp}\left(\frac{p}{q}\right)$$

This can be rearranged to give

$$\eta = -\frac{dq/q}{dp/p}$$

$$= -\frac{\text{The proportionate change in quantity demanded}}{\text{The proportionate change in price}}$$

It can be seen that, at any particular value of p, if the proportionate change in quantity demanded is numerically greater than the proportionate change in price then $\eta > 1$. In such a case we speak of demand being *elastic* with regard to price. Conversely, if the proportionate change in price is numerically greater than the proportionate change in quantity demanded, then $\eta < 1$ and demand is said to be *inelastic* with regard to price. Finally, if the proportionate change in quantity demanded is numerically equal to the proportionate change in price, then $\eta = 1$ and we speak of *unit elasticity*, which is the dividing line between the elastic and inelastic parts of the demand curve.

If $\eta > 1$ at some price p, then a price decrease will increase the total revenue whilst a price increase will decrease the total revenue. If $\eta < 1$, a price increase will increase the total revenue whilst a price decrease will decrease the total revenue. But if $\eta = 1$, then a price increase or decrease will leave the total revenue unchanged. Note also that, the nearer η becomes to zero, the less sensitive is demand to changes in price.

MARGINAL REVENUE

Total revenue (which will be denoted by R_T) is the result of selling q units at price p, and so we can write

$$R_T = pq$$

For a linear demand function,

$$p = a - bq \tag{2.16}$$

where a and b are constants. Therefore

$$R_T = (a - bq)q$$

i.e.
$$R_T = aq - bq^2 \tag{2.17}$$

Thus total revenue is expressed as a function of quantity demanded, whereas we had it originally in terms of both price and quantity demanded.

Now marginal revenue is described as the addition to total revenue if sales are increased by an infinitesimally small amount, or the decrease in total revenue if sales are decreased by an infinitesimally small amount. Assuming the total-revenue function $(aq - bq^2)$ is continuous, we can restate marginal revenue R_M as the derivative of total revenue with respect to quantity demanded, i.e.

$$R_M = \frac{dR_T}{dq}$$

Therefore, in order to derive the marginal-revenue function, we must differentiate equation 2.17 with respect to q:

$$R_T = aq - bq^2$$

∴

$$\frac{dR_T}{dq} = a - 2bq$$

i.e.

$$R_M = a - 2bq \qquad (2.18)$$

Note carefully that the slope of the linear demand curve (equation 2.16) is $-b$, whereas that of the marginal-revenue curve (equation 2.18) is $-2b$. This leads to the basic proposition that, *when a demand curve is linear, the marginal-revenue curve slopes at twice the rate of the demand curve.* Note also that the linear demand curve and the marginal-revenue curve have the same intercept a on the vertical axis.

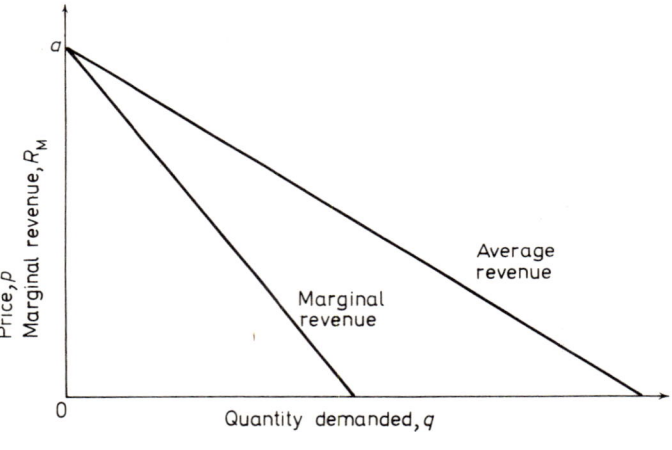

Figure 2.9

As total revenue $R_T = pq$, then average revenue R_A is defined as

$$R_A = \frac{R_T}{q} = \frac{pq}{q} = p$$

For this reason the demand curve is also known as the average-revenue curve. The usual diagrammatic presentation of the average-revenue and marginal-revenue curves is shown in Figure 2.9. If we again use our familiar linear demand function

$$p = 10 - 0.001q$$

we can more easily appreciate the relationships between the average-revenue and marginal-revenue curves (see Figure 2.10).

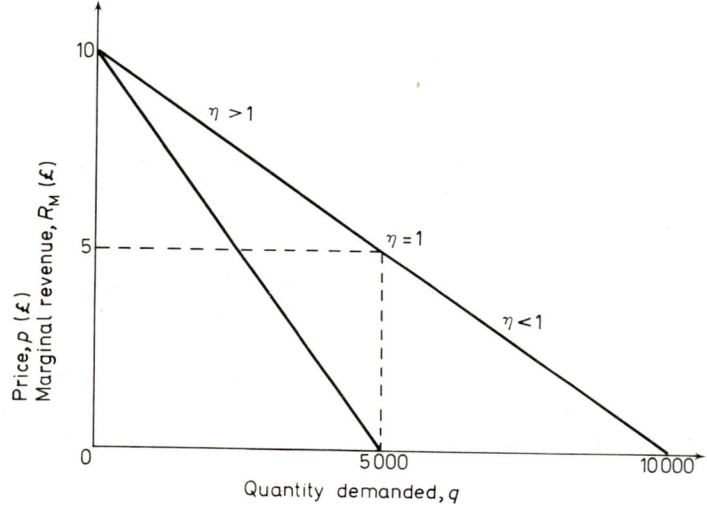

Figure 2.10

Since $p = 10 - 0.001q$, the total revenue is given by

$$R_T = pq$$

$$= (10 - 0.001q)q$$

$$= 10q - 0.001q^2$$

and therefore marginal revenue is given by

$$R_M = \frac{dR_T}{dq}$$

i.e.
$$R_M = 10 - 0.002q \qquad (2.19)$$

Again we can see that the marginal-revenue curve slopes at twice the rate of the average-revenue curve; but at what level of demand will the marginal revenue be zero? In order to find this level, $R_M = 0$ is substituted into equation 2.19 and the equation solved for q. Thus

$$0 = 10 - 0.002q$$

$\therefore$
$$0.002q = 10$$

$\therefore$
$$q = \frac{10}{0.002}$$

$$= 5000$$

Therefore marginal revenue is zero when the quantity demanded per time period is 5000: this point is halfway along the horizontal axis between $q = 0$ and $q = 10\,000$ (the point at which average revenue is zero).

When marginal revenue is zero, the associated price is that at which $\eta = 1$. This is because marginal revenue is the change in total revenue given an infinitesimally small change in demand, and this change in demand will occur if there is an infinitesimally small change in price. If $R_M = 0$ at a demand level of 5000 per time period, then we can find the price associated with this level of demand by substituting $q = 5000$ into the demand function

$$p = 10 - 0.001q$$

$\therefore$
$$p = 10 - 0.001\,(5000)$$

$$= 5$$

Thus, when the price is £5, an infinitesimally small change in this price will leave total revenue unchanged, i.e. $\eta = 1$. At prices greater than £5 then $\eta > 1$, and at prices less than £5 then $\eta < 1$.

CONSTANT-ELASTICITY CURVE AND MARGINAL REVENUE

In the case of linear demand curves, textbooks contain a familiar diagram showing a downward-sloping demand curve and a marginal-revenue curve sloping at twice the rate of the average-revenue curve. In the case of the non-linear demand curve with a constant unit elasticity there is no accompanying marginal-revenue curve. This is because such a curve represents a constant total revenue on the commodity and consequently marginal revenue is zero. This is so by definition, but we can demonstrate it by using our numerical example

$$pq = 6000$$

But total revenue R_T equals price multiplied by quantity demanded, i.e.

$$R_T = pq$$

$$\therefore \qquad R_T = 6000$$

and $\qquad \dfrac{dR_T}{dq} = 0$

Thus marginal revenue, which is equal to dR_T/dq, is also zero.

SOME GENERAL POINTS CONCERNING PRICE ELASTICITY OF DEMAND AND LINEAR DEMAND CURVES

In the previous sections we calculated values of η given specific demand functions. We shall now derive a general rule that will give an easy way of comparing different demand curves in which prices are in the same currency (this is the usual textbook case). Much confusion arises in the minds of students (and teachers!) when comparing the price elasticity of two demand curves that have different intercepts and slopes. Consider each of the diagrams in Figure 2.11, where D_1 and D_2 denote linear demand curves. We need to find a general rule which will give an answer to the following question: at any particular price, is D_1 more elastic than, less elastic than, or of the same elasticity as D_2?

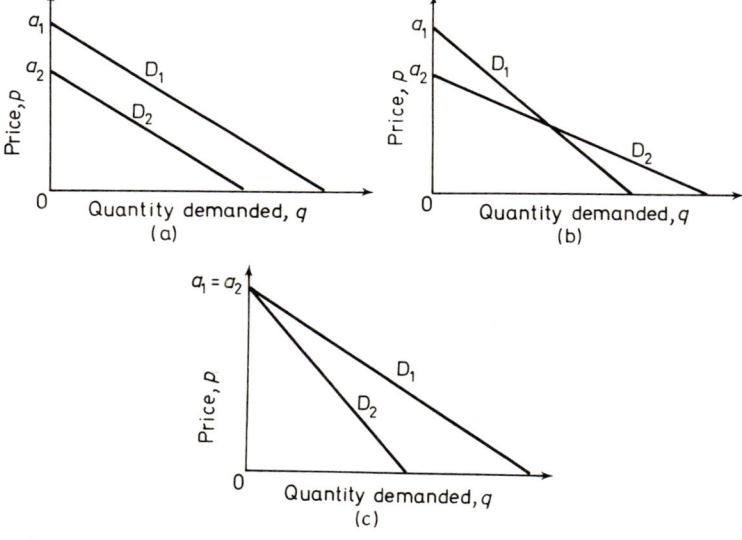

Figure 2.11

Let η_1 be the price elasticity of demand for D_1 and η_2 be the price elasticity for D_2. Similarly, let a_1 be the intercept of D_1 on the vertical axis and a_2 be the intercept of D_2 on the vertical axis. We can now make a point which frequently surprises students, namely that the rule for comparing elasticities has nothing to do with the slopes of the demand curves but is as follows. For any price p from which quantities demanded can be determined for both D_1 and D_2 [mathematically this is $p \leqslant$ minimum (a_1, a_2)]:

If $a_1 > a_2$ then $\eta_1 < \eta_2$ (D_1 is *less* elastic than D_2 at any price).

If $a_1 < a_2$ then $\eta_1 > \eta_2$ (D_1 is *more* elastic than D_2 at any price).

A SIMPLE PROOF OF THE ABOVE RULE

Consider the linear demand curve represented by the function

$$p = a - bq \qquad (2.20)$$

We have already shown that a is the intercept on the price axis and $-b$ is the slope of this demand function. Equation 2.20 can be rearranged to give q in terms of a, b, and p:

$$bq = a - p$$

$$\therefore \qquad q = \frac{a}{b} - \frac{p}{b} \qquad (2.21)$$

Therefore, differentiating with respect to p,

$$\frac{dq}{dp} = -\frac{1}{b}$$

But elasticity of demand is given by

$$\eta = -\frac{dq}{dp}\left(\frac{p}{q}\right)$$

$$= -\left(-\frac{1}{b}\right)\left(\frac{p}{q}\right)$$

Also, from equation 2.21,

$$\frac{p}{q} = \frac{p}{\dfrac{a}{b} - \dfrac{p}{b}}$$

$$= \frac{pb}{a - p}$$

$$\therefore \quad \eta = \frac{1}{b}\left(\frac{pb}{a - p}\right)$$

or $$\eta = \frac{p}{a - p} \qquad (2.22)$$

Thus we have the price elasticity of demand at any price p and can see that it is independent of the slope $-b$.

Consider now the two linear demand curves

$$p = a_1 - b_1 q$$

and $$p = a_2 - b_2 q$$

At any price $p_0 \leqslant$ minimum (a_1, a_2)

$$\eta_1 = \frac{p_0}{a_1 - p_0}$$

and $$\eta_2 = \frac{p_0}{a_2 - p_0}$$

$$\therefore \quad \frac{\eta_1}{\eta_2} = \frac{p_0}{a_1 - p_0} \div \frac{p_0}{a_2 - p_0}$$

$$= \left(\frac{p_0}{a_1 - p_0}\right)\left(\frac{a_2 - p_0}{p_0}\right)$$

$$= \frac{a_2 - p_0}{a_1 - p_0}$$

If we examine the ratio $(a_2 - p_0)/(a_1 - p_0)$ at a price $p_0 \leqslant$ minimum (a_1, a_2), it becomes clear that, if $a_1 > a_2$, then $\eta_1 < \eta_2$ at any price, and similarly, if $a_1 < a_2$, then $\eta_1 > \eta_2$ at any price. This then is the proof of the general rule for comparing elasticities. This rule can be applied to Figure 2.11a, for example, in which $a_1 > a_2$. Therefore, $\eta_1 < \eta_2$ and the demand curve D_1 is less elastic than D_2 for any price less than a_2. Similarly, in Figure 2.11b, $a_1 > a_2$ and so D_1 is less elastic than D_2 for any price less than a_2. Finally, in Figure 2.11c,

$a_1 = a_2$ and consequently D_1 has the same elasticity as D_2 at any price, even though the slopes of the curves are different.

UNIT ELASTICITY

We have already observed that the price elasticity of demand for a linear demand curve is different over the whole range of possible prices. We have also shown that $\eta = 1$ when marginal revenue is zero. In fact, equation 2.22 determined above can also provide a simple method of finding the price at which $\eta = 1$:

$$\eta = \frac{p}{a - p}$$

where p is any particular price. Therefore putting $\eta = 1$ (i.e. unit elasticity) gives

$$1 = \frac{p}{a - p}$$

$\therefore$
$$a - p = p$$

$\therefore$
$$a = 2p$$

$\therefore$
$$p = \tfrac{1}{2} a$$

Thus if we divide the price a (the intercept on the price axis) by 2, we obtain the price at which $\eta = 1$.

It is worth noting that all the above results flow from the basic definition of η, which requires q to be differentiated with respect to p. We shall now examine some numerical examples of elasticity calculations.

Example 1

Suppose we have two linear demand curves

$$p = 10 - 0.1q \qquad (= a_1 - b_1 q) \qquad (2.23)$$

and
$$p = 8 - 0.05q \qquad (= a_2 - b_2 q) \qquad (2.24)$$

The rule for comparing elasticities states that, if $a_1 > a_2$, then $\eta_1 < \eta_2$. In the equations above $a_1 = 10$ and $a_2 = 8$. Therefore $a_1 > a_2$

and at any value of p between 0 and 8 the demand curve given by equation 2.23 is less elastic than that given by equation 2.24. Let us now check this at a particular price, say $p = 6$, for each equation.

Consider, first, equation 2.23:

$$p = 10 - 0.1q$$

$$\therefore \quad q = \frac{10}{0.1} - \frac{p}{0.1}$$

$$\therefore \quad \frac{dq}{dp} = \frac{-1}{0.1}$$

$$\therefore \quad \eta = -\frac{dq}{dp}\left(\frac{p}{q}\right)$$

$$= -\left(\frac{-1}{0.1}\right)\left(\frac{6}{q}\right)$$

But the quantity demanded when $p = 6$ is given by substitution into the demand curve:

$$6 = 10 - 0.1q$$

$$\therefore \quad 0.1q = 4$$

$$\therefore \quad q = 40$$

Thus

$$\eta = -\left(\frac{-1}{0.1}\right)\left(\frac{6}{40}\right)$$

$$= \frac{6}{4}$$

i.e.

$$\eta = 1\tfrac{1}{2}$$

We can now repeat this procedure for equation 2.24:

$$p = 8 - 0.05q$$

$$\therefore \quad q = \frac{8}{0.05} - \frac{p}{0.05}$$

$$\therefore \quad \frac{dq}{dp} = \frac{-1}{0.05}$$

Now

$$\eta = -\frac{dq}{dp}\left(\frac{p}{q}\right)$$

$$= -\left(\frac{-1}{0.05}\right)\left(\frac{6}{q}\right)$$

Substituting $p = 6$ into demand equation 2.24 in order to obtain q gives

$$6 = 8 - 0.05q$$

$\therefore$
$$0.05q = 2$$

$\therefore$
$$q = 40$$

$\therefore$
$$\eta = -\left(\frac{-1}{0.05}\right)\left(\frac{6}{40}\right)$$

$$= \frac{6}{2}$$

i.e.
$$\eta = 3$$

Thus at $p = 6$ the demand curve given by equation 2.23 is less elastic than that given by equation 2.24. This is in accordance with the result obtained by applying the rule stated earlier.

Example 2

Let us take one more example, where the two demand curves have the same intercept (as in Figure 2.11c). Suppose we have the following two linear demand curves:

$$p = 10 - 0.1q \qquad (2.25)$$

and
$$p = 10 - 0.05q \qquad (2.26)$$

and we wish to compare η for the two curves at $p = 7$.

First, equation 2.25 can be rearranged to give

$$q = \frac{10}{0.1} - \frac{p}{0.1}$$

$\therefore$
$$\frac{dq}{dp} = \frac{-1}{0.1}$$

$\therefore$
$$\eta = -\frac{dq}{dp}\left(\frac{p}{q}\right)$$

$$= -\left(\frac{-1}{0.1}\right)\left(\frac{7}{q}\right)$$

Substituting $p = 7$ into equation 2.25 gives

$$7 = 10 - 0.1q$$

$\therefore$
$$q = \frac{3}{0.1}$$

$$= 30$$

$\therefore$
$$\eta = -\left(\frac{-1}{0.1}\right)\left(\frac{7}{30}\right)$$

i.e.
$$\eta = 2\tfrac{1}{3}$$

Again, this procedure can be repeated for the demand curve given by equation 2.26:

$$q = \frac{10}{0.05} - \frac{p}{0.05}$$

$\therefore$
$$\frac{dq}{dp} = \frac{-1}{0.05}$$

Also, substituting $p = 7$ into equation 2.26 gives

$$7 = 10 - 0.05q$$

$\therefore$
$$q = \frac{3}{0.05}$$

$$= 60$$

$\therefore$
$$\eta = -\left(\frac{-1}{0.05}\right)\left(\frac{7}{60}\right)$$

$$= 2\tfrac{1}{3}$$

This result conforms with the conclusion that for any $p \leqslant 10$ the elasticities of the demand curves given by equations 2.25 and 2.26 are the same.

ELASTICITY OF SUPPLY

The usual linear relationship between price and quantity supplied per time period is as shown in Figure 2.12. The intercept a indicates that, at the price a, nothing is supplied; in principle, at a price *slightly* above a, something will be supplied, and the quantity supplied is then an increasing function of price. Here price is the independent variable and quantity supplied is the dependent variable, i.e. $q = g(p)$. As with demand functions, we may need to ask the question: if there is a small change in price, what will be the response of supply? The elasticity of supply is denoted by ϵ (epsilon) and defined as

$$\epsilon = \frac{dq}{dp}\left(\frac{p}{q}\right) \qquad (2.27)$$

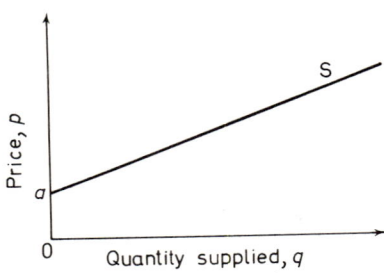

Figure 2.12

Note that this could be considered as

$$\frac{\text{The proportionate change in quantity supplied}}{\text{The proportionate change in price}}$$

Because supply is an increasing function of price, the derivative dq/dp is positive and so there is no need to introduce a minus sign to make the value of the elasticity positive (as was done for elasticity of demand).

COMPARISON OF POINT ELASTICITIES OF SUPPLY

As with demand curves, we may wish to compare elasticities of supply at the same price on different curves. The general rule developed for the demand curve applies. First, we obtain ϵ in terms of a and p, where a is the intercept on the price axis of the linear supply curve

$$p = a + bq \qquad (2.28)$$

Rearranging equation 2.28 gives

$$q = \frac{p}{b} - \frac{a}{b}$$

$\therefore$
$$\frac{dq}{dp} = \frac{1}{b}$$

$\therefore$
$$\epsilon = \frac{1}{b}\left(\frac{p}{\dfrac{p}{b} - \dfrac{a}{b}}\right)$$

$$= \frac{1}{b}\left(\frac{bp}{p - a}\right)$$

i.e.
$$\epsilon = \frac{p}{p - a} \tag{2.29}$$

If we now wish to compare the point elasticities ϵ_1 and ϵ_2 of the two linear supply curves $p = a_1 + b_1 q$ and $p = a_2 + b_2 q$ respectively, we take the ratio

$$\frac{\epsilon_1}{\epsilon_2} = \frac{p}{p - a_1} \div \frac{p}{p - a_2}$$

i.e.
$$\frac{\epsilon_1}{\epsilon_2} = \frac{p - a_2}{p - a_1}$$

If $a_1 > a_2$, then at any relevant price $\epsilon_1 < \epsilon_2$. If $a_1 < a_2$, then at any relevant price $\epsilon_1 > \epsilon_2$.

For a visual demonstration of the rule, consider the two supply curves shown in Figure 2.13. The two curves are such that the point elasticity of supply can be compared only for $p \geqslant a_1$. In accordance with our rule we conclude that, at any such price, $\epsilon_1 < \epsilon_2$ since $a_1 > a_2$. This rule can be applied to any comparison of linear supply curves on the basis of point elasticity.

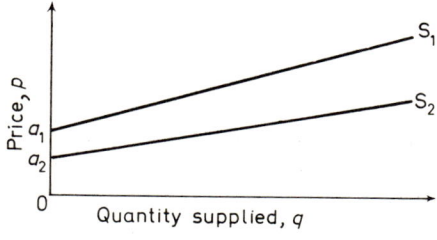

Figure 2.13

SUPPLY CURVES THROUGH THE ORIGIN — CONSTANT ELASTICITY

Any linear supply curve that goes through the origin will have an elasticity of 1, no matter what the price. In order to show this, we use equation 2.29 relating ϵ to p and a:

$$\epsilon = \frac{p}{p - a}$$

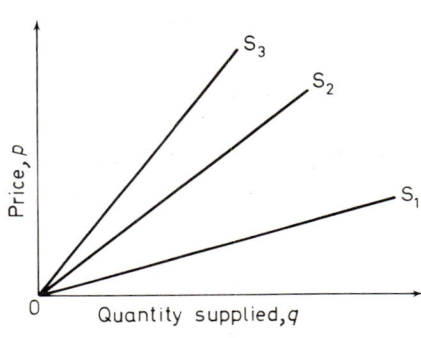

Figure 2.14

But, if the supply curve $p = a + bq$ goes through the origin, then $a = 0$ and

$$\epsilon = \frac{p}{p} = 1$$

This holds no matter what the slope b of the supply curve: elasticity of supply will equal 1 for any linear supply curve passing through the origin. Each of the supply curves in Figure 2.14, for example, has $\epsilon = 1$.

MARGINAL COST

Every economics student quickly comes upon the concept of marginal costs and is faced with the necessity of having to cope with the elementary mathematics involved. Most students find this difficult, but this is because they have to manage without the technique of differentiation. We are now in a position to use this technique in handling problems concerned with marginal costs, but before we embark on the mathematics of the problem it would be useful to revise a few basic points.

Economic theory assumes that some costs of production are fixed in that they do not vary with changes in output. For example, with a given amount of plant and equipment, depreciation charges are not related to output in that, if output rises or falls, such charges are not influenced. Rents and rates are also often treated as fixed costs. Obviously, if one increased the scale of operation, depreciation charges would increase, as might rent, rates, insurance premiums to cover property, etc., but such increases in the scale of operations take time. Similarly, one could reduce the burden of fixed costs by reducing the scale of operations, but again this takes time — hence the statement that in the long period all costs are variable. The theory of the firm given in first-year economics courses is a short-period analysis of costs, and so some costs are assumed fixed. (The categories of fixed costs are wider than those given above — they depend essentially on the particular type of business being analysed.) Variable costs in the short period are those costs which are a function of output and include such things as labour, raw materials, fuel and power, and light. At any level of output, total costs will consist of fixed costs plus the variable costs of producing that level of output.

MARGINAL COST AS THE FIRST DERIVATIVE OF THE TOTAL-COST FUNCTION

As output increases, total cost will increase. Alternatively, if output is reduced, total cost will fall. The rate at which total cost changes as output changes is known as the marginal cost. It is important to realise that, as fixed costs are not related to output, marginal cost is affected only by variable costs. This is easily seen if we examine a hypothetical cost function. Suppose a firm can produce a weekly output of q tons at a total cost (in pounds) given by

$$C_T = 300 + 3q + 0.05q^2 \qquad (2.30)$$

Notice that the fixed-cost element is £300 and so is not related to q (the quantity supplied, or output, per time period). Thus if there were no output ($q = 0$), total cost would equal £300. Graphically £300 is the intercept of the total-cost curve on the cost axis. If we wish to know the rate at which total cost changes as output changes (i.e. marginal cost), then C_T must be differentiated with respect to q (assuming the total-cost function to be continuous). Therefore

$$\frac{dC_T}{dq} = 3 + 0.05(2q)$$

i.e. $$C_M = 3 + 0.1q$$

where C_M denotes marginal cost. If output per week were 100 units, for example, then marginal cost would be given by

$$C_M = 3 + 0.1(100) = 13$$

Notice that, when the total-cost function is differentiated, the term 300 does not appear in the derivative because it is a constant. This points to an interesting conclusion. If a firm were in equilibrium and the state imposed a fixed tax on it, such a tax would not enter into marginal costs and so would not cause any change in the firm's output policy nor affect its pricing policy. (Remember a firm maximises its profits by equating marginal cost and marginal revenue, so a tax such as that suggested above would not affect this equilibrium condition.) The tax would, however, raise average total cost and so reduce total profits. Suppose the tax were £100, then the total-cost function (equation 2.30) would become

$$C_T = (300 + 100) + 3q + 0.05q^2$$

$$\therefore \qquad \frac{dC_T}{dq} = 3 + 0.1q$$

which is the same as before tax was imposed.

DERIVATIVES AND THE MULTIPLIER CONCEPT

In macro-economics it is often necessary to know what is likely to happen to the equilibrium level of national income when some autonomous change of expenditure takes place in one of the components of aggregate demand. Simple algebra and calculus enable us to examine the inner logic of income determination models more easily than relying on a graphical treatment (although graphs are pedagogically useful in dealing with some types of problems). We shall start with a simple model of income determination consisting of income and consumption as endogenous variables and investment as an exogenous variable. The model is often set out as follows:

$$Y \equiv C + I \qquad (2.31)$$

$$C = a + bY \qquad (0 < b < 1) \qquad (2.32)$$

and $\qquad I = I_0 \qquad (2.33)$

where Y is income, C is consumption expenditure, and I is business investment. The identity 2.31 is the accounting identity relating Y, C, and I. Equation 2.32 is a behavioural equation in that it indicates that consumers' planned consumption is a linear function of income: in this equation, a and b are constants reflecting consumption habits, b being the marginal propensity to consume. Equation 2.33 states that investment is a given amount I_0. As explained in Chapter 1 (see page 33), if equation 2.33 is substituted into the identity 2.31, we obtain the equilibrium relationship

$$Y = C + I_0 \qquad (2.34)$$

When the model is set out in this way, we refer to the set of equations 2.31–2.34 as structural equations as they indicate the structure of the system.

Now the two equations 2.32 and 2.34 contain two unknowns, Y and C, which can take on a whole range of possible values, whereas investment I is given (as I_0). Only one pair of values of Y and C is consistent with equations 2.32 and 2.34 at any one time. Thus, if we can find an equilibrium value for Y, we can then obtain a value for C that is consistent with that value of Y. In order to obtain the equilibrium value Y^* of Y, first substitute C from equation 2.32 into equation 2.34, i.e.

$$Y^* = a + bY^* + I_0$$

∴ $\qquad Y^* - bY^* = a + I_0$

∴ $\qquad Y^* = \dfrac{a + I_0}{1 - b} \qquad (2.35)$

Equation 2.35 is known as a reduced-form equation because it is the compressing of the model into a form in which income (an endogenous variable) is expressed in terms of an exogenous variable (investment) and parameters (a and b). It is less informative than the structural equations but is very useful for solving the system.

If we examine equation 2.35 carefully, we see that, as a and b are constants, fluctuations in income will depend on fluctuations in I_0. Suppose we ask the question: what will be the change in income, given a change in investment? The answer can be obtained by considering a change in investment from I_0 to $I_0 + \Delta I_0$. Then the corresponding change in income $\Delta Y*$ will be given by

$$Y* + \Delta Y* = \frac{a + (I_0 + \Delta I_0)}{1 - b}$$

$$= \frac{a + I_0}{1 - b} + \frac{\Delta I_0}{1 - b}$$

But

$$Y* = \frac{a + I_0}{1 - b}$$

$\therefore$

$$\Delta Y* = \Delta I_0 \left(\frac{1}{1 - b} \right) \qquad (2.36)$$

Thus income will change by an amount equal to the change in investment multiplied by $1/(1 - b)$. To show the significance of the term $1/(1 - b)$, we can rearrange equation 2.36 as follows:

$$\frac{\Delta Y*}{\Delta I_0} = \frac{1}{1 - b}$$

Thus $1/(1 - b)$ is the ratio of the change in income to the change in investment and is referred to as the multiplier. The symbol k is often used to represent the multiplier.

There are a number of points to be borne in mind when considering the multiplier. First, if ΔI_0 is very small, we can use the concept of the derivative. For example,

$$\frac{dY*}{dI_0} = \underset{\Delta I_0 \to 0}{\text{Limit}} \frac{\Delta Y*}{\Delta I_0} = \frac{1}{1 - b}$$

Thus, when we have the reduced-form equation

$$Y* = \frac{a + I_0}{1 - b}$$

then, assuming a and b are constant,

$$\frac{dY^*}{dI_0} = \frac{1}{1-b}$$

i.e. we differentiate income with respect to investment in order to obtain the multiplier.

The second point to be made is that the value of the multiplier depends on the size of b. As we have specified that $0 < b < 1$, then $1 - b$ is between 0 and 1 and the reciprocal of such a number is a number greater than 1. The greater b is, the smaller is the fraction $1 - b$, and so the greater the value of $1/(1 - b)$. Conversely, the smaller the value of b, the smaller is the value of $1/(1 - b)$.

The third point is that there are many different multipliers. For example, suppose the model includes government expenditure G as an exogenous variable:

$$Y \equiv C + I + G \tag{2.37}$$

$$C = a + bY \tag{2.38}$$

$$I = I_0 \tag{2.39}$$

and

$$G = G_0 \tag{2.40}$$

Substituting equations 2.38–2.40 into the identity 2.37 gives the equilibrium value of income as

$$Y^* = a + b\,Y^* + I_0 + G_0$$

$$\therefore \qquad Y^* - bY^* = a + I_0 + G_0$$

$$\therefore \qquad Y^* = \frac{a + I_0 + G_0}{1 - b}$$

which is the new reduced-form equation. If we now examine the rate of change of income with respect to government expenditure (assuming that I_0 remains constant and that a and b are constant), then we obtain the result

$$\frac{dY^*}{dG_0} = \frac{1}{1-b}$$

In this example the government multiplier is the same as the investment multiplier obtained above. To distinguish between them, we call them k_G and k_I respectively.

If now we introduce taxation into the model, we can derive a taxation multiplier. Suppose the new model is

$$Y \equiv C + I + G \qquad (2.41)$$

$$C = a + bY_d \qquad (2.42)$$

$$Y_d = Y - T \qquad (2.43)$$

$$I = I_0 \qquad (2.44)$$

$$G = G_0 \qquad (2.45)$$

and $\qquad T = T_0 \qquad (2.46)$

where Y is income, Y_d is disposable income, and T is a lump-sum tax. Substituting equations 2.42–2.46 into identity 2.41 will now give

$$Y^* = a + b(Y^* + T_0) + I_0 + G_0$$
$$= a + b\,Y^* - bT_0 + I_0 + G_0$$

$$\therefore \qquad Y^* - bY^* = a - bT_0 + I_0 + G_0$$

i.e. $\qquad Y^* = \dfrac{a - bT_0 + I_0 + G_0}{1 - b} \qquad (2.47)$

In order to find the multiplier effect if taxation changes, everything else remaining constant, income must be differentiated with respect to tax. Therefore, from equation 2.47,

$$\frac{dY^*}{dT_0} = \frac{-b}{1 - b}$$

Thus, if the government increased the lump-sum tax by an amount ΔT_0, then income would decline by an amount ΔY^* given by

$$\Delta Y^* = \Delta T_0 \left(\frac{-b}{1 - b} \right)$$

i.e. income would fall to a lower equilibrium level. In this case the taxation multiplier is $-b/(1 - b)$ and is designated k_T.

Let us take one last example. In the next model, taxation is made a linear function of Y, i.e. as income increases/decreases, tax revenues increase/decrease. Once again the structural equations can be set out:

$$Y \equiv C + I + G \tag{2.48}$$

$$C = a + bY_d \tag{2.49}$$

$$Y_d = Y - T \tag{2.50}$$

$$T = T_0 + hY \tag{2.51}$$

$$I = I_0 \tag{2.52}$$

and
$$G = G_0 \tag{2.53}$$

where T_0 is autonomous taxation and h is the marginal rate of taxation. Substituting equation 2.51 into equation 2.50 gives

$$Y_d = Y - (T_0 + hY)$$

i.e.
$$Y_d = Y - T_0 - hY \tag{2.54}$$

and substituting equation 2.54 into equation 2.49 gives

$$C = a + b(Y - T_0 - hY)$$

i.e.
$$C = a + bY - bT_0 - bhY \tag{2.55}$$

We can now substitute into the identity 2.48 to obtain the reduced-form equation:

$$Y^* = a + bY^* - bT_0 - bhY^* + I_0 + G_0$$

$$\therefore \quad Y^* - bY^* + bhY^* = a - bT_0 + I_0 + G_0$$

$$\therefore \quad Y^*(1 - b + bh) = a - bT_0 + I_0 + G_0$$

$$\therefore \quad Y^* = \frac{a - bT_0 + I_0 + G_0}{1 - b + bh}$$

i.e.
$$Y^* = \frac{a - bT_0 + I_0 + G_0}{1 - b(1 - h)}$$

Suppose we now wish to find the rate of change of income with respect to autonomous taxation, everything else remaining constant. We therefore differentiate Y^* with respect to T_0 to give

$$\frac{dY^*}{dT_0} = \frac{-b}{1 - b(1 - h)} = k_{T_0}$$

By making taxation a function of income we have changed the multiplier, the denominator having changed from $1 - b$ to $1 - b(1 - h)$. If $h = 0.25$, for example, then the marginal retained income after taxation (equal to $1 - h$) is 0.75. Thus

$$1 - b(1 - h) > 1 - b$$

and by increasing the size of the denominator (which is the marginal propensity to save retained income) we have reduced the value of k_{T_0} compared with the multiplier for the lump-sum tax.

To conclude, a multiplier is simply the derivative of Y^* with respect to the particular exogenous variable we are interested in. By a process of substitution in the structural equations we can obtain the reduced-form equations, from which we can then derive the multiplier.

Chapter 3

FURTHER RULES OF DIFFERENTIATION

The great advantage of mathematics in economic analysis is the ease with which it enables the relationships between variables to be handled. Most economic problems involve chains of connected relationships and, if we wish to known what happens to y as x changes, then we need to use the techniques of calculus. So far we have been considering very simple relationships, of the form $y = f(x)$, between two variables, but we shall have to deal with more complicated functional relationships such as $y = f(x)g(x)$. For example, $f(x)$ might be $3x^2 + 2x$ and $g(x)$ might be $4x^3 - 1$, and so

$$y = (3x^2 + 2x)(4x^3 - 1)$$

In economic analysis it is usual to deal with a problem by using $f(x)$, $g(x)$, etc., rather than specific functions, because it is of more value to have a general conclusion than the answer to a specific numerical problem. These points are best illustrated by taking a particular example.

As we have already seen, a demand curve frequently used in elementary economics is of the general form $p = a - bq$. Thus p is a function of quantity demanded q and this can be written as

$$p = f(q)$$

By using this notation we are indicating that we are not interested in the particular values of a and b or indeed in the specific form of the relationship; we are simply stating that price is related to quantity demanded in some way. Now total revenue R_T is equal to price multiplied by quantity demanded, which can be written as

$$R_T = pq$$

We have thus expressed total revenue in terms of price and demand, but for many problems it is convenient to have total revenue in terms of quantity demanded only. This is easy to do, as $p = f(q)$ and so

$R_T = [f(q)]q$. Hence we have total revenue as the product of two functions of q. If we now wish to determine marginal revenue, we differentiate R_T with respect to q but, as R_T is expressed as the product $[f(q)]q$, we need a rule for differentiating the product of functions.

DERIVATIVES OF PRODUCTS OF FUNCTIONS

Suppose

$$y = f(x)g(x) \tag{3.1}$$

and let x increase to $x + \Delta x$. Then the new value of y is given by

$$y + \Delta y = f(x + \Delta x)g(x + \Delta x)$$
$$\therefore \qquad \Delta y = f(x + \Delta x)g(x + \Delta x) - y$$
$$= f(x + \Delta x)g(x + \Delta x) - f(x)g(x)$$
$$\therefore \qquad \frac{\Delta y}{\Delta x} = \frac{f(x + \Delta x)g(x + \Delta x) - f(x)g(x)}{\Delta x}$$

To facilitate the calculation, the term $f(x)g(x + \Delta x)$ is added to and subtracted from the top line of this expression. This procedure does not alter the value of the expression because it simply amounts to adding zero:

$$\frac{\Delta y}{\Delta x} = \frac{f(x + \Delta x)g(x + \Delta x) - f(x)g(x + \Delta x) + f(x)g(x + \Delta x) - f(x)g(x)}{\Delta x}$$

We now take the common factor $g(x + \Delta x)$ from the first two terms and the common factor $f(x)$ from the remaining two terms, i.e.

$$\frac{\Delta y}{\Delta x} = \frac{[f(x + \Delta x) - f(x)]\,g(x + \Delta x) + f(x)\,[g(x + \Delta x) - g(x)]}{\Delta x}$$

$$= \left[\frac{f(x + \Delta x) - f(x)}{\Delta x}\right]g(x + \Delta x) + f(x)\left[\frac{g(x + \Delta x) - g(x)}{\Delta x}\right]$$

Hence

$$\frac{dy}{dx} = \underset{\Delta x \to 0}{\text{Limit}} \frac{\Delta y}{\Delta x}$$

$$= \underset{\Delta x \to 0}{\text{Limit}} \left[\frac{f(x + \Delta x) - f(x)}{\Delta x} \right] \underset{\Delta x \to 0}{\text{Limit}} [g(x + \Delta x)]$$

$$+ \underset{\Delta x \to 0}{\text{Limit}} [f(x)] \underset{\Delta x \to 0}{\text{Limit}} \left[\frac{g(x + \Delta x) - g(x)}{\Delta x} \right]$$

i.e. $\dfrac{dy}{dx} = f'(x)g(x) + f(x)g'(x)$ (3.2)

Therefore the derivative of the product of two functions is equal to the derivative of the first function multiplied by the second, plus the first function multiplied by the derivative of the second.

Example 1

Suppose

$$y = (x^3 - 3)\left(\frac{1}{x} + 2x\right)$$

which can be rewritten as

$$y = (x^3 - 3)(x^{-1} + 2x)$$

Then let $\qquad$ $f(x) = x^3 - 3$

with $\qquad$ $f'(x) = 3x^2$

and let $\qquad$ $g(x) = x^{-1} + 2x$

with $\qquad$ $g'(x) = -x^{-2} + 2$

Hence

$$\frac{dy}{dx} = f'(x)g(x) + f(x)g'(x)$$

$$= 3x^2(x^{-1} + 2x) + (x^3 - 3)(-x^{-2} + 2)$$

$$= 3x^2\left(\frac{1}{x} + 2x\right) + (x^3 - 3)\left(-\frac{1}{x^2} + 2\right)$$

Example 2

We saw at the beginning of this chapter that total revenue R_T is related to quantity q by the expression

$$R_T = [f(q)]q \tag{3.3}$$

Therefore marginal revenue R_M is given by

$$R_M = \frac{dR_T}{dq}$$

i.e.
$$R_M = [f'(q)]q + f(q) \tag{3.4}$$

Note that q is the second of the factors in the product $[f(q)]q$ in equation 3.3, and that the derivative of q with respect to q is 1. Equation 3.4 for marginal revenue will be useful to us later on, but for the moment has provided an example of the derivative of a product.

DERIVATIVES OF QUOTIENTS OF FUNCTIONS

Often we come across functional relationships of the type

$$y = \frac{f(x)}{g(x)}$$

and therefore need a method of finding the derivative of the quotient of functions. Suppose then that

$$y = \frac{f(x)}{g(x)}$$

providing $g(x) \neq 0$, and let x increase to $x + \Delta x$. Then the new value of y is

$$y + \Delta y = \frac{f(x + \Delta x)}{g(x + \Delta x)}$$

$$\therefore \qquad \Delta y = \frac{f(x + \Delta x)}{g(x + \Delta x)} - y$$

$$= \frac{f(x + \Delta x)}{g(x + \Delta x)} - \frac{f(x)}{g(x)}$$

$$\therefore \qquad \frac{\Delta y}{\Delta x} = \frac{\dfrac{f(x + \Delta x)}{g(x + \Delta x)} - \dfrac{f(x)}{g(x)}}{\Delta x}$$

Putting the top line over the common denominator $g(x + \Delta x)g(x)$ gives

$$\frac{\Delta y}{\Delta x} = \frac{\dfrac{f(x + \Delta x)g(x) - f(x)g(x + \Delta x)}{g(x + \Delta x)g(x)}}{\Delta x}$$

$$= \frac{f(x + \Delta x)g(x) - f(x)g(x + \Delta x)}{(\Delta x)g(x + \Delta x)g(x)}$$

The term $f(x)g(x)$ is now added to and subtracted from the top line of this expression to give

$$\frac{\Delta y}{\Delta x} = \frac{f(x + \Delta x)g(x) - f(x)g(x) - f(x)g(x + \Delta x) + f(x)g(x)}{(\Delta x)g(x + \Delta x)g(x)}$$

Rearrange the top line of this expression by taking a common factor $g(x)$ from the first two terms and a common factor $-f(x)$ from the remaining two terms:

$$\frac{\Delta y}{\Delta x} = \frac{[f(x + \Delta x) - f(x)]\, g(x) - f(x)\, [g(x + \Delta x) - g(x)]}{(\Delta x)g(x + \Delta x)g(x)}$$

This means that the top line of this quotient has to be divided by Δx, by $g(x + \Delta x)$, and by $g(x)$. Let us do the division by Δx first, i.e.

$$\frac{\Delta y}{\Delta x} = \frac{\left[\dfrac{f(x + \Delta x) - f(x)}{\Delta x}\right] g(x) - f(x) \left[\dfrac{g(x + \Delta x) - g(x)}{\Delta x}\right]}{g(x + \Delta x)g(x)}$$

Therefore

$$\frac{dy}{dx} = \underset{\Delta x \to 0}{\text{Limit}} \frac{\Delta y}{\Delta x}$$

$$= \frac{\underset{\Delta x \to 0}{\text{Limit}}\left[\dfrac{f(x + \Delta x) - f(x)}{\Delta x}\right] \underset{\Delta x \to 0}{\text{Limit}} [g(x)] - \underset{\Delta x \to 0}{\text{Limit}} [f(x)] \underset{\Delta x \to 0}{\text{Limit}}\left[\dfrac{g(x + \Delta x) - g(x)}{\Delta x}\right]}{\underset{\Delta x \to 0}{\text{Limit}} [g(x + \Delta x)] \underset{\Delta x \to 0}{\text{Limit}} [g(x)]}$$

$$= \frac{f'(x)g(x) - f(x)g'(x)}{g(x)g(x)}$$

Hence

$$\frac{dy}{dx} = \frac{f'(x)g(x) - f(x)g'(x)}{[g(x)]^2} \tag{3.5}$$

Therefore the derivative of the quotient of two functions is equal to the derivative of the top function multiplied by the bottom function, minus the top function multiplied by the derivative of the bottom function, all divided by the square of the bottom function.

Example

Suppose

$$y = \frac{x^3 - 1}{x^2 + 3x + 1}$$

Then let $f(x) = x^3 - 1$

with $f'(x) = 3x^2$

and let $g(x) = x^2 + 3x + 1$

with $g'(x) = 2x + 3$

Hence

$$\frac{dy}{dx} = \frac{3x^2(x^2 + 3x + 1) - (x^3 - 1)(2x + 3)}{(x^2 + 3x + 1)^2}$$

$$= \frac{(3x^4 + 9x^3 + 3x^2) - (2x^4 + 3x^3 - 2x - 3)}{(x^2 + 3x + 1)^2}$$

$$= \frac{3x^4 + 9x^3 + 3x^2 - 2x^4 - 3x^3 + 2x + 3}{(x^2 + 3x + 1)^2}$$

$$= \frac{x^4 + 6x^3 + 3x^2 + 2x + 3}{(x^2 + 3x + 1)^2}$$

ECONOMIC APPLICATION

The relationship between marginal and average cost is one the student comes upon early in his economics course. The assumed shapes of these curves are as shown in Figure 3.1 and reflect assumptions about the operation of diminishing returns in the short period. The point usually stressed in textbooks is that the marginal-cost curve cuts the average-cost curve at the lowest point of the latter. Intuitive explanations are often given in terms of cricketers' scoring records over a season (!), but using the rule for differentiating quotients we can prove the relationship between average-cost curves and marginal-cost curves.

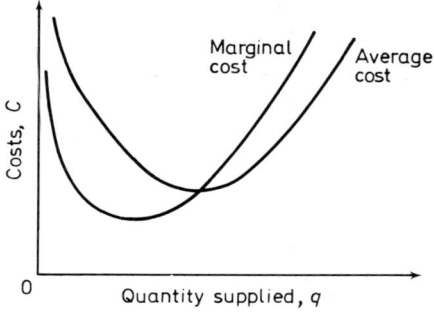

Figure 3.1

Let C_T be total cost and let q be quantity supplied (output). Then marginal cost C_M is given by the equation

$$C_M = \frac{dC_T}{dq} \qquad (3.6)$$

Average cost C_A is given by dividing total cost by output, i.e.

$$C_A = \frac{C_T}{q} \qquad (3.7)$$

The important point to note is that we have now expressed both marginal cost and average cost as functions of output. Suppose we obtain the gradient of the average-cost curve, which is the derivative of the average-cost function with respect to q. As average cost is given by the ratio C_T/q, we need to use the quotient rule as follows:

$$\frac{dC_A}{dq} = \frac{d}{dq}\left(\frac{C_T}{q}\right)$$

$$= \frac{\left(\frac{dC_T}{dq}\right)q - C_T\left(\frac{dq}{dq}\right)}{q^2}$$

$$= \frac{1}{q^2}\left[q\left(\frac{dC_T}{dq}\right) - C_T\right]$$

$$= \frac{1}{q}\left(\frac{dC_T}{dq} - \frac{C_T}{q}\right)$$

But, from equations 3.6 and 3.7, $dC_T/dq = C_M$ and $C_T/q = C_A$. Therefore

$$\frac{dC_A}{dq} = \frac{1}{q}(C_M - C_A) \qquad (3.8)$$

If we assume that the curves have the conventional U-shape given in the textbooks, then certain facts follow. When the average-cost curve is sloping downwards, the gradient (derivative) of the average-cost curve is negative, i.e.

$$\frac{1}{q}(C_M - C_A) < 0$$

Therefore, since output q is positive,

$$C_M - C_A < 0$$

i.e. $$C_M < C_A$$

Thus, when the average-cost curve is sloping downwards, marginal costs are less than average costs. Similarly, at the lowest point on the average-cost curve the gradient is zero (this is dealt with in detail at the beginning of Chapter 4). Hence

$$\frac{1}{q}(C_M - C_A) = 0$$

∴ $$C_M - C_A = 0$$

i.e. $$C_M = C_A$$

Thus, at the lowest point on the average-cost curve, marginal costs are equal to average costs. Finally, when the average-cost curve is rising, the gradient is positive, i.e.

$$\frac{1}{q}(C_M - C_A) > 0$$

∴ $$C_M > C_A$$

i.e. marginal costs are greater than average costs.

FUNCTION OF A FUNCTION

In the marginal productivity theory of wages, a firm's demand curve for labour is stated to be the marginal revenue product curve. The model assumes that, with a given amount of capital equipment, output depends on the amount used of the variable factor, labour. Thus we could say that output is a function of labour. Using q to represent output and L to represent labour we can write

$$q = g(L)$$

and the marginal physical product of labour as dq/dL or $g'(L)$. However, as the labour input changes, output changes. If the firm or industry is facing a downward-sloping demand curve, then an increased output can be sold only if price falls and price rises if output declines. This means that, as labour input changes, output changes and so the price of the product changes. We can see therefore that price is related to labour input and so also is total revenue, which is given by price times output. Alternatively, if the firm is in a perfectly competitive industry, it faces a horizontal demand curve for its product, i.e. the price at which it sells its output is constant. In either case the firm is assumed to employ labour up to the point where the addition to total revenue equals the cost of employing the marginal unit of labour, and so the firm wants to know how total revenue changes as labour input changes. To cope with this kind of problem we need to be able to differentiate a function of a function.

To differentiate a function such as

$$y = (x^2 + 2)^2$$

we could expand the terms in the brackets and write the function as

$$y = x^4 + 4x^2 + 4$$

We could then differentiate each term as we have done previously. The same procedure could be adopted for the equation $y = (x^2 + 2)^4$, but the expansion is becoming more difficult. Once we start dealing with such functions as $y = (x^2 + 2)^{12}$ the complexity of expanding the expression becomes prohibitive. It is much more convenient to consider $y = (x^2 + 2)^{12}$ as a combination of two functions, one inside the other. For example, if we are given the equation

$$y = (x^2 + 2)^{12}$$

the function *inside* the brackets could be represented by u, i.e.

$$u = x^2 + 2$$

and the *outside* function would be $y = u^{12}$. We could express other functions in a similar way. For instance, if

$$y = (x^3 + x^2 + 1)^{-3}$$

and we let

$$u = x^3 + x^2 + 1$$

then

$$y = u^{-3}$$

Expressions of this type are called functions of a function. There are many different kinds of these, but we shall normally be concerned with functions of the form

$$y = [f(x)]^n$$

where n is a positive or negative whole number or fraction. In general, then, consider

$$y = g[f(x)]$$

i.e. y is some function g of a function f of x. Let $u = f(x)$ and hence $y = g(u)$. We can then find

$$\frac{du}{dx} = f'(x) \quad \text{and} \quad \frac{dy}{du} = g'(u)$$

But we require dy/dx and must therefore use a result called the *chain rule,* which states that

$$\frac{dy}{dx} = \frac{dy}{du}\frac{du}{dx}$$

i.e.

$$\frac{dy}{dx} = g'(u) \, f'(x)$$

This formula can be demonstrated as follows:

$$\frac{dy}{dx} = \underset{\Delta x \to 0}{\text{Limit}} \left\{ \frac{g[f(x + \Delta x)] - g[f(x)]}{\Delta x} \right\}$$

$$= \underset{\Delta x \to 0}{\text{Limit}} \left\{ \frac{g[f(x + \Delta x)] - g[f(x)]}{f(x + \Delta x) - f(x)} \frac{f(x + \Delta x) - f(x)}{\Delta x} \right\}$$

We have multiplied top and bottom by $f(x + \Delta x) - f(x)$, which has the effect of multiplying by 1. Now let $u = f(x)$ and then

$$\Delta u = f(x + \Delta x) - f(x)$$

Hence

$$\frac{dy}{dx} = \underset{\Delta x \to 0}{\text{Limit}} \left[\frac{g(u + \Delta u) - g(u)}{\Delta u} \; \frac{f(x + \Delta x) - f(x)}{\Delta x} \right]$$

Now as $\Delta x \to 0$ then $\Delta u \to 0$, and so

$$\frac{dy}{dx} = \underset{\Delta u \to 0}{\text{Limit}} \left[\frac{g(u + \Delta u) - g(u)}{\Delta u} \right] \underset{\Delta x \to 0}{\text{Limit}} \left[\frac{f(x + \Delta x) - f(x)}{\Delta x} \right]$$

$$= g'(u) f'(x)$$

$$\therefore \qquad \frac{dy}{dx} = g'[f(x)] f'(x) \qquad (3.9)$$

or $\qquad \dfrac{dy}{dx} = \dfrac{dy}{du} \dfrac{du}{dx}$

Therefore, to differentiate a function of a function we differentiate the outside function (leaving the inside function alone) and then multiply by the derivative of the inside function.

Consider again the relationship

$$y = [f(x)]^n$$

If we call the function inside the square brackets u, i.e. $u = f(x)$, then y is related to u by the function g, say. Thus we could write $y = g(u)$. In this particular case $g(u) = u^n$ and so

$$y = u^n$$

and $\qquad \dfrac{dy}{du} = nu^{n-1}$

Hence $\qquad \dfrac{dy}{dx} = \dfrac{dy}{du} \dfrac{du}{dx}$

$$= nu^{n-1} f'(x)$$

i.e. $\qquad \dfrac{dy}{dx} = n[f(x)]^{n-1} f'(x) \qquad (3.10)$

It is worth noting that the chain rule leads to a result that is often useful, namely

$$\frac{dx}{dy} = \frac{1}{dy/dx}$$

(see, for example, page 61, where we could have used this formula instead of rearranging equation 2.11). We may use the chain rule to write

$$\frac{dx}{dx} = \frac{dx}{dy}\frac{dy}{dx}$$

But $dx/dx = 1$, i.e.

$$1 = \frac{dx}{dy}\frac{dy}{dx}$$

$\therefore$

$$\frac{1}{dy/dx} = \frac{dx}{dy}$$

Example 1

Suppose

$$y = (x^2 + 2)^{12}$$

Then we can apply equation 3.10 to this function to give

$$\frac{dy}{dx} = 12(x^2 + 2)^{11}(2x)$$

i.e.

$$\frac{dy}{dx} = 24x(x^2 + 2)^{11}$$

Example 2

Let

$$y = \sqrt{(2x + 1)}$$

This can be rewritten as

$$y = (2x + 1)^{1/2}$$

$\therefore$

$$\frac{dy}{dx} = \frac{1}{2}(2x + 1)^{-1/2}(2)$$

i.e.

$$\frac{dy}{dx} = \frac{1}{\sqrt{(2x + 1)}}$$

Example 3

Let
$$y = \frac{1}{(x^3 + x^2 + 1)^3}$$

i.e.
$$y = (x^3 + x^2 + 1)^{-3}$$

∴
$$\frac{dy}{dx} = -3(x^3 + x^2 + 1)^{-4}(3x^2 + 2x)$$

i.e.
$$\frac{dy}{dx} = \frac{-3(3x^2 + 2x)}{(x^3 + x^2 + 1)^4}$$

Example 4

In the above examples we directly applied the chain rule to numerical relationships. Now we shall give a general rather than numerical example from economics. In the simple marginal-product model we assume that, with a given amount of capital, output depends on labour input. Thus we can write

$$q = g(L) \tag{3.11}$$

where q is output, L is labour input, and g is the function relating output to labour input (this is given by the underlying production function). We also know that in a less than perfectly competitive market the price of the firm's product is related to output, and so we could write

$$p = f(q) \tag{3.12}$$

where p is price and f is the function relating output to price. Now it becomes clear the price is related to labour input through output, and to express price as a function of labour input we can proceed as follows.

Since $p = f(q)$ and $q = g(L)$, we can write

$$p = f[g(L)] \tag{3.13}$$

This indicates that p is a function f of the function g of L. When L is known, the function g enables us to determine q; and when q is known, p is determined by the function f.

If we wish to know the rate of change of price p with respect to labour input L, we need to obtain dp/dL. This can be found by applying the chain rule:

$$\frac{dp}{dL} = \frac{dp}{dq}\frac{dq}{dL}$$ (3.14)

But by differentiating equation 3.11 we know that

$$\frac{dq}{dL} = g'(L)$$ (3.15)

which is known as the marginal physical product of labour (i.e. the change in total product given a very small change in labour input). Similarly, by differentiating equation 3.12,

$$\frac{dp}{dq} = f'(q)$$ (3.16)

Therefore, substituting equations 3.15 and 3.16 into equation 3.14,

$$\frac{dp}{dL} = f'(q)g'(L)$$

$$= f'[g(L)]\,g'(L)$$

So again we apply the rule of differentiating the outside function (leaving the inside function alone) and multiplying by the derivative of the inside function.

MARGINAL REVENUE AND ELASTICITY OF DEMAND

On pages 87–88 we showed that total revenue R_T is related to demand q by the expression

$$R_T = [f(q)]\,q$$

and on page 90 that marginal revenue R_M is given by

$$R_M = \frac{dR_T}{dq}$$

i.e. $$R_M = [f'(q)]\,q + f(q)$$

Marginal revenue could be left in this form or can be restated in a number of different ways: it is a matter of choosing the formulation that meets the particular needs.

As an example we shall now express marginal revenue in terms of price and elasticity. We already know that

$$p = f(q)$$

$$\frac{dp}{dq} = f'(q)$$

and

$$R_M = [f'(q)]q + f(q)$$

∴

$$R_M = \frac{dp}{dq} q + p \qquad (3.17)$$

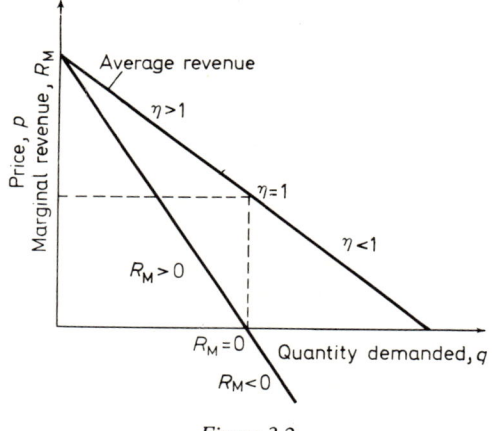

Figure 3.2

If we now put brackets around the terms on the right-hand side and take p outside the brackets, we can write

$$R_M = p \left[\frac{dp}{dq} \left(\frac{q}{p} \right) + 1 \right] \qquad (3.18)$$

But by definition the elasticity of demand η is given by

$$\eta = -\frac{dq}{dp} \left(\frac{p}{q} \right)$$

∴

$$-\eta = \frac{dq}{dp} \left(\frac{p}{q} \right)$$

and

$$-\frac{1}{\eta} = \frac{dp}{dq} \left(\frac{q}{p} \right)$$

Therefore by substituting this in equation 3.18 we obtain

$$R_M = p \left(-\frac{1}{\eta} + 1 \right)$$

i.e.
$$R_M = p \left(1 - \frac{1}{\eta} \right) \qquad (3.19)$$

This formulation of marginal revenue is useful. It shows directly that, if $\eta = 1$, then marginal revenue is zero at any price p. If $\eta < 1$ then marginal revenue would be negative at any price, while if $\eta > 1$ marginal revenue would be positive at any price. It might be reassuring to look at a familiar diagram to see that these results are what we would expect (see Figure 3.2).

DISCRIMINATING MONOPOLIST

Suppose a firm is producing a product which can be sold in two different markets, in each of which demand conditions vary. This situation often arises in international trade. In the simple model used in economic theory the question arises as to what ought to be the policy pursued by the firm with regard to maximising profits. As the firm sells more in each market, marginal revenue from each market will fall. As we assume the marginal costs of the units sold in each market are the same, then profits will be maximised by producing and selling up to the point where marginal cost equals marginal revenue; also, the marginal revenue must be the same from sales in each market, otherwise it would pay the firm to reduce sales in the market where marginal revenue was lower and sell in the market where marginal revenue was higher. Thus, the equilibrium condition for the firm involves marginal revenue being equal in both markets. In which market should the firm charge the higher price? It can easily be shown that the price must be lower in the market with the higher elasticity of demand.

Consider the statement of marginal revenue given in equation 3.19:

$$R_M = p \left(1 - \frac{1}{\eta} \right)$$

The marginal revenues in both markets must be the same, and we shall assume the elasticity in the two markets is different. Let R_{M1} represent marginal revenue in one market, p_1 the price in this market, and η_1 the elasticity of demand at price p_1. Similarly, let R_{M2} represent the marginal revenue in the other market, p_2 the price, and η_2 the elasticity of demand at price p_2. Then in equilibrium

$$R_{M1} = R_{M2}$$

and hence
$$p_1 \left(1 - \frac{1}{\eta_1}\right) = p_2 \left(1 - \frac{1}{\eta_2}\right)$$

If $\eta_1 = \eta_2$ then obviously $p_1 = p_2$ and there is no chance of discriminating between markets, but if $\eta_1 > \eta_2$ then p_1 must be less than p_2 if R_{M1} is to equal R_{M2}.

MARGINAL REVENUE PRODUCT CURVE

The usual model dealing with a firm's demand for labour assumes that the firm has a fixed amount of capital and that the variable factor in the short period is labour. We have already introduced the idea of output as a function of labour input and also the idea of price as a function of labour input. We are not concerned here with the precise conditions necessary to give the shape of total-product and marginal-product curves found in textbooks. The attraction of mathematical notation is that general results can be applied to specific cases. The firm, it is assumed, will employ labour up to the point where the addition to its total revenue equals the cost of the marginal unit of labour. This means it wants to know the rate of change of total revenue with respect to labour input, i.e. its marginal revenue product.

To begin, we must state total revenue as a function of labour input (we have already prepared the way for this in some of the examples above). We have written price p as a function of output q, i.e.

$$p = f(q)$$

and
$$\frac{dp}{dq} = f'(q)$$

and have written output as a function of labour input L, i.e.

$$q = g(L)$$

and
$$\frac{dq}{dL} = g'(L)$$

where $g'(L)$ is the marginal physical product of labour. Therefore

$$p = f[g(L)]$$

and total revenue $R_T = pq$ is given by

$$R_T = f[g(L)]\, g(L)$$

Thus we now have total revenue in terms of labour input. Notice that the first of the two terms on the right-hand side is the function of a

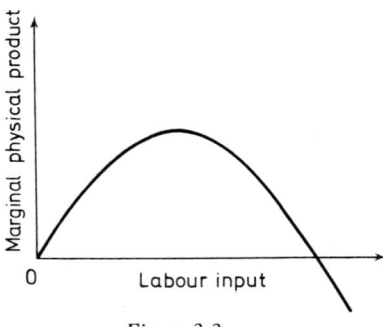

Figure 3.3

function we have already dealt with, and that it is multiplied by another function, $g(L)$. This means that we have to use the rule for differentiating a product and that for differentiating a function of a function in order to obtain dR_T/dL (the marginal revenue product).

Using the rule for a product first gives

$$\frac{dR_T}{dL} = \frac{d\{f[g(L)]\}}{dL}g(L) + g'(L)f[g(L)]$$

and using the rule for a function of a function to find df/dL gives

$$\frac{dR_T}{dL} = f'[g(L)]\, g'(L)g(L) + g'(L)f[g(L)]$$

$$= g'(L)\left\{f'[g(L)]\, g(L) + f[g(L)]\right\}$$

since $g'(L)$ is common to both terms. Therefore

$$\frac{dR_T}{dL} = g'(L)\left(\frac{dp}{dq}\, q + p\right)$$

But $g'(L)$ is the marginal physical product of labour, and from equation 3.17 marginal revenue is given by

$$R_M = \frac{dp}{dq}q + p$$

Therefore

Marginal revenue product = marginal physical product × marginal revenue

In the case of perfect competition, marginal revenue and price are the same so marginal revenue product equals price times marginal physical product. (With perfect competition, the firm faces a horizontal demand curve, i.e. $p = a$, and so $dp/dq = 0$ and $R_M = p$ from equation 3.17.)

It is worth noting that the use of mathematical notation removes the need to specify the precise production function and the consequent marginal-product function. The result stands, irrespective of the particular production function in question. Given a fixed amount of capital, we simply state that $q = g(L)$, where the function g will be determined by technology (i.e. the way output behaves for given changes in the labour input is a matter of technology, but whatever the relationship is we describe it by the function g). Also, the behaviour of the marginal physical product reflects the particular production function; $g'(L)$ is the marginal physical product of labour, stated generally. In most textbooks, the marginal physical product curve is as shown in Figure 3.3 because of the assumption of diminishing returns to a factor. In this case, the function $g'(L)$ has specific characteristics, which raises the point that the imposition of economic, technical, or physical conditions will restrict the forms that a function will take.

Chapter 4

MAXIMUM AND MINIMUM POINTS OF A FUNCTION

A point on a curve where it changes from increasing to decreasing, or from decreasing to increasing, is called a *stationary point* or an *extreme point*. The first type of these extreme points is called a maximum and the second type is called a minimum (see Figure 4.1). It can be seen

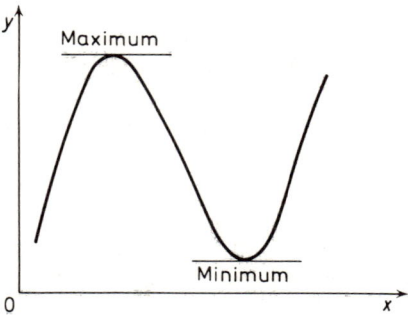

Figure 4.1

that the tangent to the curve at either a maximum or a minimum point is a line parallel to the horizontal axis. Since the gradient of such a line is zero, the gradient to the curve at this point is also zero. Therefore, to find the position of extreme points of a function

$$y = f(x)$$

we must differentiate y with respect to x and solve the equation

$$\frac{dy}{dx} = 0$$

Consider, for example, the function

$$y = 2x^3 + 3x^2 - 12x + 5$$

106

Differentiating with respect to x gives .

$$\frac{dy}{dx} = 6x^2 + 6x - 12$$

Therefore an extreme point will occur when

$$6x^2 + 6x - 12 = 0$$

i.e. $$x^2 + x - 2 = 0$$

or $$(x - 1)(x + 2) = 0$$

Hence there are two extreme points, one at $x = 1$ and one at $x = -2$.

Once the positions of the extreme points have been found, we must determine some way of identifying which of them are maxima and which are minima.

Suppose a *maximum* is at $x = M$ and the curve near to $x = M$ is as shown in Figure 4.2a. We know that, at $x = M$, $dy/dx = 0$. Further, y is

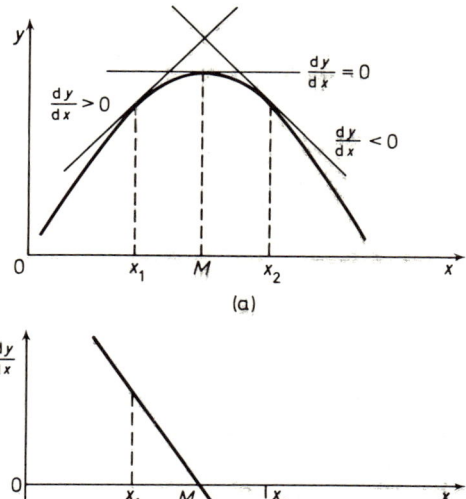

(a)

(b)

Figure 4.2

increasing for values of x near but less than M, i.e. dy/dx is positive for all such values of x. Also, the closer x becomes to $x = M$, the flatter the tangent line becomes and so the closer dy/dx becomes to zero. For values of x near but greater than M, y is decreasing, i.e. dy/dx is negative for all such values of x. Again, the closer x becomes to $x = M$, the nearer dy/dx becomes to zero.

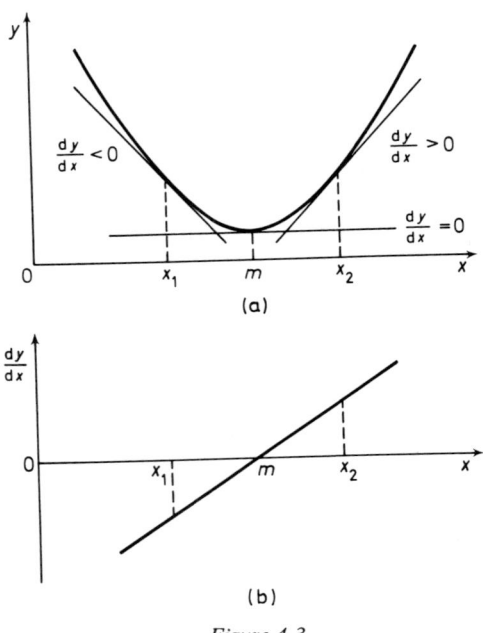

Figure 4.3

If a graph of dy/dx against x is plotted (Figure 4.2b), we can see that, around $x = M$, dy/dx is a *decreasing* function of x. Remember that the derivative of a decreasing function is negative, and so here the derivative of dy/dx is negative, i.e. at $x = M$

$$\frac{d}{dx}\left(\frac{dy}{dx}\right) < 0$$

or

$$\frac{d^2y}{dx^2} < 0$$

Suppose now that a *minimum* is at $x = m$ and that the curve near $x = m$ is as shown in Figure 4.3a. We know that, at $x = m$, $dy/dx = 0$.

For values of x near but less than m, y is decreasing and so dy/dx is negative for all such values of x. Again, the closer x becomes to m, the nearer dy/dx becomes to zero. Also, for values of x near but greater than m, y is increasing and so dy/dx is positive for all such values of x. And again, the closer x is to m, the nearer dy/dx is to zero. If a graph of dy/dx against x is plotted (as in Figure 4.3b), we can see that dy/dx is an *increasing* function of x around $x = m$. The derivative of an increasing function is positive, and so here the derivative of dy/dx must be positive, i.e. at $x = m$

$$\frac{d}{dx}\left(\frac{dy}{dx}\right) > 0$$

or

$$\frac{d^2y}{dx^2} > 0$$

A third situation can arise, namely when

$$\frac{d^2y}{dx^2} = 0$$

Such a point will be neither a maximum nor a minimum, but a point of inflection. However, such points are not likely to concern students of this book.

NOTATION

As shown above, the differentiation of dy/dx with respect to x is denoted by

$$\frac{d}{dx}\left(\frac{dy}{dx}\right) = \frac{d^2y}{dx^2}$$

Therefore d^2y/dx^2 is found by differentiating y with respect to x *twice*. If $y = f(x)$, we have seen before that we can write dy/dx as $f'(x)$. Similarly, we can continue this process and write

$$\frac{d^2y}{dx^2} = f''(x)$$

As an example, let

$$y = x^3 + 2x + 1$$

Then $$\frac{dy}{dx} = 3x^2 + 2$$

and $$\frac{d^2y}{dx^2} = 6x$$

Similarly, suppose that

$$f(x) = x^4$$

Then $$f'(x) = 4x^3$$

and $$f''(x) = 12x^2$$

Hence $$f''(2) = 12(2 \times 2) = 48$$

SUMMARY

To find extreme points of a function, first solve the equation

$$\frac{dy}{dx} = 0$$

To identify the extreme points, calculate d^2y/dx^2 and evaluate this at each of the extreme points. Then:

(1) If $\dfrac{d^2y}{dx^2} > 0$, the point is a minimum point.

(2) If $\dfrac{d^2y}{dx^2} < 0$, the point is a maximum point.

As an example, we can consider further the function

$$y = 2x^3 + 3x^2 - 12x + 5 \tag{4.1}$$

given at the beginning of this chapter. We have already shown that

$$\frac{dy}{dx} = 6x^2 + 6x - 12 \tag{4.2}$$

and that extreme points occur at $x = 1$ and $x = -2$. If we differentiate equation 4.2 with respect to x, then we obtain

$$\frac{d^2y}{dx^2} = 12x + 6 \qquad (4.3)$$

We can now substitute $x = 1$ into equation 4.3 to give

$$\frac{d^2y}{dx^2} = 12(1) + 6$$

$$= 18$$

Hence
$$\frac{d^2y}{dx^2} > 0$$

and so $x = 1$ gives a minimum point. The corresponding minimum value of y is given by substituting $x = 1$ into equation 4.1:

$$y = 2(1)^3 + 3(1)^2 - 12(1) + 5$$

$$= 2 + 3 - 12 + 5$$

$$= -2$$

Thus a minimum point occurs at $x = 1, y = -2$.

Consider now the extreme point at $x = -2$ and substitute this value of x into equation 4.3. Then

$$\frac{d^2y}{dx^2} = 12(-2) + 6$$

$$= -24 + 6$$

$$= -18$$

Hence
$$\frac{d^2y}{dx^2} < 0$$

and so $x = -2$ gives a maximum point. The corresponding maximum value of y is now given by substituting $x = -2$ into equation 4.1:

$$y = 2(-2)^3 + 3(-2)^2 - 12(-2) + 5$$

$$= 2(-8) + 3(4) + 24 + 5$$

$$= -16 + 12 + 24 + 5$$

$$= 25$$

Thus a maximum point occurs at $x = -2, y = 25$.

ECONOMIC APPLICATIONS

Much of conventional economic analysis is concerned with the actions of individuals, business units, and governments trying to maximise or minimise something. Consumers are assumed to try to maximise their total utility when spending their income, business units are assumed to be making decisions that will maximise their profits (or minimise their losses), whilst governments may want to maximise the national level of employment (minimise unemployment) or minimise the rate at which the general price level rises. When we express one variable as a function of another, we often want to know at what point the function has a maximum or minimum value. Consider the case of the profit-maximising firm that arises in what is known as the theory of the firm. We have already established that total revenue equals price times number sold per time period, and that total revenue can be expressed as a function of output. Similarly, total cost consists of fixed costs, and of variable costs which are a function of output. If we define profits to be total revenue minus total cost, then profits also can be expressed as a function of output.

Consider the following example. Let the demand function be

$$p = 10 - 0.001q$$

the total-revenue function be

$$pq = 10q - 0.001q^2$$

and the total-cost function be

$$C_T = 100 + 7q + 0.002q^2$$

where p is price and q is output. Then

Total profits = total revenue − total cost

i.e.
$$P_T = (10q - 0.001q^2) - (100 + 7q + 0.002q^2)$$

or
$$P_T = 3q - 0.003q^2 - 100 \qquad (4.4)$$

where P_T denotes total profits. Thus we have expressed total profits as a function of output and we could, if necessary, draw the curve of total profits against output and find the values of q at which the curve had a maximum or minimum point. However, this would be a tiresome business and it would be simpler to use the differentiation technique developed at the beginning of this chapter.

The first step is to differentiate total profits with respect to output, i.e. differentiate equation 4.4:

$$\frac{dP_T}{dq} = 3 - 0.006q \qquad (4.5)$$

At an extreme point

$$\frac{dP_T}{dq} = 0$$

i.e.

$$3 - 0.006q = 0$$

∴

$$q = \frac{3}{0.006}$$

$$= 500$$

Thus, at an output of 500 units per time period the profits function has a turning point. In order to find out whether it is a point of maximum or minimum profits, we must differentiate dP_T/dq with respect to q and see if the result is negative or positive for $q = 500$. Remember that the derivative of dP_T/dq can be written as d^2P_T/dq^2 and, if this is negative, then the function has a maximum value at $q = 500$. If the value of d^2P_T/dq^2 is positive, then the function has a minimum value at $q = 500$.

Differentiating equation 4.5 gives

$$\frac{d^2P_T}{dq^2} = -0.006$$

which is obviously negative for all values of q. The negative value means that, at an output of 500 units per time period, profits are maximised. If we wish to know the price at which the profit-maximising output is sold, we substitute $q = 500$ into the demand function

$$p = 10 - 0.001q$$

Therefore at profit-maximising output

$$p = 10 - 0.001\,(500)$$

$$= 9.5$$

The firm's output will be sold at £9.50 per unit (assuming pounds to be the unit of currency).

Notice that the firm in this example faced a downward-sloping demand curve. In other words, the firm had some degree of monopoly power. Such a firm can either put output on the market and let the given demand conditions determine the price, or fix the price and see how many units of output it can sell. Here we assumed known demand and cost conditions and established the *output* at which profits would be maximised. The price was then determined by the given demand conditions.

IMPORTANT PROPOSITIONS ABOUT THE PROFIT-MAXIMISING BEHAVIOUR OF FIRMS

The numerical example above simply established the output at which a firm would maximise its total profits, given known demand and cost conditions. We now wish to demonstrate the power of mathematics to derive important propositions about the behaviour of firms without confining ourselves to particular examples. These propositions are: first, that in order to maximise profits, a firm must produce that output at which marginal cost equals marginal revenue; and secondly, that the marginal-cost curve must cut the marginal-revenue curve from below. In the intermediate textbooks these propositions are usually not proved; they are simply shown by drawing the graphs that give this result. We shall now proceed to derive these results formally.

Let R_T stand for total revenue, C_T for total cost, P_T for total profits, and q for output. Total profits are defined as total revenue minus total cost, i.e.

$$P_T = R_T - C_T \tag{4.6}$$

Thus we want to maximise the function $R_T - C_T$. Both R_T and C_T are functions of q, and so we must differentiate $R_T - C_T$ with respect to q and set the derivative equal to zero, i.e.

$$\frac{\mathrm{d}(R_T - C_T)}{\mathrm{d}q} = 0$$

But

$$\frac{\mathrm{d}(R_T - C_T)}{\mathrm{d}q} = \frac{\mathrm{d}R_T}{\mathrm{d}q} - \frac{\mathrm{d}C_T}{\mathrm{d}q}$$

$\therefore$

$$\frac{\mathrm{d}R_T}{\mathrm{d}q} = \frac{\mathrm{d}C_T}{\mathrm{d}q}$$

which is a *necessary* condition for profits to be maximised. But as was shown in Chapter 2, the derivative of total revenue with respect to output is marginal revenue (page 65) whilst the derivative of total cost with respect to output is marginal cost (page 79). We have, therefore, established that a necessary condition for the firm to maximise profits is that *marginal cost equals marginal revenue.* We have not used any specific cost and revenue functions and, therefore, the proposition holds in general.

Not only must the first derivative of a function equal zero for a turning point to exist, but additionally, for a maximum, $d^2(R_T - C_T)/dq^2$ must be negative. The equality of marginal cost and marginal revenue is, therefore, a necessary but *not* sufficient condition for a maximum. The sufficient conditions can be derived as follows. For a maximum point

$$\frac{d^2(R_T - C_T)}{dq^2} < 0$$

which can be rewritten as

$$\frac{d^2 R_T}{dq^2} - \frac{d^2 C_T}{dq^2} < 0$$

Adding $d^2 C_T/dq^2$ to each side does not change the validity of the inequality, so we can write

$$\frac{d^2 R_T}{dq^2} - \frac{d^2 C_T}{dq^2} + \frac{d^2 C_T}{dq^2} < \frac{d^2 C_T}{dq^2}$$

$$\therefore \qquad \frac{d^2 R_T}{dq^2} < \frac{d^2 C_T}{dq^2}$$

We are now stating that, not only must marginal cost equal marginal revenue at the output giving maximum profits, but in addition *the derivative of marginal revenue with respect to output must be less than the derivative of marginal cost.*

From the point of view of calculations alone, this second condition is easy to establish: with given revenue and cost functions we would simply calculate $d^2 R_T/dq^2$ and $d^2 C_T/dq^2$ and see whether the former is less than the latter. From the point of view of economic theory, however, we need to understand the full implications of the condition. Remember that $d^2 R_T/dq^2$ is the derivative of the marginal-revenue function and therefore gives the slope of the marginal-revenue function.

Similarly d^2C_T/dq^2 is the derivative of the marginal-cost function and so gives the slope of the marginal-cost function. This means that the condition

$$\frac{d^2R_T}{dq^2} < \frac{d^2C_T}{dq^2}$$

states that, at the profit-maximising output, the marginal-cost curve has a steeper slope than the marginal-revenue curve.

It is important to remember that, though this proposition has been derived mathematically and holds no matter what the shape of the functions involved, the particular functions that one meets in elementary economic analysis are determined by assumptions concerning the behaviour of consumers and firms, market structures, and technical conditions of production. For example, in a perfectly competitive market, the demand curve facing a firm is horizontal and marginal revenue equals price. In a less than perfectly competitive market, the

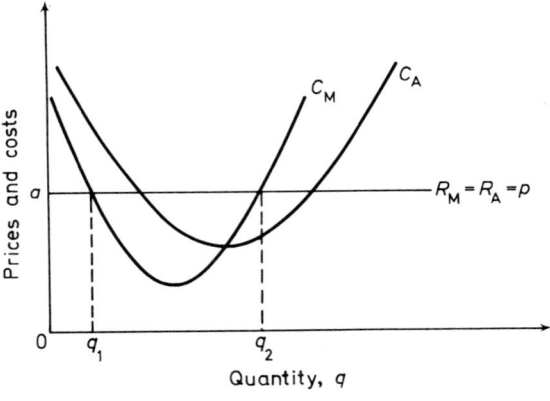

Figure 4.4

demand curve is downward sloping and marginal revenue is a decreasing function of output. In the case of cost curves, the short-period analysis assumes that the firm has a fixed amount of plant and equipment and so output takes place under conditions of eventually diminishing returns, giving rise to the familiar U-shaped marginal-cost and average-cost curves.

All of this means that the sufficient condition

$$\frac{d^2 R_T}{dq^2} < \frac{d^2 C_T}{dq^2}$$

for a maximum profit leads to the statement that, at the profit-maximising output, the marginal-cost curve cuts the marginal-revenue curve from below. This will be more recognisable if we refer to the type of diagram seen in all introductory texts (Figure 4.4), where C_M is marginal cost, C_A is average cost, R_M is marginal revenue, and R_A is average revenue. The firm is assumed to face a horizontal demand curve at a price p because its contribution to the market output is insignificant. Thus the demand curve is of the form $p = a$ where a is the intercept of the demand curve with the vertical axis. Total revenue R_T is given by

$$R_T = pq = aq$$

and therefore

$$R_M = \frac{dR_T}{dq} = a$$

and

$$\frac{d^2 R_T}{dq^2} = 0$$

Thus marginal revenue equals price, and the slope of the marginal revenue curve is zero. It can be seen that $C_M = R_M$ at the outputs q_1 and q_2 in Figure 4.4. At the output q_1, the marginal-cost curve is a decreasing function of q and so

$$\frac{dC_M}{dq} = \frac{d^2 C_T}{dq^2}$$

is negative. This means that at output q_1

$$\frac{d^2 R_T}{dq^2} > \frac{d^2 C_T}{dq^2}$$

since zero is greater than a negative number. Similarly, at output q_2, marginal cost is an increasing function of q and so $d^2 C_T/dq^2$ is positive. Therefore at q_2

$$\frac{d^2 R_T}{dq^2} < \frac{d^2 C_T}{dq^2}$$

since zero is less than a positive number; as we showed above, this is the condition for profit maximisation. (Note that the situation at q_1, where

$$\frac{\mathrm{d}^2 R_T}{\mathrm{d}q^2} > \frac{\mathrm{d}^2 C_T}{\mathrm{d}q^2}$$

is indicative of minimum profits.)

We have therefore proved what we can deduce from the diagram, namely that the equality of marginal cost and marginal revenue at a particular output is a necessary, but not sufficient, condition for profits to be maximised.

LESS THAN PERFECT COMPETITION

If competition is less than perfect, a firm is assumed to face a downward-sloping demand curve. Marginal revenue is then a decreasing function of output and so the derivative of the marginal-revenue function is also negative. The average-cost and marginal-cost curves are assumed to have

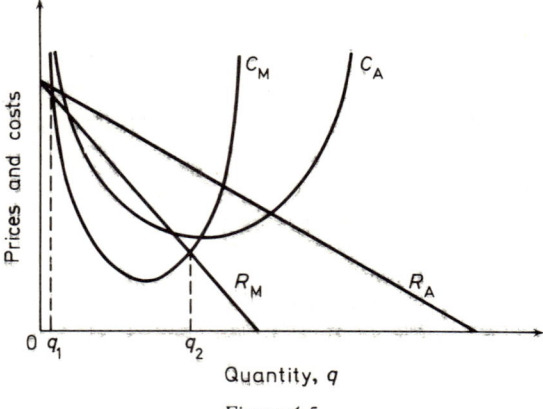

Figure 4.5

the normal shape, which means that over low ranges of output marginal cost is a decreasing function of output whilst over larger ranges marginal cost becomes an increasing function of output. The usual diagrammatic presentation is as shown in Figure 4.5.

At the output q_1 the marginal-cost curve and the marginal-revenue curve are equal and are *both* of negative slope, but the marginal-cost curve has a steeper slope than the marginal-revenue curve. Thus

$$\frac{d^2 R_T}{dq^2} > \frac{d^2 C_T}{dq^2}$$

(because a numerically smaller negative number is greater than a numerically larger negative number): consequently, this cannot be a position of profit-maximising output. At q_2 the marginal-cost curve is an increasing function of output whilst the marginal-revenue function is a decreasing function of output, and therefore

$$\frac{d^2 R_T}{dq^2} < \frac{d^2 C_T}{dq^2}$$

which we have shown to be a sufficient condition for profit maximisation.

Often the condition that $C_M = R_M$ is spoken of as the first-order condition for profit maximisation, and the condition that

$$\frac{d^2 R_T}{dq^2} < \frac{d^2 C_T}{dq^2}$$

is said to be the second-order condition.

CONSTRAINED MAXIMA AND MINIMA

Most economic problems reflect the fact that the resources capable of satisfying human wants are scarce relative to the demand for them and so the necessity of choosing between alternatives arises. The choosing agent, be it individual, firm, or country, is assumed to aim at maximising something, be it total utility, profits, or national income, and in all cases will be faced with constraints. For example, the individual consumer will be faced with a variety of goods and services that he wishes to enjoy. In the market system, these relatively scarce resources will have prices such that the ability of the consumer to maximise his total utility will be subject to the constraint of a limited amount of purchasing power available to him and the prices of the goods. Alternatively, a firm may wish to maximise profits, and profits may be a function of output. However, in the short period, given a fixed amount of some factors, the firm is faced with the operation of diminishing returns when output is increased beyond a certain level, with the result that marginal costs will rise. Thus in the case of perfect competition the firm is faced with rising marginal costs as a constraint on profit maximisation, whilst in the case of the less than perfectly competitive market there is the additional constraint of falling prices as output increases. In a sense, the example of the profit-maximising firm that we have already dealt with is an example of maximisation subject to a constraint, but the problem of constrained maxima and minima can be presented more clearly in respect of consumer behaviour and production theory. Before this, we shall deal with functions of more than one variable and some related problems.

Chapter 5

FUNCTIONS OF TWO OR MORE VARIABLES – PARTIAL DIFFERENTIATION

We have so far been concerned with functions of one variable, such as price as a function of output $[p = f(q)]$, total revenue as a function of output $[R_T = g(q)]$, and consumption as a function of income $[C = h(Y)]$. It is clearly unrealistic to assume that most of the functions met in economic analysis do in fact depend on only one variable. The total utility of the consumer is a function of a large number of goods and services he consumes; the demand for a commodity is a function of its price, the price of substitutes, tastes of the consumers, income per head, etc. The usual presentation of the theory of production involves output as a function of labour and capital. Therefore in this chapter we shall mainly consider functions of two variables, but the concepts and theorems here can easily be extended to functions of any number of variables.

A general expression for a function of two variables is

$$z = f(x, y)$$

Here, the value of the variable z depends on the values of both variables x and y. We normally suppose that x and y are independent variables, which means that the value of x can be altered without affecting the value of y, and vice versa. However, note that a change in the value of x, or of y, or of both can produce a change in the value of z.

The reader will by now be familiar with the fact that the graphical representation of a function of one variable (when it is possible to draw one) is a *curve*. This is, of course, two dimensional. For example, the function

$$y = \sqrt{(1 - x^2)}$$

(taking the positive square root) is represented by a curve which is the upper half of a circle of radius 1 and centred at the origin ($x = 0, y = 0$) (see Figure 5.1).

Considering now functions of two independent variables, the first thing to note is that any graphical representation will require an extra dimension. When $y = f(x)$, values of y are read from the vertical axis and values of x from the horizontal axis. However, when we have a

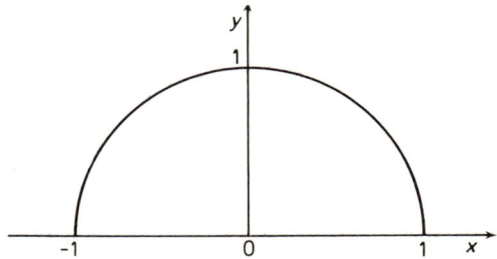

Figure 5.1

function such as $z = f(x, y)$, we need an axis for the dependent variable z, and an axis for each of the independent variables x and y. Thus any possible graph will be a 'three-dimensional' figure. For example, if we plot the points of the function

$$z = \sqrt{(1 - x^2 - y^2)}$$

(again taking the positive square root), we construct not a curve but a *surface*. This particular surface is the upper half of a sphere of radius 1 and centred at the origin ($x = 0, y = 0, z = 0$) (see Figure 5.2).

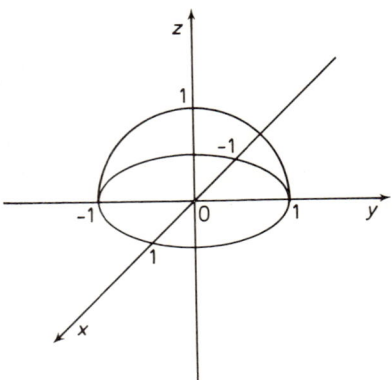

Figure 5.2

So that graphs of functions used in this chapter can be visualised, we shall normally restrict ourselves to functions of two independent variables. If a third independent variable were introduced, then the function

$$z = f(x, y, w)$$

would need four dimensions to be plotted on a graph, which is not of course possible.

Assuming, as with the one-variable functions, that our two-variable functions are continuous, how then are we to differentiate them? The first thing to consider is how a derivative is to be interpreted. For the function

$$y = f(x)$$

the derivative was the rate of change of y with respect to x. For the function

$$z = f(x, y)$$

the derivative will be the rate of change of z, but with respect to what: will it be x, or y, or both x and y together? We shall immediately leave alone the discussion of x and y both changing together, and suppose that y is to remain constant and x will vary.

Let us consider the specific example

$$z = 1 - x^2 + 3xy - 2y^2 \tag{5.1}$$

Suppose, first, that y is constant with the value 1. Then substituting $y = 1$ into equation 5.1 gives

$$z = 1 - x^2 + 3x(1) - 2(1)^2$$
$$= 1 - x^2 + 3x - 2$$

i.e.
$$z = -1 - x^2 + 3x \tag{5.2}$$

Thus z is now a function of one variable and can be plotted on a graph, as shown in Figure 5.3a. We can also differentiate this function of one variable, thus

$$\frac{dz}{dx} = -2x + 3 \tag{5.3}$$

However, we had no reason for supposing that the constant value of

y was 1. Consider, for example, what would have happened if the value of y had been 2. Then, by substituting $y = 2$ into equation 5.1,

$$z = 1 - x^2 + 3x(2) - 2(2)^2$$
$$= 1 - x^2 + 6x - 8$$

i.e.
$$z = -7 - x^2 + 6x \qquad (5.4)$$

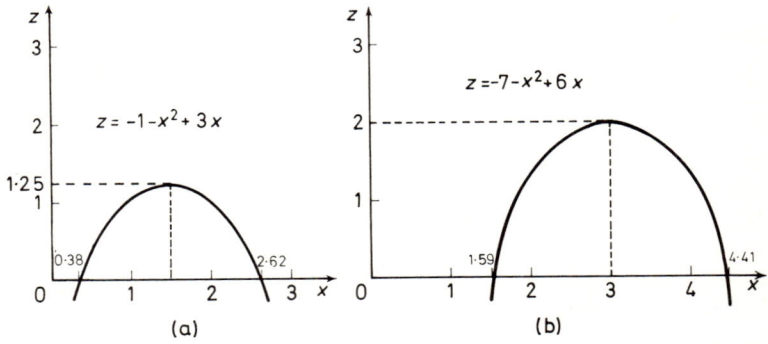

Figure 5.3

This can be plotted as shown in Figure 5.3b, which is obviously a different curve from that in Figure 5.3a. Also, we can again differentiate:

$$\frac{dz}{dx} = -2x + 6 \qquad (5.5)$$

Thus the derivative is also different from that obtained when y had the value 1. It is therefore essential to note what value y has each time we differentiate. The following notation can be used:

$$\left.\frac{dz}{dx}\right|_{y=1} = -2x + 3$$

and
$$\left.\frac{dz}{dx}\right|_{y=2} = -2x + 6$$

If we were to repeat the process for $y = 4$, we would get

$$z = 1 - x^2 + 3x(4) - 2(4)^2$$
$$= 1 - x^2 + 12x - 32$$

i.e.

$$z = -31 - x^2 + 12x \tag{5.6}$$

and

$$\left.\frac{dz}{dx}\right|_{y=4} = -2x + 12 \tag{5.7}$$

Now, instead of giving y a particular constant value, suppose it has a general constant value c, say. Then at $y = c$

$$z = 1 - x^2 + 3x(c) - 2(c)^2$$

i.e.

$$z = 1 - x^2 + 3cx - 2c^2 \tag{5.8}$$

and

$$\left.\frac{dz}{dx}\right|_{y=c} = -2x + 3c \tag{5.9}$$

If we substitute the values 1, 2, and 4 for c in equations 5.8 and 5.9, we obtain the results already found in equations 5.2–5.7. Note carefully that to obtain equation 5.8 we simply replaced y by c. However, this is making unnecessary work since we had already stated that y had a constant value; replacing y by c just repeats this statement. We can obtain the same results as before by differentiating equation 5.1, *remembering that y is a constant.* Thus

$$z = 1 - x^2 + 3xy - 2y^2$$

and

$$\left.\frac{dz}{dx}\right|_{y \text{ constant}} = -2x + 3y \tag{5.10}$$

Again this result can be checked by putting $y = 1$, $y = 2$, and $y = 4$ and comparing it with equations 5.3, 5.5, and 5.7.

Instead of differentiating as above, we could have kept x constant and varied y. Then

$$\left.\frac{dz}{dy}\right|_{x \text{ constant}} = 3x - 4y$$

Instead of writing

$$\left.\frac{dz}{dx}\right|_{y \text{ constant}} \quad \text{and} \quad \left.\frac{dz}{dy}\right|_{x \text{ constant}}$$

every time, we abbreviate these to

$$\frac{\partial z}{\partial x} \quad \text{and} \quad \frac{\partial z}{\partial y}$$

respectively. This particular form of differentiation is called *partial differentiation* and $\partial z/\partial x$ and $\partial z/\partial y$ are called *partial derivatives*. Thus if $z = f(x, y)$, then:

$\dfrac{\partial z}{\partial x}$ is the derivative of z with respect to x when y is held constant.

$\dfrac{\partial z}{\partial y}$ is the derivative of z with respect to y when x is held constant.

The implication of these definitions ought to be clear if we consider the following example from micro-economics.

An indifference curve shows the various combinations of two goods that yield the consumer a given amount of utility. As the indifference curves move out from the origin, each curve represents a higher level of utility. If U represents utility, q_1 the quantity of commodity 1, and q_2 the quantity of commodity 2, then we could state that

$$U = f(q_1, q_2)$$

i.e. utility is some function of q_1 and q_2. Further, $\partial U/\partial q_1$ is the marginal utility of commodity 1 in that it is the rate of change in the consumer's total utility given an infinitesimal change in his consumption of commodity 1, his consumption of commodity 2 being held constant.* Similarly, $\partial U/\partial q_2$ is the marginal utility of commodity 2, i.e. the rate of change in the consumer's total utility given an infinitesimal change in the consumer's consumption of commodity 2, his consumption of commodity 1 being held constant.

In production theory the same conceptual apparatus applies. The usual example given is the production function in which physical output X is some function of inputs, usually capital K and labour L. This is written as

$$X = f(K, L)$$

and $\partial X/\partial L$ is the marginal product of labour, i.e. the rate of change of output with respect to labour, capital being held constant. Similarly, $\partial X/\partial K$ is the marginal product of capital, i.e. the rate of change of output with respect to capital, labour input being held constant.

---

* The precise meaning that one can asign to the concept of marginal utility in the context of ordinal analysis is to be treated with care: see J. M. Henderson and R. E. Quandt, *Microeconomic Theory*, 2nd edn, McGraw-Hill, New York (1958).

In Chapter 2, total revenue and total cost were expressed as functions of output (i.e. functions of one variable) and so marginal revenue and marginal cost were straightforward derivatives of one variable. Now we have utility as a function of two variables and output as a function of two variables, and so marginal utility of any one commodity or marginal product of any one factor is a partial derivative.

EXTENSION TO FUNCTIONS OF MORE THAN TWO VARIABLES

Consider the function

$$z = f(x, y, u, v, w)$$

then $\partial z/\partial x$ is the derivative of z with respect to x when *all* the other variables are held constant. The derivatives $\partial z/\partial y$, $\partial z/\partial u$, $\partial z/\partial v$, and $\partial z/\partial w$, are similarly defined.

For example, if

$$z = 2 - 3xyu + u^3 - 3x^2uv + w$$

then

$$\frac{\partial z}{\partial x} = -3yu - 6xuv$$

$$\frac{\partial z}{\partial y} = -3xu$$

$$\frac{\partial z}{\partial u} = -3xy + 3u^2 - 3x^2v$$

$$\frac{\partial z}{\partial v} = -3x^2u$$

and

$$\frac{\partial z}{\partial w} = 1$$

NOTATION

If $z = f(x, y)$, the partial derivative with respect to x is sometimes written as $\partial f/\partial x$ instead of $\partial z/\partial x$. However, a more useful notation is

$$\frac{\partial z}{\partial x} = f_x(x, y)$$

and

$$\frac{\partial z}{\partial y} = f_y(x, y)$$

which enables any particular point at which the partial derivatives are calculated to be denoted easily. Note that this notation is analogous to

$$\frac{dy}{dx} = f'(x)$$

for a function of one variable. Thus $f_x(a, b)$ is the partial derivative of z with respect to x at the point $x = a$, $y = b$. As another example, if

$$f(x, y) = 1 - x^2 + 3xy - 2y^2$$

then $f_x(x, y) = -2x + 3y$

and $f_y(x, y) = 3x - 4y$

Hence $f_x(2, 1) = -2(2) + 3(1) = -4 + 3 = -1$

and $f_y(5, 3) = 3(5) - 4(3) = 15 - 12 = 3$

Quite often in economic analysis we are not concerned with specific functions and values of variables and so the notation indicated above is used in a general way. For example, given a utility function

$$U = f(q_1, q_2)$$

then $\partial U/\partial q_1$ is written as $f_1(q_1, q_2)$ or simply f_1 (the marginal utility of commodity 1). Similarly, $\partial U/\partial q_2$ is written as $f_2(q_1, q_2)$ or simply f_2 (the marginal utility of commodity 2).

The same points concerning notation apply to production theory. Suppose we had a production function in which output X is a function of two variable inputs, labour L and capital K (in the long term all factors are variable), i.e.

$$X = f(L, K)$$

then $\partial X/\partial L$ is the marginal product of labour and can be written as f_L, whilst $\partial X/\partial K$ is the marginal product of capital and can be written as f_K.

RULES

All of the rules given earlier for differentiating sums, products, and quotients also apply for functions of more than one variable. Thus:

(1) If $z = cf(x, y)$ where c is a constant, then

$$\frac{\partial z}{\partial x} = cf_x(x, y)$$

(2) If $z = f(x, y) + g(x, y)$, then

$$\frac{\partial z}{\partial x} = f_x(x, y) + g_x(x, y)$$

(3) If $z = f(x, y)g(x, y)$, then

$$\frac{\partial z}{\partial x} = f_x(x, y)g(x, y) + f(x, y)g_x(x, y)$$

(4) If $z = f(x, y)/g(x, y)$ at points where $g(x, y) \neq 0$, then

$$\frac{\partial z}{\partial x} = \frac{f_x(x, y)g(x, y) - f(x, y)g_x(x, y)}{[g(x, y)]^2}$$

(5) If $z = [f(x, y)]^n$, then

$$\frac{\partial z}{\partial x} = n[f(x, y)]^{n-1} f_x(x, y)$$

Each of these rules would give a similar result for $\partial z / \partial y$.

SECOND DERIVATIVES

Given a simple production function

$$X = f(K, L)$$

we know that $\partial X / \partial L$ is the derivative of output with respect to labour, capital being held constant, i.e. the marginal product of labour. In most elementary models of this type, capital is taken to be fixed in the short period and so output becomes a function of labour input only. A further point emphasised is that, as the labour input is increased, output will increase up to a maximum and then it will decrease (this is explained in terms of the 'law' of diminishing returns to the variable factor). Figure 5.4 shows the type of diagram used to illustrate the relationship between total product (output) and the variable factor, say labour.

The gradient of the total-product curve at any particular value of L is actually the partial derivative of X with respect to labour (capital held constant), i.e. the marginal product of labour. The gradient of the total-product curve at labour inputs L_1, L_2, and L_3 is given by the gradient of the tangent to the curve at each of these points, and it can be seen that the gradient is changing over all the possible values of labour input. At L_1 the marginal product of labour is positive, at L_2 it is zero, and at L_3 it is negative. In other words, $\partial X/\partial L$ is changing in value as L changes. We would expect this when given the assertions

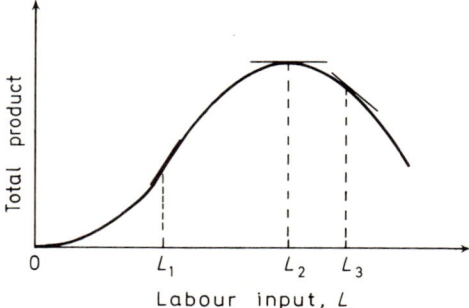

Figure 5.4

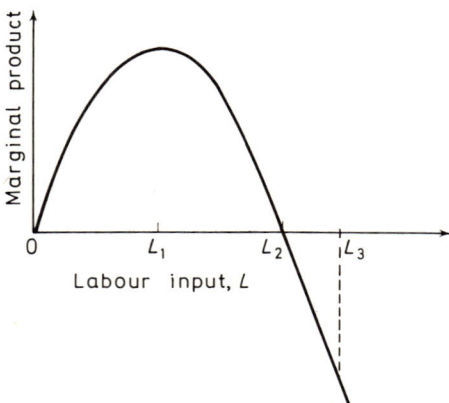

Figure 5.5

in economic theory about the law of diminishing returns, the marginal-product curve having the shape shown in Figure 5.5. At labour input L_2 the marginal product of labour is zero, i.e.

$$\frac{\partial X}{\partial L} = 0$$

(at this point total product has reached a maximum). If the labour input is increased from L_2, capital being held constant, then $\partial X/\partial L$ is negative and so total product falls (it is important to remember that this behaviour of the marginal-product curve reflects our hypothesis that factors are not perfect substitutes and hence the prediction of diminishing returns – it has nothing to do with mathematics, which helps in exploring the logical implications of these hypotheses). It now becomes clear that we shall want to measure the rate of change of marginal product as labour input varies, and hence we need the derivative of $\partial X/\partial L$ with respect to L, capital K being held constant. Alternatively, we may be dealing with the marginal product of capital and want the derivative of $\partial X/\partial K$ with respect to K, labour input L being held constant. Thus, we need to know how to calculate the second derivative of a partial first derivative. This technique is useful not only in production theory but throughout the whole of economic analysis.

CALCULATION OF SECOND DERIVATIVES

Returning to the example

$$z = 1 - x^2 + 3xy - 2y^2$$

we have already shown that

$$\frac{\partial z}{\partial x} = -2x + 3y$$

and

$$\frac{\partial z}{\partial y} = 3x - 4y$$

Note that $\partial z/\partial x$ is a function of x and y, and so we can also find the rate of change of $\partial z/\partial x$ if x changes, y being held constant. This is done by partially differentiating $\partial z/\partial x$ with respect to x:

$$\frac{\partial}{\partial x}\left(\frac{\partial z}{\partial x}\right) = \frac{\partial^2 z}{\partial x^2} = -2$$

Similarly, we can partially differentiate $\partial z/\partial y$ with respect to y:

$$\frac{\partial}{\partial y}\left(\frac{\partial z}{\partial y}\right) = \frac{\partial^2 z}{\partial y^2} = -4$$

In economic terms, if we consider the production function $X = f(K, L)$, then $\partial X/\partial L$ is the marginal product of labour. If we wish to know what happens to the marginal product of labour as the labour input is varied, then we must determine $\partial^2 X/\partial L^2$, which is in effect the slope of the marginal-product curve. If $\partial^2 X/\partial L^2$ is positive, then the marginal product of labour is rising; if $\partial^2 X/\partial L^2$ is zero, then the marginal product of labour has reached a maximum (by assertion it will not be a minimum because we are normally concerned only with positive marginal products); and if $\partial^2 X/\partial L^2$ is negative, the marginal product of labour is falling. Similar results would apply to the curve showing the marginal product of capital, $\partial^2 X/\partial K^2$.

Note that the second partial derivatives $\partial^2 X/\partial L^2$ and $\partial^2 X/\partial K^2$ can be written as f_{LL} and f_{KK} respectively.

CROSS-PARTIAL DERIVATIVES

Returning to the numerical example

$$z = 1 - x^2 + 3xy - 2y^2$$

we can see that the second partial derivatives $\partial^2 z/\partial x^2$ and $\partial^2 z/\partial y^2$ are not the only ones which can be obtained. Just as z is a function of the two variables x and y, so also are $\partial z/\partial x$ and $\partial z/\partial y$. We can therefore find the partial derivative of $\partial z/\partial x$ with respect to y:

$$\frac{\partial}{\partial y}\left(\frac{\partial z}{\partial x}\right) = \frac{\partial^2 z}{\partial y \partial x} = 3$$

Similarly, we can find the partial derivative of $\partial z/\partial y$ with respect to x:

$$\frac{\partial}{\partial x}\left(\frac{\partial z}{\partial y}\right) = \frac{\partial^2 z}{\partial x \partial y} = 3$$

The derivatives

$$\frac{\partial^2 z}{\partial x \partial y} \quad \text{and} \quad \frac{\partial^2 z}{\partial y \partial x}$$

are called the *cross-partial* derivatives. Note that each of these cross-partial derivatives is equal to 3 in this particular example, and that it is no coincidence that they are equal. Examples can be found in mathematics where the cross-partial derivatives are not equal, but the student can take it as almost certain that, for every function he will meet in economics,

$$\frac{\partial^2 z}{\partial x \partial y} = \frac{\partial^2 z}{\partial y \partial x}$$

We shall assume from now on that this is so.

Let us consider the following example:

$$z = x^2 y + y^3$$

Then $\qquad \dfrac{\partial z}{\partial x} = 2xy \qquad \dfrac{\partial z}{\partial y} = x^2 + 3y^2$

$$\frac{\partial^2 z}{\partial x^2} = 2y \qquad \frac{\partial^2 z}{\partial y^2} = 6y$$

and $\qquad \dfrac{\partial^2 z}{\partial y \partial x} = 2x \qquad \dfrac{\partial^2 z}{\partial x \partial y} = 2x$

Thus again $\qquad \dfrac{\partial^2 z}{\partial y \partial x} = \dfrac{\partial^2 z}{\partial x \partial y}$

TOTAL, MARGINAL, AND AVERAGE PRODUCT

The familiar U-shaped cost curves of elementary economic theory reflect certain assumed characteristics of the underlying production function. Let us retain our previous example of a production function in which output X is some function of the input of the two factors, labour L and capital K. Thus

$$X = f(L, K)$$

Remember that X is the *maximum* output that any combination of the two factors can produce, in other words we assume technical efficiency. There are three questions we may wish to ask concerning the production function:

(1) What happens to output if the factor inputs are increased by the same proportion, i.e. what will happen to X if we double, treble, halve, etc., any particular combination of L and K? We shall postpone a discussion of this until Chapter 6.

   (2) Assuming that the function is continuous (which implies both factors can be combined in an infinite number of ways) and we wish to produce a given output, at what rate must we substitute labour for capital and still maintain the desired output level? This question will also be postponed until Chapter 6.

   (3) If one factor is fixed in amount, what happens to output as the other factor is varied? This is the situation usually postulated in the 'theory of the firm'. Capital is assumed to be a fixed factor in the short period, whilst labour input is treated as the variable factor. This means that output changes as the labour input is changed. It is this situation we shall deal with first.

We have already introduced the ideas of a total-product curve and of a marginal-product curve. Given the assumption of eventually diminishing returns to the variable factor, the total-product curve has the shape indicated in Figure 5.4. Three questions arise concerning the variable factor and output. Firstly, what is the total product associated with any given labour input (remember that, though labour is treated as a variable factor, any particular labour input, given a fixed stock of capital, represents a particular combination of capital and labour)? The second question we can ask with reference to a particular input of labour is: what is the rate of change in total product, given a change in the variable factor (i.e. what is the marginal product of the variable factor)? Lastly, given any particular labour input, what is the average product of labour (i.e. the total product divided by the labour input)?

In Figure 5.4 we gave an example of a total-product curve, emphasising that the gradient of the curve at any particular point was the marginal product of the variable factor at the input associated with that point. The average product of labour is defined to be X/L, where L is any labour input. This is given by the slope of a line drawn from the origin to the point on the curve associated with the labour input at which the average product of labour is to be measured (see Figure 5.6). The vertical distance AL_1 indicates the total product associated with a labour input L_1, and the horizontal distance OL_1 indicates the labour input. If P_A stands for average product, then the average product at a labour input L_1 is given by

$$P_A = \frac{X_1}{L_1} = \frac{AL_1}{OL_1}$$

which is the slope of the line OA. Average product reaches a maximum when the slope of any such line is steepest. For example, the slope of the line OB in Figure 5.6 is less than the slope of OA. Therefore, the average product at labour input L_2 is less than that at L_1.

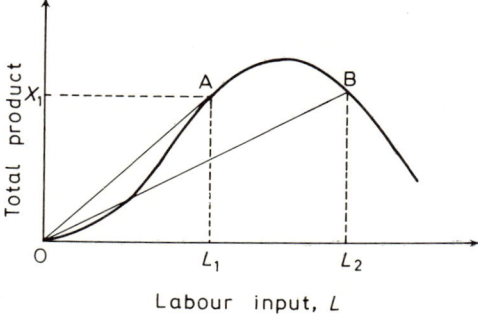

Labour input, L

Figure 5.6

Most students are acquainted with the drawing of marginal-product and average-product curves showing the following characteristics:

(1) As long as marginal product P_M is greater than average product P_A, then average product will continue to rise.
(2) Marginal product P_M is equal to average product P_A at the maximum value of average product.
(3) Marginal product reaches a maximum to the left of the average-product maximum.

Figure 5.7 illustrates these relationships.

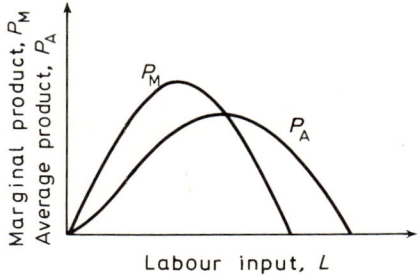

Labour input, L

Figure 5.7

With regard to the first characteristic, we can refer back to Figure 5.6. The point A represents the labour input at which the average product of labour is at a maximum. The student should demonstrate for himself that the slope of a line from the origin to any point on the curve to the left or right of A in Figure 5.6 would produce a less steep slope, and hence a lower average product of labour. However, remember that the gradient of the total-product curve itself at any point is the marginal product of labour at the associated labour input. At any point to the left of A, the gradient of the total-product curve is greater than the slope of the line drawn from the origin to this point, i.e. $P_M > P_A$. Similarly, at any point to the right of A, and up to the turning point of the total-product curve, the gradient of the total-product curve is less than the slope of the line drawn from the origin to that point. (At the maximum value of the total-product curve, $P_M = 0$.)

The second point, that $P_M = P_A$ when P_A is a maximum, is related to the first. This can be proved by using partial derivatives and the quotient rule. The production function can be written as

$$X = f(L, \bar{K})$$

where $\bar{K}$ is a constant amount of capital. Then

$$P_A = \frac{X}{L} \tag{5.11}$$

and

$$P_M = \frac{\partial X}{\partial L} = f_L(L, \bar{K})$$

As $X = f(L, \bar{K})$, we can rewrite equation 5.11 as

$$P_A = \frac{f(L, \bar{K})}{L} \tag{5.12}$$

We know that the gradient of the average-product curve is given by the partial derivative $\partial P_A / \partial L$, and on page 129 the rule for partially differentiating quotients was given: namely, when

$$z = \frac{f(x, y)}{g(x, y)}$$

then

$$\frac{\partial z}{\partial x} = \frac{f_x(x, y)g(x, y) - f(x, y)g_x(x, y)}{[g(x, y)]^2}$$

Therefore from equation 5.12

$$\frac{\partial P_A}{\partial L} = \frac{f_L(L, \overline{K})L - f(L, \overline{K})}{L^2}$$

since $\partial L/\partial L = 1$. We know that $\partial P_A/\partial L = 0$ when P_A is at a maximum, so

$$\frac{f_L(L, \overline{K})L - f(L, \overline{K})}{L^2} = 0$$

$\therefore \qquad\qquad f_L(L, \overline{K})L - f(L, \overline{K}) = 0$

i.e. $\qquad\qquad f_L(L, \overline{K})L = f(L, \overline{K})$

or $\qquad\qquad f_L(L, \overline{K}) = \dfrac{f(L, \overline{K})}{L}$

But $\qquad\qquad f_L(L, \overline{K}) = P_M$

and $\qquad\qquad \dfrac{f(L, \overline{K})}{L} = P_A$

and therefore $P_M = P_A$ when P_A is at a maximum.

TOTAL PRODUCT, AND CHANGES IN THE STOCK OF FIXED CAPITAL

It is beyond the scope of this book to examine all the questions raised by the law of variable proportions, and we have chosen to examine those issues that are most likely to face students on traditional economics courses. Our discussion so far has been of a production function with output as a function of two variables, labour and capital. Further, we have treated capital as the fixed factor and labour as the variable factor. This could have been reversed, and the conclusions regarding the behaviour and interrelationships of total, average, and marginal products would be unchanged. In terms of calculus, we have $\partial X/\partial L$ as the marginal product of labour and $\partial^2 X/\partial L^2$ as the rate of change of marginal product with respect to labour, but we could have dealt with $\partial X/\partial K$ as the marginal product of capital (L constant at $\overline{L}$), and $\partial^2 X/\partial K^2$ as the gradient of the marginal product of capital curve.

One question we have not investigated is what happens to the marginal product of labour if the fixed amount of capital is increased?

This means we must examine the cross-partial derivative $\partial^2 X/\partial K \partial L$. One would expect an increase or decrease in the stock of fixed capital to affect the total, average, and marginal products of labour, as total product is a function of both fixed and variable factors. Under normal conditions we would expect an increase in K to move the total-product curve to the left, which means that any particular level of output can now be produced with a smaller labour input. This is shown in Figure 5.8, where P_{T1} is the total product with a capital stock $\overline{K}_1$, P_{T2} is the total product with a capital stock $\overline{K}_2$, and so on $(\overline{K}_3 > \overline{K}_2 > \overline{K}_1)$. With the original stock of capital $\overline{K}_1$, an output X_1 was produced with a labour input L_1; given an increase in capital to $\overline{K}_2$, the same output can be produced with a smaller input of labour L_2, whilst with a further increase in capital the output can be produced with labour input L_3. In principle, we could plot a mass of total-product curves reflecting very small changes in the stock of capital. With each total-product curve there would be associated marginal-product and average-product curves.

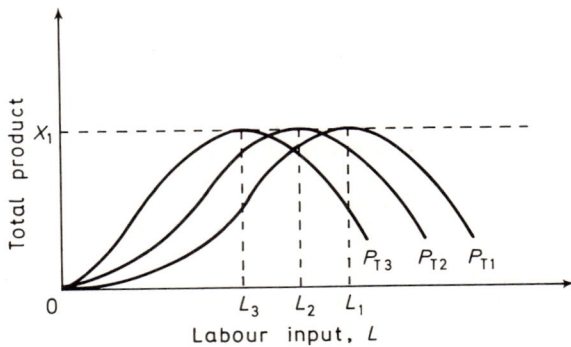

Figure 5.8

Concentrating on marginal product (given by $\partial X/\partial L$), we can see that at any specific labour input, such as L_1, $\partial X/\partial L$ changes as the capital stock is increased from one constant value to another. For example, given P_{T1}, $\partial X/\partial L = 0$ at L_1, whereas, given P_{T2}, $\partial X/\partial L$ is negative at L_1. Similarly, at L_2, $\partial X/\partial L$ is positive given P_{T1}, $\partial X/\partial L = 0$ given P_{T2}, and $\partial X/\partial L$ is negative given P_{T3}. Thus at any value of L, marginal product changes as $\overline{K}$ changes.

We have here stressed the second cross-partial derivative $\partial^2 X/\partial K \partial L$ because, quite apart from the fact that it occurs in economic analysis, it is easy to forget that, given a function of two variables, a partial derivative can still be a function of the two variables and that the 'constant' variable can have a number of possible values. We have used the production function to introduce partial derivatives in economic analysis, but we could, and shall, use partial derivatives in consumer analysis. Here also the second cross-partial derivative has an economic significance. The marginal utility of commodity Z to the consumer is the change in his total utility given a change in his consumption of Z, *the consumption of other commodities being held constant.* If consumption of these other commodities is held constant but at a *higher* level, then it will affect the marginal utility of Z. Thus if $U = f(q_1, q_2)$ is the consumer's utility function, then $\partial U/\partial q_1$ is the marginal utility of commodity 1, consumption of commodity 2 being held constant; also, $\partial^2 U/\partial q_2 \partial q_1$ is the change in $\partial U/\partial q_1$ given a change in q_2. This cross-partial is often written as f_{12}.

Chapter 6

PARTIAL DIFFERENTIATION – SIMULTANEOUS CHANGE OF INDEPENDENT VARIABLES

Let us pause and consider the ground covered so far in this book. We have shown that, given continuous functions, then economic concepts such as marginal revenue, marginal cost, and multipliers are in fact derivatives of the appropriate functions. Further, the translation of economic concepts into a mathematical form enables the hypothesised relationships between the variables of economic theory to be examined more easily. We dealt first with functions of one variable, such as price, total cost, and profit each as a function of output. In the last chapter we introduced the idea of functions of two variables, taking the consumer's utility function and the firm's production function as examples. We then introduced marginal utility and marginal products as partial derivatives.

The differentiation discussed so far may seem rather limited in use because, for a function of two or more variables, it is not realistic to confine ourselves to problems in which one variable remains constant. For example, we may need to know what happens to output if both capital and labour inputs change simultaneously, and a similar question could be asked concerning a consumer's utility function. Likewise, a firm's profits may be a function of its sales of two products, and we may wish to know what happens to profits if the sales of both products change simultaneously? We must now acquire the mathematics appropriate to such problems.

Consider a production function such as

$$X = 3KL^2 \tag{6.1}$$

where X is output, K is the input of capital, and L is the labour input. Suppose that the input of capital is increased by a small amount ΔK, and at the same time the labour input is increased by a small amount ΔL. Then X will increase to a new value $X + \Delta X$, where

$$X + \Delta X = 3(K + \Delta K)(L + \Delta L)^2$$

Thus output will have increased by ΔX, where

$$\Delta X = 3(K + \Delta K)(L + \Delta L)^2 - X$$
$$= 3(K + \Delta K)[L^2 + 2L(\Delta L) + (\Delta L)^2] - 3KL^2$$
$$= 3[KL^2 + 2KL(\Delta L) + K(\Delta L)^2 + L^2(\Delta K) + 2L(\Delta K)(\Delta L)$$
$$+ (\Delta K)(\Delta L)^2] - 3KL^2$$
$$= 3KL^2 + 6KL(\Delta L) + 3K(\Delta L)^2 + 3L^2(\Delta K) + 6L(\Delta K)(\Delta L)$$
$$+ 3(\Delta K)(\Delta L)^2 - 3KL^2$$
$$= 6KL(\Delta L) + 3K(\Delta L)^2 + 3L^2(\Delta K) + 6L(\Delta K)(\Delta L) + 3(\Delta K)(\Delta L)^2$$

But we have assumed that the changes ΔL and ΔK in factor inputs are small amounts. Thus $(\Delta L)^2$ and $(\Delta K)(\Delta L)$ are very small, whilst $(\Delta K)(\Delta L)^2$ is even smaller. For example, if $\Delta K = 0.01$ and $\Delta L = 0.01$, then

$$(\Delta L)^2 = 0.0001$$
$$(\Delta K)(\Delta L) = 0.0001$$

and
$$(\Delta K)(\Delta L)^2 = 0.000\,001$$

Thus we shall assume that these terms are small enough to ignore and so we obtain the approximate expression for ΔX:

$$\Delta X = 6KL(\Delta L) + 3L^2(\Delta K) \tag{6.2}$$

Note that the smaller are ΔK and ΔL, the better is the approximation to ΔX.

If we now return to equation 6.1 and partially differentiate, we obtain for the marginal product of capital

$$\frac{\partial X}{\partial K} = 3L^2$$

and for the marginal product of labour

$$\frac{\partial X}{\partial L} = 6KL$$

Thus we have shown that the change in output, given simultaneous small changes in inputs, is *approximately* equal to the respective marginal products multiplied by the incremental change in factor inputs, i.e.

$$\Delta X = \frac{\partial X}{\partial K} \Delta K + \frac{\partial X}{\partial L} \Delta L \tag{6.3}$$

This result can be generalised to give, for the function $z = f(x, y)$,

$$\Delta z = \frac{\partial z}{\partial x} \Delta x + \frac{\partial z}{\partial y} \Delta y \qquad (6.4)$$

Remember that $\partial z/\partial x$ can be written as f_x and that $\partial z/\partial y$ can be written as f_y. From now on we shall in general use this notation for partial derivatives.

Equation 6.4 can be applied to the consumer's utility function

$$U = f(q_1, q_2)$$

The approximate change in total utility, given simultaneous small changes in the consumption of both commodities, is given as

$$\Delta U = f_1 \Delta q_1 + f_2 \Delta q_2$$

The general result can also easily be extended to functions of more than two variables. For example, the function

$$z = f(x, y, u, v, w)$$

would give $\qquad \Delta z = f_x \Delta x + f_y \Delta y + f_u \Delta u + f_v \Delta v + f_w \Delta w$

TOTAL DERIVATIVE AND THE CHAIN RULE

In the preceding section we considered such questions as what happens to total output if the inputs of both capital and labour change by small amounts, and what happens to total utility if the consumer's consumption of both commodities changes by small amounts. The answers were indicated by an *approximate* determination of ΔX and ΔU. However, we may wish to know the *precise* change in output and utility, given changes in the quantities of factor inputs and the quantities consumed, and to obtain the precise *rate* of change, we need a further result.

Suppose we have a function

$$z = f(x, y)$$

but, in addition, both x and y are themselves functions of another variable, which for convenience we shall call t. Thus, if t varies, both x and y will vary and so z will change. Under these circumstances we could replace all the x's and y's with t and obtain z as a function of t; then, on differentiating, we could find dz/dt (note that this would be a full derivative as we are not holding any variable constant). However, there is another, and easier, way of obtaining dz/dt, as follows.

Let an increase Δt in t produce a change Δx in x and a change Δy in y, and let these in turn produce a change Δz in z. Then, from equation 6.4,

$$\Delta z = f_x \Delta x + f_y \Delta y$$

Now, dividing each side by Δt,

$$\frac{\Delta z}{\Delta t} = f_x \frac{\Delta x}{\Delta t} + f_y \frac{\Delta y}{\Delta t} \tag{6.5}$$

Let $\Delta t \to 0$, and then

$$\underset{\Delta t \to 0}{\text{Limit}} \frac{\Delta z}{\Delta t} = \underset{\Delta t \to 0}{\text{Limit}} \left(f_x \frac{\Delta x}{\Delta t} + f_y \frac{\Delta y}{\Delta t} \right)$$

$$= f_x \left(\underset{\Delta t \to 0}{\text{Limit}} \frac{\Delta x}{\Delta t} \right) + f_y \left(\underset{\Delta t \to 0}{\text{Limit}} \frac{\Delta y}{\Delta t} \right) \tag{6.6}$$

But

$$\underset{\Delta t \to 0}{\text{Limit}} \frac{\Delta z}{\Delta t} = \frac{dz}{dt}$$

$$\underset{\Delta t \to 0}{\text{Limit}} \frac{\Delta x}{\Delta t} = \frac{dx}{dt}$$

and

$$\underset{\Delta t \to 0}{\text{Limit}} \frac{\Delta y}{\Delta t} = \frac{dy}{dt}$$

Hence equation 6.6 becomes

$$\frac{dz}{dt} = f_x \frac{dx}{dt} + f_y \frac{dy}{dt} \tag{6.7}$$

Remember that equation 6.4 was an *approximation* for Δx that became better as Δt became nearer zero. Now we have let $\Delta t \to 0$, and so equation 6.7 is an *exact* expression for dz/dt. The result is one form of the chain rule and is very useful indeed, as can be shown if we first look at a numerical example.

Let $$z = 3x^2 - 4y^5 \tag{6.8}$$

$$x = 10 + 3t \tag{6.9}$$

and $$y = 4 - 2t^2 \tag{6.10}$$

Therefore, substituting for x and y,

$$z = 3(10 + 3t)^2 - 4(4 - 2t^2)^5$$

It is easy to see that a very cumbersome calculation would be needed to give dz/dt directly. However, using the total derivative we need only two partial derivatives and two derivatives, all easily obtained. Thus

$$\frac{dz}{dt} = \frac{\partial z}{\partial x}\frac{dx}{dt} + \frac{\partial z}{\partial y}\frac{dy}{dt}$$

where, from equations 6.8–6.10,

$$\frac{\partial z}{\partial x} = 6x \qquad \frac{\partial z}{\partial y} = -20y^4$$

and

$$\frac{dx}{dt} = 3 \qquad \frac{dy}{dt} = -4t$$

$\therefore$

$$\frac{dz}{dt} = 6x(3) + (-20y^4)(-4t)$$

$$= 18x + 80y^4t$$

Thus, given specific values of x, y, and t, we can find dz/dt by substitution.

Equation 6.7 is very useful in economics in those problems in which the independent variables are themselves related to a third variable. There is no special significance in the choice of the letter t to denote the third variable. In those problems where two variables both happen to be related to time, then we say they are both functions of t, where in this particular case t stands for time, but the letter t can stand for any variable we choose. A common example often quoted is that in which we have a production function of the form

$$X = f(K, L)$$

which relates an economy's output to its stock of capital K and its supply of labour L. If we further assume that both K and L are functions of time, i.e. as time passes both K and L change, then X also changes with time. It might, for example, be the case that capital accumulation takes place over time and that population growth due to natural increase or immigration takes place over time. Therefore we would write $K = g(t)$ and $L = h(t)$, where here t denotes time. The rate of change of output with respect to time would be

$$\frac{dX}{dt} = \frac{\partial X}{\partial K}\frac{dK}{dt} + \frac{\partial X}{\partial L}\frac{dL}{dt}$$

Thus, given specific functions, we would need to obtain only two marginal products and two derivatives.

Quite often, we are not interested in the specific functional forms but use the total derivative in its general form to carry out further operations within a piece of analysis in order to obtain a general conclusion.* In the present text we shall deal with a *special* case of the total derivative because it will enable us to prove some important propositions of elementary economic theory.

THE CHAIN RULE FOR A FUNCTION OF TWO DEPENDENT VARIABLES

So far we have assumed that for the function

$$z = f(x, y)$$

the variables x and y have been independent (see page 121). However, equation 6.4 still holds if x and y are not independent, i.e. if x *cannot* be varied while y is held constant; a change in x automatically produces a change in y. The distinction between independent and dependent variables may be clearer if we refer to economic analysis. In the analysis of consumer behaviour, indifference curves represent an ordering of levels of utility and, if a line is drawn from the origin of the indifference map through the indifference curves, we can say that the further any point on that line is from the origin the higher is the level of utility represented by the curve at this point. Thus utility itself is assumed to be a function of the quantities consumed of two goods. If an individual consumes *more* of one commodity and *no less* of the other, he is, automatically, on a higher indifference curve and hence a higher level of satisfaction. Thus we must stress that the consumption of each of the goods is independent of the consumption of the other when we

---

* Often this occurs in analysis beyond the level of an intermediate principles course in economics. For those interested in an application, see R. Solow, 'Technical Change and the Aggregate Production Function', *Review of Economics and Statistics*, Aug. (1957).

discuss movements from one indifference curve to another, but the problem changes when we discuss movements along a given indifference curve. In this case a change in the consumption of one commodity necessarily involves a change in the consumption of the other. Thus, if we state that for a given level of utility $\bar{U} = \mathrm{f}(q_1, q_2)$, where q_1 and q_2 are the amounts consumed of the two goods, then q_1 and q_2 are related — they are not independent.

Suppose we have a function

$$z = \mathrm{f}(x, y)$$

and y is a function of x. This means that we can replace t by x in equation 6.7 to give

$$\frac{dz}{dx} = \frac{\partial z}{\partial x}\frac{dx}{dx} + \frac{\partial z}{\partial y}\frac{dy}{dx}$$

but

$$\frac{dx}{dx} = 1$$

and so

$$\frac{dz}{dx} = \frac{\partial z}{\partial x} + \frac{\partial z}{\partial y}\frac{dy}{dx} \tag{6.11}$$

which can be written as

$$\frac{dz}{dx} = f_x + f_y\frac{dy}{dx} \tag{6.12}$$

That this is a very important result will be best appreciated if we go on to use it immediately.

INDIFFERENCE CURVES AND THE RATE OF COMMODITY SUBSTITUTION

The analysis of consumer behaviour using indifference curves assumes that the consumer (or household) can indicate which of various combinations of two commodities will give him more or less utility. Additionally, it is assumed that he can indicate the various combinations of the two goods that will yield him the same level of utility. When he ranks various combinations equally as yielding the same level of satisfaction, we say he is indifferent in terms of choosing between them. Graphically, an indifference curve is the locus of all the various combinations of the two goods that yield a constant but unspecified level of utility. The usual diagrammatic presentation of indifference curves is shown in Figure 6.1.

In the figure, C_1 is an indifference curve and is the locus of all the combinations of the two commodities that yield the consumer the same amount of utility. On the vertical axis q_2 represents the quantity of commodity 2 consumed, whilst on the horizontal axis q_1 represents the quantity of commodity 1 consumed. Thus point A represents the

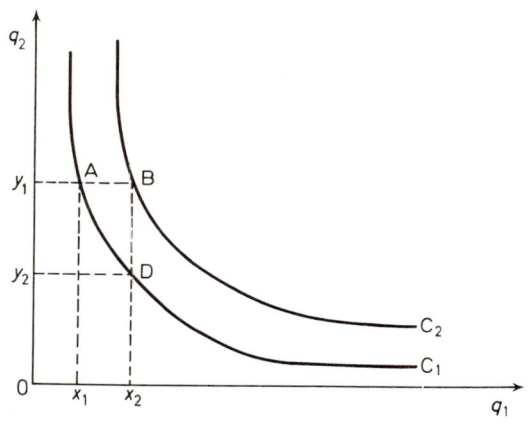

Figure 6.1

combination y_1 of commodity 2 and x_1 of commodity 1, whilst point D represents the combination y_2 of commodity 2 and x_2 of commodity 1. Both combinations yield the consumer the same amount of utility. Curve C_2 is another indifference curve, further from the origin, and represents a higher level of utility than C_1. Thus the combination at B of y_1 of commodity 2 and x_2 of commodity 1 represents a higher level of utility than any point on C_1.

In principle we could have an infinite number of indifference curves on the diagram, which would be known as an indifference map. There are several points worth stressing with regard to indifference curves. The curves are convex to the origin, reflecting an economic hypothesis that, as the consumer reduces his consumption of commodity 2 and consumes more of commodity 1, then the *rate* at which commodity 1 is substituted for commodity 2 in order to maintain the consumer's level of utility will have to increase (conversely, if commodity 1 is being given up for increased consumption of commodity 2, then the rate at which commodity 2 is substituted for commodity 1 will increase). This seems intuitively plausible because, the less the consumer has of a commodity, the higher will be its marginal utility. A further point is the assumption that the commodities are divisible, i.e. variations in the quantities consumed can be infinitesimally small. This, in effect, is the familiar continuity assumption.

We now need to prove an important theoretical proposition concerning the rate of commodity substitution, and will use the chain rule for a function of two dependent variables. The word 'rate' implies something to do with the slope of the indifference curve at a point. Remember that, as we move along an indifference curve, the level of utility it represents is unchanged. Additionally, if the consumer reduces his consumption of commodity 1, he increases his consumption of commodity 2, so q_1 and q_2 are not independent of each other. This means that with respect to a particular indifference curve we can speak of the rate of change of q_2 with respect to q_1, and vice versa.

Suppose we have the utility function

$$U = f(q_1, q_2)$$

i.e. utility is a function of the quantities consumed of commodity 1 and commodity 2. However, as we are discussing movements *along* an indifference curve, there is no change in the level of utility as the consumption of q_1 and q_2 varies. Thus using the total derivative (equation 6.7) and letting $t = q_2$, we obtain

$$\frac{dU}{dq_2} = f_1 \frac{dq_1}{dq_2} + f_2 \frac{dq_2}{dq_2}$$

But $dq_2/dq_2 = 1$ and therefore

$$\frac{dU}{dq_2} = f_1 \frac{dq_1}{dq_2} + f_2 \tag{6.13}$$

Thus, the *precise* rate of change of utility with respect to a change in q_2 is given by

$$f_1 \frac{dq_1}{dq_2} + f_2$$

However, as $dU/dq_2 = 0$ by definition, we have

$$0 = f_1 \frac{dq_1}{dq_2} + f_2$$

$$\therefore \qquad -f_1 \frac{dq_1}{dq_2} = f_2$$

or
$$\frac{f_2}{f_1} = -\frac{dq_1}{dq_2} \qquad\qquad (6.14)$$

Remember that f_1 denotes $\partial U/\partial q_1$, a partial derivative which is the marginal utility of commodity 1, whilst f_2 is $\partial U/\partial q_2$, the marginal utility of commodity 2.

The term on the right-hand side of equation 6.14 ($-dq_1/dq_2$) is known as the rate of commodity substitution and it equals the ratio of the marginal utilities. This is an important result in the micro-economic theory of consumer behaviour and takes us some way towards establishing the conditions for consumer equilibrium. Although we have defined $-dq_1/dq_2$ as the rate of commodity substitution, in fact it gives the rate of substitution of commodity 1 for commodity 2. It should be clear (see page 97) that we could equally state

$$\frac{f_1}{f_2} = -\frac{dq_2}{dq_1}$$

The negative sign precedes the derivative as the indifference curve slopes downward to the right. Obviously, if we move up the indifference curve (Figure 6.1), commodity 2 is being substituted for commodity 1 whereas, if we move down the indifference curve, commodity 1 is being substituted for commodity 2.

At a point of the indifference curve we can simply talk about the rate of commodity substitution. This result will be useful later when we examine the conditions under which a consumer will be in equilibrium, in terms of maximising his utility, subject to constraints. For the moment we shall emphasise the mathematics involved by establishing another important proposition in the field of production theory.

ISOQUANTS AND THE RATE OF TECHNICAL SUBSTITUTION

Earlier, in dealing with partial derivatives, we introduced the idea of the marginal product of labour as the rate of change of output with respect to the labour input, capital held constant, and also the marginal product of capital as the rate of change of output with respect to capital input, labour held constant. Then we introduced the idea of a change in output given a change in *both* factor inputs. More of both factors puts the firm on a higher isoquant and hence a higher level of output. In this case capital and labour are independent factors.

The concept of the isoquant has some parallel features with the indifference curve in that an isoquant is the locus of all the combinations of the two factor inputs which will yield a constant level of output, thus making the factor inputs dependent for any particular

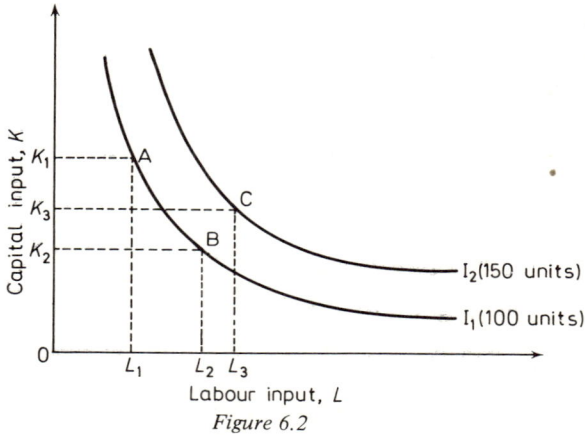

Figure 6.2

isoquant. The assumption that factor inputs are divisible, i.e. can be varied by infinitely small amounts, means that the isoquant is a continuous curve, which implies that there is an infinite number of combinations of factors that will yield a given level of output (unlike utility, output can be measured and so, in this respect, indifference curves and isoquants differ). Like the indifference curve, the isoquant is convex to the origin. This reflects the empirical hypothesis that factors of production are not perfect substitutes for each other with the result that if, for example, less and less capital is used and more labour is substituted for capital, the *rate* at which labour is substituted for capital will have to increase in order to maintain the constant level of output (the argument holds in reverse when capital is substituted for labour).

Figure 6.2 shows an isoquant map, assuming two factor inputs, capital and labour. The further away from the origin is an isoquant, the higher is the level of output yielded by the factor combinations it represents. The isoquant I_1 shows the various combinations of capital and labour that will yield a given volume of output, say 100 units (each particular combination can be called a process). Thus the point A on I_1 is the combination (K_1, L_1) and it produces 100 units of output, as does the combination (K_2, L_2) at point B. The combination at A uses more capital and less labour than the combination at point B (all the points on an isoquant represent technically efficient processes). The isoquant I_2 represents combinations of capital and labour that will produce a greater volume of output that those on I_1. Thus point C represents the combination (K_3, L_3), which produces 150 units.

We shall now use the mathematics explained earlier in this chapter to establish certain propositions about the slope of an isoquant at any particular point on it. Remember that, as we move along an isoquant, the change in output is zero, i.e. no matter which combination of factors are used on I_1, the output will be 100 units. It is the rate of technical substitution of factors which is of interest.

Suppose we have the production function

$$X = f(K, L)$$

Then
$$\frac{dX}{dL} = \frac{\partial f}{\partial K}\frac{dK}{dL} + \frac{\partial f}{\partial L}\frac{dL}{dL}$$

But
$$\frac{\partial f}{\partial K} = f_K$$

$$\frac{\partial f}{\partial L} = f_L$$

$$\frac{dL}{dL} = 1$$

and so
$$\frac{dX}{dL} = f_K \frac{dK}{dL} + f_L$$

Also, since output X is constant on any isoquant, $dX/dL = 0$ and therefore

$$0 = f_K \frac{dK}{dL} + f_L$$

∴
$$-f_K \frac{dK}{dL} = f_L$$

or
$$-\frac{dK}{dL} = \frac{f_L}{f_K} \qquad (6.15)$$

The term on the left-hand side $(-\mathrm{d}K/\mathrm{d}L)$ is the slope of the isoquant at a point and is known as the *rate of technical substitution* (or the marginal rate of factor substitution). Equation 6.15 indicates that the rate of technical substitution of one factor for the other, at any particular point on the curve, equals the ratio of their marginal products. Since f_K is the partial derivative $\partial X/\partial K$ whilst f_L is $\partial X/\partial L$, equation 6.15 could be written as

$$-\frac{\mathrm{d}K}{\mathrm{d}L} = \frac{\partial X/\partial L}{\partial X/\partial K}$$

The student should prove to himself that

$$-\frac{\mathrm{d}L}{\mathrm{d}K} = \frac{f_K}{f_L} \tag{6.16}$$

As in the analogous case of indifference curves, it does not matter whether we use equation 6.15 or equation 6.16, since the rate of technical substitution refers to a movement in either direction from a point. Both this result and that of the rate of commodity substitution are derived by the use of calculus and cannot be established by graphical methods. Note that the concepts of marginal utility and marginal product used by economists are defined as partial derivatives. In considering the rate of commodity substitution and the rate of technical substitution, we have established two important propositions which are relevant in examining such problems as the conditions under which a consumer will maximise his total utility when spending his income, and the conditions under which a firm will maximise its output given a specified cost outlay. This class of problem is often referred to as one of constrained maxima and minima and will be dealt with in the next chapter.

$z = f(x, y)$ WHERE x AND y ARE EACH A FUNCTION OF u AND v

So far we have considered the function $z = f(x, y)$ where x and y are independent, and then the situation where x and y are related to each other. There is another possibility to be introduced now, namely $z = f(x, y)$ where

$$x = g(u, v)$$

and

$$y = h(u, v)$$

By substituting for x and y in z we would express z as a function of u and v, and differentiating we would obtain the partial derivatives $\partial z/\partial u$ and $\partial z/\partial v$. These can be found by a similar process to that used before.

Suppose v is kept constant and let u increase by Δu. This will produce changes Δx in x and Δy in y, and these will produce a change Δz in z. From equation 6.5

$$\frac{\Delta z}{\Delta u} = \frac{\partial z}{\partial x}\frac{\Delta x}{\Delta u} + \frac{\partial z}{\partial y}\frac{\Delta y}{\Delta u}$$

which in the limit $\Delta u \to 0$ becomes

$$\frac{\partial z}{\partial u} = \frac{\partial z}{\partial x}\frac{\partial x}{\partial u} + \frac{\partial z}{\partial y}\frac{\partial y}{\partial u} \qquad (6.17)$$

Alternatively, if u were kept constant and v changed, we would have

$$\frac{\partial z}{\partial v} = \frac{\partial z}{\partial x}\frac{\partial x}{\partial v} + \frac{\partial z}{\partial y}\frac{\partial y}{\partial v} \qquad (6.18)$$

Equations 6.7, 6.17, and 6.18 are known as *chain rules.*

This kind of partial derivative will now be demonstrated with reference to a problem in economics. We shall introduce the problem without carrying it through to a solution, as that will have to be delayed until the next chapter. A student would not meet this economics problem in an introductory principles course, or even a second-year course, but we feel that it might usefully be tackled here as the mathematics is not difficult, given our progression so far. The problem is often associated with a nineteenth-century economist by the name of Cournot.

A MONOPOLIST PRODUCING TWO COMMODITIES

Suppose that a firm produces two goods X_1 and X_2, and let q_1 be the amount of X_1 produced whilst q_2 is the amount of X_2. Similarly, let p_1 be the price of X_1 and p_2 the price of X_2. We now assume that the sales of these two goods are related (they could be complementary or substitutes). Thus the demand for X_1 is a function of p_1 *and* p_2, and similarly the demand for X_2 is a function of p_2 *and* p_1. Thus we could state these demand functions as

$$q_1 = \mathrm{h}(p_1, p_2)$$

and

$$q_2 = \mathrm{k}(p_1, p_2)$$

If R_T represents the total revenue, then

$$R_T = p_1 q_1 + p_2 q_2 \qquad (6.19)$$

Suppose we now wish to consider what happens to total revenue if the firm changes p_1, holding p_2 constant. We are now looking for marginal revenue with respect to p_1, but two facts must be remembered. First, as q_1 and q_2 are related in consumption (let us assume they are substitutes), then a change in p_1 will affect q_1 *and* q_2; secondly, the rate of change of total revenue with respect to p_1 will be a partial derivative. Thus marginal revenue with respect to p_1 is given by

$$\frac{\partial R_T}{\partial p_1} = q_1 + p_1 \frac{\partial q_1}{\partial p_1} + p_2 \frac{\partial q_2}{\partial p_1} \qquad (6.20)$$

Note that in differentiating $p_1 q_1$ we used the product rule, with $\partial p_1 / \partial p_1 = 1$; also, in differentiating $p_2 q_2$ we used the product rule, but $\partial p_2 / \partial p_1 = 0$ because p_2 is constant. Alternatively, we could have assumed the firm changes p_2 leaving p_1 constant, in which case we would have

$$\frac{\partial R_T}{\partial p_2} = q_2 + p_1 \frac{\partial q_1}{\partial p_2} + p_2 \frac{\partial q_2}{\partial p_2} \qquad (6.21)$$

The formulation of the problem becomes more interesting if costs and profits are introduced. Suppose that total cost C_T is given by

$$C_T = f(q_1, q_2) \qquad (6.22)$$

i.e. cost is given as a function of output. As q_1 and q_2 are each a function of p_1 and p_2, total cost is also a function of p_1 and p_2. To find what happens to total cost if the firm changes p_1, holding p_2 constant, we can apply equation 6.17 or 6.18. Hence

$$\frac{\partial C_T}{\partial p_1} = \frac{\partial C_T}{\partial q_1} \frac{\partial q_1}{\partial p_1} + \frac{\partial C_T}{\partial q_2} \frac{\partial q_2}{\partial p_1} \qquad (6.23)$$

and similarly, if the firm changes p_2, holding p_1 constant, then

$$\frac{\partial C_T}{\partial p_2} = \frac{\partial C_T}{\partial q_1} \frac{\partial q_1}{\partial p_2} + \frac{\partial C_T}{\partial q_2} \frac{\partial q_2}{\partial p_2}$$

Thus we can obtain both marginal cost and marginal revenue with respect to p_1 and p_2.

Since, at any level of output, total profits equal total revenue minus total costs, we can obtain total profits as a function of p_1 and p_2 only. If P_T denotes total profits, then

$$P_T = R_T - C_T \qquad (6.24)$$

Therefore, from equations 6.19 and 6.22,

$$P_T = p_1 q_1 + p_2 q_2 - f(q_1, q_2) \qquad (6.25)$$

We thus have P_T as a function of q_1 and q_2 and of p_1 and p_2. But as q_1 and q_2 are each a function of p_1 and p_2, we could express total profits as a function of prices only, i.e.

$$P_T = g(p_1, p_2)$$

If the demand functions were given, we could find the profit-maximising prices and hence the profit-maximising outputs. Remember that, when we examined the simple case of profits being a function of one variable, output, the conditions for maximum profit were quite simple, namely

$$\frac{dP_T}{dq} = 0$$

and

$$\frac{d^2 P_T}{dq^2} < 0$$

Our present problem is much more difficult because profits are a function of the two outputs q_1 and q_2, which in turn are each a function of two prices. However, we are well on the way to being able to handle this problem. Its final solution will have to wait until the next chapter, but the analysis given above is a necessary part of the solution. For the moment, we shall concentrate on differentiating the total-profits function first partially with respect to p_1 and then with respect to p_2.

Thus from equation 6.24

$$\frac{\partial P_T}{\partial p_1} = \frac{\partial R_T}{\partial p_1} - \frac{\partial C_T}{\partial p_1}$$

and from equations 6.20 and 6.23

$$\frac{\partial P_T}{\partial p_1} = \left(q_1 + p_1 \frac{\partial q_1}{\partial p_1} + p_2 \frac{\partial q_2}{\partial p_1} \right) - \left(\frac{\partial C_T}{\partial q_1} \frac{\partial q_1}{\partial p_1} + \frac{\partial C_T}{\partial q_2} \frac{\partial q_2}{\partial p_1} \right)$$

i.e.

$$\frac{\partial P_T}{\partial p_1} = q_1 + p_1 \frac{\partial q_1}{\partial p_1} + p_2 \frac{\partial q_2}{\partial p_1} - \frac{\partial C_T}{\partial q_1} \frac{\partial q_1}{\partial p_1} - \frac{\partial C_T}{\partial q_2} \frac{\partial q_2}{\partial p_1} \qquad (6.26)$$

Similarly, the partial derivative of P_T with respect to p_2 is given by

$$\frac{\partial P_T}{\partial p_2} = q_2 + p_1 \frac{\partial q_1}{\partial p_2} + p_2 \frac{\partial q_2}{\partial p_2} - \frac{\partial C_T}{\partial q_1} \frac{\partial q_1}{\partial p_2} - \frac{\partial C_T}{\partial q_2} \frac{\partial q_2}{\partial p_2} \qquad (6.27)$$

To establish the prices at which total profits will be a maximum, we must set

$$\frac{\partial P_T}{\partial p_1} = \frac{\partial P_T}{\partial p_2} = 0$$

Why this is so we shall have to leave until the next chapter.

HOMOGENEOUS FUNCTIONS

We have frequently referred to production functions, isoquants, and the marginal products of factors of production. A production function reflects all the technically efficient means of producing any level of output, and an isoquant map reflects the characteristics of the particular production function concerned. So far, we have considered the following concepts:

(1) The marginal product of a factor, i.e. the change in output when one factor is varied whilst the other (or others) is held constant. This involves the idea of a marginal product as a partial derivative and appears in economics textbooks under the heading of 'returns to a factor'.

(2) The marginal rate of technical substitution (or the marginal rate of factor substitution). Here we considered the rate at which one factor would be substituted for another in order to maintain a given level of output, in other words, the rate of factor substitution at a point on an isoquant.

A question that arises early on in an economics course is what happens to output if all factors of production are increased or decreased in proportion? For example, if all factors are doubled, will output double, more than double, or increase less than double? This is the familiar problem of returns to scale (not to be confused with returns to a factor). The answer depends on the nature of the production function, and this leads us to an examination of a class of functions particularly important in economic analysis, namely the homogeneous function.

It might be helpful to consider first a numerical example of what we wish to convey, and then give a formal statement. Suppose we had the function

$$z = f(x, y)$$

where

$$f(x, y) = x^2 + 2y^2$$

Let us now multiply each of the variables x and y by a non-zero constant λ (lambda). Thus

$$
\begin{aligned}
f(\lambda x, \lambda y) &= (\lambda x)^2 + 2(\lambda y)^2 \\
&= \lambda^2 x^2 + 2\lambda^2 y^2 \\
&= \lambda^2 (x^2 + 2y^2) \\
&= \lambda^2 f(x, y) \\
&= \lambda^2 z
\end{aligned}
$$

Thus λ^2 can be taken out of $f(\lambda x, \lambda y)$ as a common factor, and we would therefore describe $f(x, y)$ as a homogeneous function of degree two.

To state the general result formally, suppose we had the function

$$z = f(x, y)$$

If each variable x and y is multiplied by a non-zero constant and the function is evaluated at the point $(\lambda x, \lambda y)$, i.e. we evaluate $f(\lambda x, \lambda y)$, and if we find that

$$f(\lambda x, \lambda y) = \lambda^n f(x, y)$$

then $z = f(x, y)$ is called a homogeneous function of degree n.

Let us consider now the numerical example

$$f(x, y) = \frac{3x^3 - xy^2}{\sqrt{(x + y)}}$$

Then, if λ is a non-zero constant,

$$f(\lambda x, \lambda y) = \frac{3(\lambda x)^3 - (\lambda x)(\lambda y)^2}{\sqrt{(\lambda x + \lambda y)}}$$

$$= \frac{3\lambda^3 x^3 - \lambda x \lambda^2 y^2}{\sqrt{[\lambda(x + y)]}}$$

$$= \frac{\lambda^3 (3x^3 - xy^2)}{\sqrt{\lambda}\sqrt{(x + y)}}$$

$$= \frac{\lambda^3 (3x^3 - xy^2)}{\lambda^{1/2}\sqrt{(x + y)}}$$

$$= \lambda^{5/2} \left[\frac{3x^2 - xy^2}{\sqrt{(x + y)}} \right]$$

Therefore $f(x, y)$ is homogeneous of degree $\frac{5}{2}$.

Now suppose

$$X = AL^\alpha K^\beta$$

where X is output, A is a constant, L is the labour input, K is the capital input, and α and β are parameters with the property that

$$\alpha + \beta = 1$$

As L and K are variables, we can examine what happens to X if L and K are each multiplied by some non-zero constant λ. Thus

$$A(\lambda L)^\alpha (\lambda K)^\beta = A\lambda^\alpha L^\alpha \lambda^\beta K^\beta$$

$$= \lambda^{\alpha + \beta} AL^\alpha K^\beta$$

Therefore, since $\alpha + \beta = 1$,

$$A(\lambda L)^\alpha (\lambda K)^\beta = \lambda(AL^\alpha K^\beta)$$

$$= \lambda X$$

Thus the effect of multiplying the variables L and K by λ has been to increase output by a factor λ. Suppose $\lambda = 2$, then we are saying that doubling the factor inputs will double output. This is the condition of *constant returns to scale*.

This concept leads to the important point that constant returns to scale occur only when the production function is homogeneous of degree one. This will be clear if we examine the production function

$$X = 3KL^2$$

Multiplying the variables on the right-hand side by λ gives

$$3(\lambda K)(\lambda L)^2 = 3\lambda K \lambda^2 L^2$$
$$= \lambda^3(3KL^2)$$
$$= \lambda^3 X$$

Thus, if $\lambda = 2$, then the factor inputs are being doubled, which in this particular case will multiply output by the factor $2^3 = 8$. This is an example of *increasing returns to scale*.

Suppose now we had a production function

$$X = 10K^{1/4}L^{1/4}$$

Multiplying the variables on the right-hand side by λ gives

$$10(\lambda K)^{1/4}(\lambda L)^{1/4} = 10\lambda^{1/4}K^{1/4}\lambda^{1/4}L^{1/4}$$
$$= \lambda^{1/2}(10K^{1/4}L^{1/4})$$
$$= \lambda^{1/2}X$$

Thus, if $\lambda = 9$, then the factor inputs are being increased ninefold, which in this case will multiply output by the factor $9^{1/2} = 3$. Consequently the increase in output is less than ninefold, and this is an example of *decreasing returns to scale*.

The conclusions reached so far could be summarised as follows:

(1) If a production function is homogeneous of degree less than one, output is subject to decreasing returns to scale.
(2) If a production function is homogeneous of degree one, output is subject to constant returns to scale.
(3) If a production function is homogeneous of degree greater than one, output is subject to increasing returns to scale.

EULER'S FIRST THEOREM

We shall now state and prove a very useful theorem concerned with homogeneous functions, as follows. If $z = f(x, y)$ is homogeneous of degree n, then

$$x\frac{\partial f}{\partial x} + y\frac{\partial f}{\partial y} = nf(x, y)$$

Proof

If λ is any non-zero constant, put $X = \lambda x$ and $Y = \lambda y$. Then

$$\frac{\partial X}{\partial \lambda} = x$$

and
$$\frac{\partial Y}{\partial \lambda} = y$$

If we consider the function evaluated at the point (X, Y), then

$$f(X, Y) = f(\lambda x, \lambda y)$$

or, since $f(x, y)$ is a homogeneous function of degree n,

$$f(X, Y) = \lambda^n f(x, y) \tag{6.28}$$

Partially differentiating the left-hand side of equation 6.28 with respect to λ gives (using equation 6.17)

$$\frac{\partial}{\partial \lambda} [f(X, Y)] = \frac{\partial f}{\partial X} \frac{\partial X}{\partial \lambda} + \frac{\partial f}{\partial Y} \frac{\partial Y}{\partial \lambda}$$

Therefore, since $\partial X/\partial \lambda = x$ and $\partial Y/\partial \lambda = y$,

$$\frac{\partial}{\partial \lambda} [f(X, Y)] = \frac{\partial f}{\partial X} x + \frac{\partial f}{\partial Y} y \tag{6.29}$$

Also, partially differentiating the right-hand side of equation 6.28 with respect to λ gives

$$\frac{\partial}{\partial \lambda} [\lambda^n f(x, y)] = n\lambda^{n-1} f(x, y) \tag{6.30}$$

Therefore, equating the right-hand sides of equations 6.29 and 6.30,

$$x \frac{\partial f}{\partial X} + y \frac{\partial f}{\partial Y} = n\lambda^{n-1} f(x, y) \tag{6.31}$$

But remember that $X = \lambda x$ and $Y = \lambda y$, and so equation 6.31 becomes

$$x \frac{\partial f}{\partial(\lambda x)} + y \frac{\partial f}{\partial(\lambda y)} = n\lambda^{n-1} f(x, y) \tag{6.32}$$

This holds for any non-zero value of λ, and so it will hold for $\lambda = 1$.

Therefore, putting $\lambda = 1$,

$$x\frac{\partial f}{\partial x} + y\frac{\partial f}{\partial y} = nf(x, y) \tag{6.33}$$

This result is widely used in economic analysis.

FACTOR SHARES OF TOTAL PRODUCT

Suppose we have a production function

$$X = f(K, L)$$

that is homogeneous of degree n. Then Euler's theorem states that

$$K\frac{\partial X}{\partial K} + L\frac{\partial X}{\partial L} = nf(K, L)$$

If the function is homogeneous of degree one, then $n = 1$ and so

$$K\frac{\partial X}{\partial K} + L\frac{\partial X}{\partial L} = f(K, L)$$

i.e.

$$K\frac{\partial X}{\partial K} + L\frac{\partial X}{\partial L} = X \tag{6.34}$$

We are now saying that the input of capital times the marginal product of capital, plus the input of labour times the marginal product of labour, equals the total product.

Suppose we started an analysis based on the following assumptions:

(1) Factors of production are rewarded according to their marginal product.
(2) The shares of the products going to each factor add up to the total product.

These two conditions will not be met under all circumstances. The share of output going to labour is given by $L(\partial X/\partial L)$, whilst that going to capital is $K(\partial X/\partial K)$. Thus labour's share is its marginal product times the number of units of labour used, and capital's share is the marginal product of capital times the units of capital used. It is thus quite in order to argue that factors are paid according to their marginal products *and* that their shares of the product add up to the total amount as long as the production function is homogeneous of degree one, i.e. there are constant returns to scale. Equation 6.34, for a homogeneous function of degree one, is then met.

But suppose that the production function is homogeneous of degree two, then

$$K \frac{\partial X}{\partial K} + L \frac{\partial X}{\partial L} = 2f(K, L) = 2X \qquad (6.35)$$

We cannot now argue that assumptions 1 and 2 above hold because equation 6.35 implies that the shares of the factors of production, if they receive their marginal products, add up to twice the output — a result which is clearly nonsensical. Similarly, suppose that the production function is homogeneous of degree less than one, i.e. production is subject to decreasing returns to scale. If it is homogeneous of degree $\frac{1}{2}$, for example, then

$$K \frac{\partial X}{\partial K} + L \frac{\partial X}{\partial L} = \frac{1}{2} f(K, L) = \frac{1}{2} X$$

We are saying here that factor shares do not exhaust the total product but that they equal half the product, and so assumption 2 above does not hold. Additionally, we would need an economic explanation of what happens to the half of the output that does not go to labour and capital. In the late nineteenth century there was a great deal of interest in theoretical propositions concerning the share of national output that went to the various factors, and the Marginal Productivity Theory of Distribution draws heavily on the type of mathematics we have introduced. We have carried out the above analysis in terms of physical inputs and outputs, but if the price of a product were introduced it would not change the results as long as we are speaking of perfect competition. As the analysis of factor shares of total product is a much-discussed area of economic analysis, Euler's theorem is extremely useful in checking on the logical consistency of models.

Chapter 7

OPTIMISATION OF FUNCTIONS OF MORE THAN ONE VARIABLE

For functions of more than one variable, optimisation (the finding of maximum or minimum values) follows broadly the same methods as those used for functions of one variable, but there are a few extensions, some predictable, others not quite so. In economics we wish to consider such theoretical problems as: 'Given a consumer's utility function, under what conditions will the consumer maximise his total utility?' and 'Given a firm's or industry's production function, under what conditions will the firm or industry maximise its output?' However, the form in which these questions have been put is not very useful, for consumers and firms will be operating under constraints and so we shall ultimately be concerned with constrained maximisation (or minimisation, of costs for example). Before considering such problems, we must tackle the mathematics necessary to cope with them. The results obtained here should be compared with those of Chapter 4. Proof of most of these results is beyond the scope of this book, but the more mathematically inclined reader could obtain proofs from Chapters 9 and 10 of *A Course of Analysis* by E. G. Phillips (Cambridge University Press, 1960).

STATIONARY POINTS

For the continuous function of one variable given by

$$y = f(x)$$

stationary points were found at all values of x satisfying the equation

$$\frac{dy}{dx} = 0$$

We are now concerned with continuous functions of the form

$$z = f(x, y)$$

163

This has two variables, and partial derivatives can be determined. A stationary point will then be found where x and y satisfy simultaneously the equations

$$\frac{\partial z}{\partial x} = 0 \quad \text{and} \quad \frac{\partial z}{\partial y} = 0$$

If the stationary point occurs where $x = a$ and $y = b$, for example, the stationary value of the function is given by $z = f(a, b)$.

We shall not prove this result, but it should seem logical. Suppose for example, that a maximum point occurs when $x = a$ and $y = b$, as shown in Figure 7.1a. If we were to plot the function $z = f(x, b)$, i.e. the

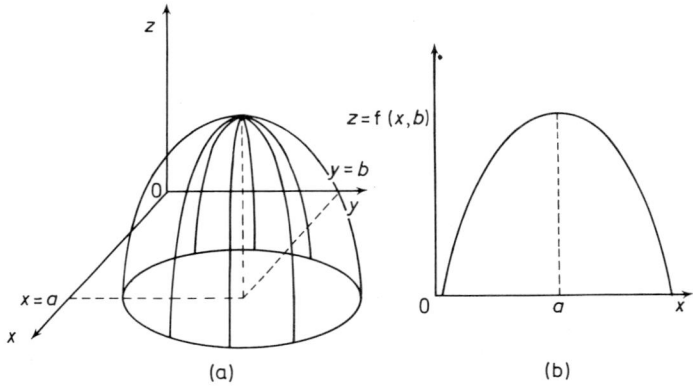

(a)   (b)

Figure 7.1

function $z = f(x, y)$ with y having the constant value b, we would produce the curve shown in Figure 7.1b. We would expect this curve to have its maximum at $x = a$, i.e. we would expect

$$\frac{dz}{dx}\bigg|_{y=b} = 0$$

to be satisfied when $x = a$. In other words,

$$\frac{\partial z}{\partial x} = 0$$

would be satisfied when $x = a$ and $y = b$. Similarly, we could have given

x the constant value a, leading to the curve $z = f(a, y)$ which we would expect to have its maximum at $y = b$. In other words,

$$\frac{dz}{dy}\bigg|_{x=a} = 0$$

or

$$\frac{\partial z}{\partial y} = 0$$

when $x = a$ and $y = b$. It thus seems reasonable that, at the maximum point,

$$\frac{\partial z}{\partial x} = 0 \quad \text{and} \quad \frac{\partial z}{\partial y} = 0$$

We could have produced this same argument for a minimum point, such as the one shown in Figure 7.2.

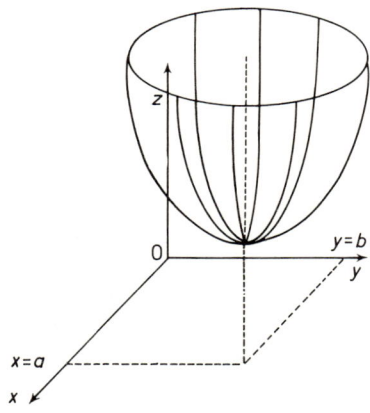

Figure 7.2

CLASSIFICATION OF STATIONARY POINTS

As in Chapter 4, having found the stationary points we are still left with the problem of determining whether they are maxima or minima. In the one-variable case

$$y = f(x)$$

We had at a minimum

$$\frac{d^2y}{dx^2} > 0$$

and at a maximum

$$\frac{d^2y}{dx^2} < 0$$

These results are closely followed here for the two-variable case, but again no proof is attempted.

For a *minimum* to occur at a stationary point where $x = a$ and $y = b$, we require that

$$\frac{\partial^2 z}{\partial x^2} > 0 \quad \text{and} \quad \frac{\partial^2 z}{\partial y^2} > 0$$

when $x = a$ and $y = b$, i.e.

$$f_{xx}(a, b) > 0 \quad \text{and} \quad f_{yy}(a, b) > 0$$

For a *maximum* to occur at a stationary point where $x = a$ and $y = b$, we require that

$$\frac{\partial^2 z}{\partial x^2} < 0 \quad \text{and} \quad \frac{\partial^2 z}{\partial y^2} < 0$$

when $x = a$ and $y = b$, i.e.

$$f_{xx}(a, b) < 0 \quad \text{and} \quad f_{yy}(a, b) < 0$$

This is as far as the similarity with Chapter 4 goes for, in addition to these conditions, for either a maximum or a minimum, an *extra* condition must be satisfied, namely

$$\left(\frac{\partial^2 z}{\partial x^2}\right)\left(\frac{\partial^2 z}{\partial y^2}\right) - \left(\frac{\partial^2 z}{\partial x \partial y}\right)^2 > 0$$

when $x = a$ and $y = b$, i.e.

$$f_{xx}(a, b) f_{yy}(a, b) - [f_{xy}(a, b)]^2 > 0$$

This leads us to the question of what happens if a stationary point occurs where

$$\left(\frac{\partial^2 z}{\partial x^2}\right)\left(\frac{\partial^2 z}{\partial y^2}\right) - \left(\frac{\partial^2 z}{\partial x \partial y}\right)^2 < 0$$

We know that this stationary point could not be a maximum or minimum, and there must therefore be a third type of stationary point. This is called a *saddle point* because of its property of appearing to be a minimum in one plane (view of a saddle from the side) and a maximum in another plane (view of a saddle from the end) (see Figure 7.3).

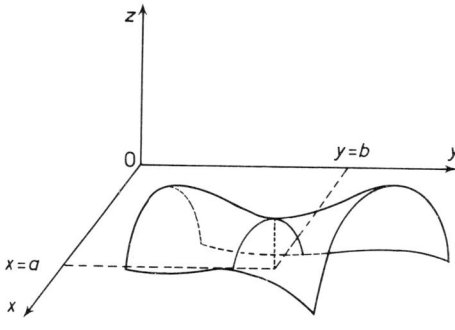

Figure 7.3

We can summarise the steps in finding and classifying the stationary points of the function $z = f(x, y)$ in the following way:

(1) Solve simultaneously the equations

$$f_x(x, y) = 0$$

and $$f_y(x, y) = 0$$

This will give the values of x and y at the stationary points, and hence the stationary values of the function.

(2) For each stationary point where $x = a$ and $y = b$, evaluate

$$\Delta = f_{xx}(a, b) f_{yy}(a, b) - [f_{xy}(a, b)]^2 \qquad (7.1)$$

(3) If $\Delta < 0$ then the stationary point is a saddle point.

(4) If $\Delta > 0$ then the stationary point is either a maximum or minimum, and $f_{xx}(a, b)$ and $f_{yy}(a, b)$ must be evaluated to determine which.

(5) If $f_{xx}(a, b) > 0$ and $f_{yy}(a, b) > 0$, then the point is a minimum.

(6) If $f_{xx}(a, b) < 0$ and $f_{yy}(a, b) < 0$, then the point is a maximum.

Example 1

Suppose

$$f(x, y) = x^2 + 2xy - 2y^2 - 2x + 4y \qquad (7.2)$$

then

$$f_x(x, y) = 2x + 2y - 2 \qquad (7.3)$$

and

$$f_y(x, y) = 2x - 4y + 4 \qquad (7.4)$$

We must therefore solve the simultaneous equations

$$2x + 2y - 2 = 0$$

and

$$2x - 4y + 4 = 0$$

i.e.

$$x + y - 1 = 0 \qquad (7.5)$$

and

$$x - 2y + 2 = 0 \qquad (7.6)$$

Subtracting equation 7.6 from equation 7.5 gives

$$3y - 3 = 0$$

$$\therefore \qquad y = 1$$

Substituting $y = 1$ in equation 7.5 gives

$$x + 1 - 1 = 0$$

$$\therefore \qquad x = 0$$

Therefore the function has only one stationary point Y, which occurs when $x = 0$ and $y = 1$. The stationary value of the function is found by substituting $x = 0$ and $y = 1$ into equation 7.2, i.e.

$$f(0, 1) = (0)^2 + 2(0)(1) - 2(1)^2 - 2(0) + 4(1)$$

$$= 0 + 0 - 2 - 0 + 4$$

$$= 2$$

In order to classify the stationary point, we must find Δ as defined in equation 7.1. From equations 7.3 and 7.4

$$f_{xx} = 2$$

$$f_{yy} = -4$$

and

$$f_{xy} = 2$$

Note that none of these partial derivatives contain either of the terms x and y, so the values $x = 0$ and $y = 1$ do not have to be substituted in this particular example. Thus, from equation 7.1,

$$\Delta = 2(-4) - 2^2$$
$$= -8 - 4$$
$$= -12$$

Thus $\Delta < 0$ and the stationary point is a saddle point.

Example 2

Suppose $f(x, y) = x^2 + 2y^2 - 2xy - 4y$ (7.7)

Then $f_x(x, y) = 2x - 2y$ (7.8)

and $f_y(x, y) = 4y - 2x - 4$ (7.9)

We must therefore solve the simultaneous equations

$$2x - 2y = 0$$

and $$4y - 2x - 4 = 0$$

i.e. $$x - y = 0$$ (7.10)

and $$2y - x - 2 = 0$$ (7.11)

From equation 7.10, $y = x$ and this can be substituted into equation 7.11 to give

$$2x - x - 2 = 0$$

∴ $$x - 2 = 0$$

∴ $$x = 2$$

and so $$y = 2$$

Again there is only one stationary point, and this occurs at $x = 2, y = 2$. The stationary value of $f(x, y)$ is found by substituting $x = y = 2$ into equation 7.7, thus

$$f(2, 2) = (2)^2 + 2(2)^2 - 2(2)(2) - 4(2)$$
$$= 4 + 8 - 8 - 8$$
$$= -4$$

From equations 7.8 and 7.9

$$f_{xx} = 2$$
$$f_{yy} = 4$$

and
$$f_{xy} = -2$$

∴
$$\Delta = 2(4) - (-2)^2$$
$$= 8 - 4$$
$$= 4$$

Thus $\Delta > 0$ and the stationary point is either a maximum or a minimum. But $f_{xx} > 0$ and $f_{yy} > 0$, and therefore the stationary point is a minimum.

A MONOPOLIST PRODUCING TWO COMMODITIES RELATED IN CONSUMPTION

In Chapter 6 we showed how to differentiate the function $z = f(x, y)$ when x and y are each a function of u and v. To show how these rules might be applied in the context of economic analysis, we considered the case of a monopolist producing two goods X_1 and X_2 that were related in consumption. Thus the demand for X_1 was a function of the prices p_1 and p_2 of X_1 and X_2 respectively, whilst the demand for X_2 was also a function of p_1 and p_2. Given the cost as a function of q_1 and q_2, the quantities produced of X_1 and X_2 respectively, we obtained total profits P_T as a function of p_1 and p_2 only, i.e.

$$P_T = g(p_1, p_2)$$

In order to demonstrate the rule concerning differentiation of this type of function, we obtained the following partial derivatives (see equations 6.26 and 6.27):

$$\frac{\partial P_T}{\partial p_1} = q_1 + p_1 \frac{\partial q_1}{\partial p_1} + p_2 \frac{\partial q_2}{\partial p_1} - \frac{\partial C_T}{\partial q_1}\frac{\partial q_1}{\partial p_1} - \frac{\partial C_T}{\partial q_2}\frac{\partial q_2}{\partial p_1} \qquad (7.12)$$

and
$$\frac{\partial P_T}{\partial p_2} = q_2 + p_1 \frac{\partial q_1}{\partial p_2} + p_2 \frac{\partial q_2}{\partial p_2} - \frac{\partial C_T}{\partial q_1}\frac{\partial q_1}{\partial p_2} - \frac{\partial C_T}{\partial q_2}\frac{\partial q_2}{\partial p_2} \qquad (7.13)$$

We stopped at this point but were leading up the question: what are the values of p_1 and p_2 that will maximise profits? Now

$$P_T = g(p_1, p_2)$$

is a similar function to $z = f(x, y)$ which we have been discussing. We stated at the beginning of this chapter that a stationary point will be found at any point where the values $x = a$ and $y = b$ satisfy simultaneously the equations

$$\frac{\partial z}{\partial x} = 0 \quad \text{and} \quad \frac{\partial z}{\partial y} = 0$$

Similarly, given $P_T = g(p_1, p_2)$, a stationary point will be found at any point where the values $p_1 = a$ and $p_2 = b$ satisfy simultaneously the equations

$$\frac{\partial P_T}{\partial p_1} = 0 \tag{7.14}$$

and

$$\frac{\partial P_T}{\partial p_2} = 0 \tag{7.15}$$

Solutions of these two equations will give the values of p_1 and p_2 at which the profits function has a stationary point, but such a point could be a saddle point or a maximum or a minimum.

For a maximum or minimum, the further condition

$$\left(\frac{\partial^2 P_T}{\partial p_1{}^2}\right)\left(\frac{\partial^2 P_T}{\partial p_2{}^2}\right) - \left(\frac{\partial^2 P_T}{\partial p_1 \partial p_2}\right)^2 > 0 \tag{7.16}$$

must also be met. If it is met, then the last stage of the operation is to determine whether any stationary point is a maximum or a minimum. In order to do this, the second partial derivatives

$$\frac{\partial^2 P_T}{\partial p_1{}^2} \quad \text{and} \quad \frac{\partial^2 P_T}{\partial p_2{}^2}$$

must be evaluated. If they are both negative, then profits will be *maximised* at the particular values of p_1 and p_2. If positive, then profits are a *minimum*. Suppose that, in a particular example, profits were found to be a maximum. Then, given specific demand functions, the values of p_1 and p_2 can be substituted to give outputs at which profits are maximised.

This may all seem rather complicated, but the following numerical example should convince the reader that the actual operation is easier than it at first appears. Although this example of the monopolist producing two goods related in consumption has been used to demonstrate the mathematics developed in Chapter 6 and in this chapter, it serves an additional purpose. It shows how the constituent elements of a problem can be rearranged in order to facilitate mathematical treatment. Thus, given $q_1 = h(p_1, p_2)$, $q_2 = k(p_1, p_2)$, and $C_T = f(q_1, q_2)$, we can set up the problem with total profits as a function of only p_1 and p_2, which makes it much easier to handle. It is very important to realise that problems can usually be restated in a more manageable and convenient form.

Example

Let q_1 represent the quantity demanded of X_1 whilst q_2 is the quantity demanded of X_2. Suppose we have the demand functions

$$q_1 = 10 - 2p_1 + p_2 \tag{7.17}$$
$$q_2 = 20 + p_1 - 3p_2 \tag{7.18}$$

and the total-cost function

$$C_T = 4q_1 + 2q_2 \tag{7.19}$$

where p_1 and p_2 are the prices of X_1 and X_2 respectively. We now wish to obtain total profits explicitly in terms of p_1 and p_2.

First, the equation for total profit P_T is

$$P_T = R_T - C_T \tag{7.20}$$

where R_T is total revenue, given by

$$R_T = p_1 q_1 + p_2 q_2 \tag{7.21}$$

Substituting equations 7.17 and 7.18 into equation 7.21 gives

$$R_T = p_1(10 - 2p_1 + p_2) + p_2(20 + p_1 - 3p_2)$$
$$\therefore \quad R_T = 10p_1 - 2p_1^2 + p_1p_2 + 20p_2 + p_1p_2 - 3p_2^2$$
$$\text{i.e.} \quad R_T = 10p_1 + 20p_2 - 2p_1^2 + 2p_1p_2 - 3p_2^2 \tag{7.22}$$

Now, in order to find C_T in terms of p_1 and p_2, equations 7.17 and 7.18 are substituted into equation 7.19:

$$C_T = 4(10 - 2p_1 + p_2) + 2(20 + p_1 - 3p_2)$$
$$\therefore \quad C_T = 40 - 8p_1 + 4p_2 + 40 + 2p_1 - 6p_2$$
$$\text{i.e.} \quad C_T = 80 - 6p_1 - 2p_2 \tag{7.23}$$

Therefore, substituting equations 7.22 and 7.23 into equation 7.20 gives

$$P_T = 10p_1 + 20p_2 - 2p_1^2 + 2p_1p_2 - 3p_2^2 - (80 - 6p_1 - 2p_2)$$

$$\therefore \quad P_T = 10p_1 + 20p_2 - 2p_1^2 + 2p_1p_2 - 3p_2^2 - 80 + 6p_1 + 2p_2$$

i.e. $P_T = 16p_1 + 22p_2 - 2p_1^2 + 2p_1p_2 - 3p_2^2 - 80$ (7.24)

Thus we have total profits P_T as a function of p_1 and p_2 only. The next step is to find the values of p_1 and p_2 at which P_T will have a maximum value. The first-order conditions are that

$$\frac{\partial P_T}{\partial p_1} = \frac{\partial P_T}{\partial p_2} = 0$$

Partially differentiating equation 7.24 and setting the derivatives equal to zero therefore gives

$$\frac{\partial P_T}{\partial p_1} = 16 - 4p_1 + 2p_2 = 0 \qquad (7.25)$$

and
$$\frac{\partial P_T}{\partial p_2} = 22 + 2p_1 - 6p_2 = 0 \qquad (7.26)$$

i.e. we must solve the equations

$$8 - 2p_1 + p_2 = 0 \qquad (7.27)$$

and $11 + p_1 - 3p_2 = 0$ (7.28)

Multiplying equation 7.27 by 3 gives

$$24 - 6p_1 + 3p_2 = 0$$

which can be added to equation 7.28 to give

$$35 - 5p_1 = 0$$

$$\therefore \qquad\qquad 35 = 5p_1$$

i.e. $p_1 = 7$

Substituting this value into equation 7.27 gives

$$8 - 2(7) + p_2 = 0$$

i.e. $8 - 14 + p_2 = 0$

$$\therefore \qquad\qquad p_2 = 6$$

Thus the values of p_1 and p_2 that will give a stationary point are $p_1 = 7$ and $p_2 = 6$.

In order to establish if the profit is a maximum or a minimum value, condition 7.16 above must be satisfied. But from equations 7.25 and 7.26

$$\frac{\partial^2 P_T}{\partial p_1{}^2} = -4 \qquad (7.29)$$

$$\frac{\partial^2 P_T}{\partial p_2{}^2} = -6 \qquad (7.30)$$

and

$$\frac{\partial^2 P_T}{\partial p_1 \partial p_2} = 2$$

∴

$$\left(\frac{\partial^2 P_T}{\partial p_1{}^2}\right)\left(\frac{\partial^2 P_T}{\partial p_2{}^2}\right) - \left(\frac{\partial^2 P_T}{\partial p_1 \partial p_2}\right)^2 = (-4)(-6) - 2^2$$
$$= 24 - 4$$
$$= 20$$

Thus condition 7.16 is satisfied and the profits function has a maximum or a minimum when $p_1 = 7$ and $p_2 = 6$. But from equations 7.29 and 7.30, $\partial^2 P_T/\partial p_1{}^2$ and $\partial^2 P_T/\partial p_2{}^2$ are both negative. Thus profits will be *maximised* when $p_1 = 7$ and $p_2 = 6$.

If the quantities q_1 and q_2 are required, the values of p_1 and p_2 are simply substituted into the demand functions as follows. From equation 7.17

$$q_1 = 10 - 2(7) + 6$$

i.e.

$$q_1 = 10 - 14 + 6$$

∴

$$q_1 = 2$$

and from equation 7.18

$$q_2 = 20 + 7 - 3(6)$$

i.e.

$$q_2 = 27 - 18$$

∴

$$q_2 = 9$$

CONSTRAINED MAXIMA AND MINIMA

Many economics problems are concerned with situations in which some choosing agent, be it consumer, household, firm or government, seeks to achieve an objective, subject to constraints. Usually, it is hypothesised that the consumer wishes to maximise his total utility; the firm wishes to maximise profits; and the government wishes to maximise employment. In each case the choosing agent is subject to constraints.

Let us first deal with the analysis of consumer behaviour that appears in many intermediate economics courses. Here, we assert that the consumer wishes to maximise his total utility, which in turn is a function of the amounts of the goods and services he consumes. The constituent features of the utility maximisation problem are:

(1) The goods and services consumed have differing marginal utilities for the consumer.
(2) They have prices, i.e. they are not free.
(3) The consumer has a limited income.

Thus prices and a limited income place constraints on the individual's consumption in that he cannot consume everything he wants up to the point of satiation and so he has to choose between possible alternative combinations of goods and services. The theory of consumer behaviour seeks to establish the conditions under which the consumer is maximising his utility, subject to the above-mentioned constraints. It goes further in analysing what happens to the individual's demand for goods if prices and/or income changes. Returning to indifference curves, we shall first examine the problem of consumer equilibrium. The conditions for maximising the consumer's utility, subject to the constraints, can be established using a model with two commodities, given prices for these two goods and a fixed amount of income. The usual analysis assumes, in addition to convex indifference curves, that the consumer spends all of his income (he does not save) and that satiation of his wants does not occur, i.e. the higher the indifference curve he can reach, the better off he is.

Consider the indifference curves shown in Figure 7.4. Given the price p_1 of commodity 1, the spending of all of a consumer's income on this commodity would buy the quantity OX per time period. If he were to spend all of his income on commodity 2, given the assumed price p_2, he could buy OY units per time period. However, he does not need to spend all of his income entirely on one or the other and typically he will buy combinations of the two goods. The line XY shows the various combinations open to him, given the prices and his limited income. This line is known as the *budget* line and is a constraint on his ability to consume the two commodities. The analysis assumes that goods are divisible, so the budget line represents an infinitely large number of possible combinations of the two goods that he could buy. The budget line further implies that the consumption of the two goods is related because more of one means less of the other.

Any combination of goods to the right of the line XY is not available to the consumer because, given the prices and his income, he cannot afford them. Thus in Figure 7.4 the combination of the two

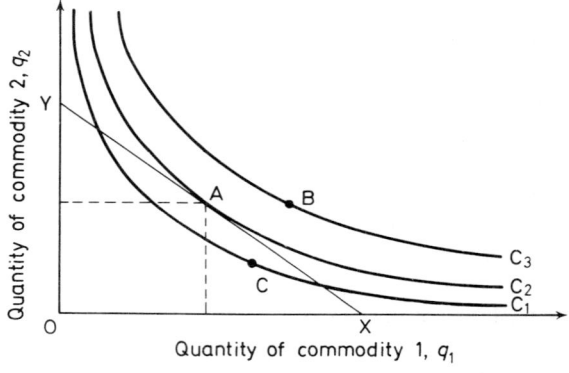

Figure 7.4

goods at point B is not in his feasible set of choices. The point C represents a combination open to him, but it would leave him with unspent income and so he would not be maximising his utility. Any point on the line XY represents a combination of the two commodities available to him whilst meeting the condition of spending all his income, and the combination at point A maximises his utility in that it yields him the highest level of utility available to him. At this point, the budget line XY is tangential to the indifference curve C_2. Intuitively, point A appears to be a position of maximum utility because, at this point, C_2 is the indifference curve which represents the highest level of utility that the budget line makes available. In principle, an indifference map is completely covered with indifference curves and so any point on XY, other than A, must be on an indifference curve that represents a lower level of utility.

We shall now use calculus to examine this constrained maximisation problem a little closer. This is necessary for the derivation of an important proposition about consumer equilibrium — a proposition that cannot be proved using graphs.

MAXIMISATION OF UTILITY SUBJECT TO CONSTRAINTS

Assuming the consumer wishes to maximise his utility U, the function to be maximised is

$$U = f(q_1, q_2) \tag{7.31}$$

subject to the constraint

$$Y = p_1 q_1 + p_2 q_2 \tag{7.32}$$

where Y is the given fixed level of income, p_1 is the price of commodity 1, q_1 is the quantity of commodity 1 consumed, p_2 is the price of commodity 2, and q_2 is the quantity of commodity 2 consumed.

Given the fact of constant prices and a specific level of income, then q_1 and q_2 are *not* independent variables. If the consumer buys more of commodity 1, he must buy less of commodity 2. There is also a maximum quantity of either commodity that he can buy by spending all of his income on one or other, and so the budget constraint is placing a limit on the range of values that q_1 and q_2 can take. In order to see how q_1 and q_2 are related, we can take the budget constraint and obtain q_2 in terms of q_1, i.e.

$$Y = p_1 q_1 + p_2 q_2$$

$$\therefore \qquad q_2 = \frac{Y}{p_2} - \frac{p_1 q_1}{p_2} \tag{7.33}$$

Thus q_2 is a linear function of q_1, and in fact this is the equation of the budget line XY in Figure 7.4. We now differentiate and obtain the rate of change of q_2 with respect to q_1, i.e.

$$\frac{dq_2}{dq_1} = -\frac{p_1}{p_2}$$

or

$$-\frac{dq_2}{dq_1} = \frac{p_1}{p_2} \tag{7.34}$$

Since q_2 and q_1 are related, we maximise U with respect to one of them, say q_1. The requirement for a maximum or a minimum is

$$\frac{dU}{dq_1} = 0$$

Differentiation (see equations 6.11 and 6.12) gives

$$\frac{dU}{dq_1} = \frac{\partial U}{\partial q_1} + \frac{\partial U}{\partial q_2} \frac{dq_2}{dq_1}$$

or

$$\frac{dU}{dq_1} = f_1 + f_2 \frac{dq_2}{dq_1} \tag{7.35}$$

Thus for a maximum or a minimum

$$f_1 + f_2 \frac{dq_2}{dq_1} = 0$$

i.e.

$$-\frac{dq_2}{dq_1} = \frac{f_1}{f_2} \tag{7.36}$$

From equations 7.34 and 7.36 it can be seen that the condition for a maximum or a minimum is

$$\frac{p_1}{p_2} = \frac{f_1}{f_2} \tag{7.37}$$

This is an important result in micro-economic theory. A necessary condition for the maximisation of the consumer's utility is that he purchases that combination of goods at which the ratio of their prices equals the ratio of their marginal utilities.

The condition for maximisation could be restated by rearranging the terms in equation 7.37 so that

$$\frac{f_2}{p_2} = \frac{f_1}{p_1} \tag{7.38}$$

The maximisation of the consumer's utility occurs when the consumer is purchasing that combination of goods at which the ratio of the marginal utility to price is the same for all goods purchased. In effect, we are saying that the consumer's equilibrium position is that at which the last unit of money spent on commodity 1 would yield the same utility if spent on commodity 2. This result stands if there are more than two goods in the consumer's utility function. Considering equation 7.38, it is obvious that, if p_2 were to increase whilst p_1 remained constant, then the marginal unit of money spent on commodity 2 would yield less utility than the same money spent on commodity 1. Therefore, the consumer would spend less on commodity 2 and more on commodity 1. As less of commodity 2 is consumed its marginal utility would rise, whilst that of commodity 1 would fall as more was consumed. When the ratios of marginal utility to price are again equal, the consumer is once more in equilibrium. It ought to be clear that goods yield differing marginal utilities and the equality of marginal utilities in consumption is not the issue. The point is that it is the equality of utility per marginal unit of expenditure that would maximise utility. Thus price changes affect demand. In the above case, an increase in p_2 would result in a contraction of the quantity demanded of commodity 2.

Before leaving this point it is worth drawing attention to certain features of the budget constraint. We have already obtained the equation of the budget line (equation 7.33)

$$q_2 = \frac{Y}{p_2} - \frac{p_1 q_1}{p_2}$$

Note that Y/p_2 is the intercept of the budget line with the vertical axis in Figure 7.4 and that the ratio $-p_1/p_2$ is the slope of the line. But from equation 7.34

$$-\frac{p_1}{p_2} = \frac{dq_2}{dq_1}$$

when utility is maximised. Thus the slope of the budget line is equal to the gradient of the indifference curve, i.e. the budget line is tangential to the indifference curve, when utility is maximised. It can be seen that, since the slope of the budget line is $-p_1/p_2$, price changes that change this ratio alter the slope of the budget line.

If the consumer spends all of his income on q_2 so that q_1 is zero, then

$$q_2 = \frac{Y}{p_2}$$

As Y is money income and p_2 is the price of commodity 2, then Y/p_2 represents real income. Obviously, if p_2 rises or falls whilst Y is constant, the intercept of the budget line on the vertical axis shifts. Conversely, if we assume a percentage increase in money income and the same percentage increase in price, then Y/p_2 remains the same and so the budget line is unchanged. These points are worth keeping in mind by those readers who prefer to analyse demand by using indifference maps and budget lines rather than algebra.

SECOND-ORDER CONDITIONS

We stated above that, for a maximum or minimum utility,

$$\frac{dU}{dq_1} = 0$$

and, given the constraint $Y = p_1q_1 + p_2q_2$, we derived equation 7.37:

$$\frac{p_1}{p_2} = \frac{f_1}{f_2}$$

However, this equality does not means that there is necessarily a maximum, since the further condition

$$\frac{d^2U}{dq_1^2} < 0 \qquad (7.39)$$

must also be satisfied. Given the conventional analysis, using *convex* indifference curves, the student can safely assume that the first-order condition given by equation 7.37 represents a position of maximum utility under the constraints of fixed prices and incomes. However, some types of analysis involve indifference curves that are concave: the tangency of a budget line with such indifference curves would also occur when

$$\frac{p_1}{p_2} = \frac{f_1}{f_2}$$

but this would not be a condition of maximum utility since the second-order condition above would not be met. However, such analysis would not arise in an intermediate economics course and so the reader may move directly to the example at the end of this section (page 182). For the more mathematically inclined, we shall show that

$$\frac{d^2U}{dq_1^2} = f_{11} + 2f_{12} \left(-\frac{p_1}{p_2} \right) + f_{22} \left(-\frac{p_1}{p_2} \right)^2$$

and this, of course, must be negative for a maximum. The derivation which follows involves many of the rules already given, but it is rather more complicated.

From equation 7.35,

$$\frac{d^2U}{dq_1^2} = \frac{d}{dq_1} \left(f_1 + f_2 \frac{dq_2}{dq_1} \right) \qquad (7.40)$$

i.e. in order to find the rate of change of dU/dq_1 with respect to q_1, we must obtain the derivative with respect to q_1 of each term in the brackets on the right-hand side of equation 7.40. Remember that f_1 denotes $\partial U/\partial q_1$ and is a function of q_1 and q_2, and similarly f_2 denotes $\partial U/\partial q_2$ and is a function of q_1 and q_2. Equation 7.40 could therefore be rewritten as

$$\frac{d^2 U}{dq_1{}^2} = \frac{d}{dq_1}\left(\frac{\partial U}{\partial q_1} + \frac{\partial U}{\partial q_2}\frac{dq_2}{dq_1}\right)$$

or

$$\frac{d^2 U}{dq_1{}^2} = \frac{d}{dq_1}\left(\frac{\partial U}{\partial q_1}\right) + \frac{d}{dq_1}\left(\frac{\partial U}{\partial q_2}\frac{dq_2}{dq_1}\right) \tag{7.41}$$

Dealing first with the derivative of $\partial U/\partial q_1$, we can write (from equation 6.11)

$$\frac{d}{dq_1}\left(\frac{\partial U}{\partial q_1}\right) = \frac{\partial}{\partial q_1}\left(\frac{\partial U}{\partial q_1}\right) + \frac{\partial}{\partial q_2}\left(\frac{\partial U}{\partial q_1}\right)\frac{dq_2}{dq_1}$$

$$= \frac{\partial^2 U}{\partial q_1{}^2} + \frac{\partial^2 U}{\partial q_2 \partial q_1}\frac{dq_2}{dq_1}$$

$$= f_{11} + f_{12}\frac{dq_2}{dq_1} \tag{7.42}$$

We must also obtain the derivative of

$$\frac{\partial U}{\partial q_2}\frac{dq_2}{dq_1}$$

with respect to q_1, and this involves the derivative of a product, thus

$$\frac{d}{dq_1}\left(\frac{\partial U}{\partial q_2}\frac{dq_2}{dq_1}\right) = \frac{d}{dq_1}\left(\frac{\partial U}{\partial q_2}\right)\frac{dq_2}{dq_1} + \frac{\partial U}{\partial q_2}\frac{d}{dq_1}\left(\frac{dq_2}{dq_1}\right)$$

$$= \left[\frac{\partial}{\partial q_1}\left(\frac{\partial U}{\partial q_2}\right) + \frac{\partial}{\partial q_2}\left(\frac{\partial U}{\partial q_2}\right)\frac{dq_2}{dq_1}\right]\frac{dq_2}{dq_1} + \frac{\partial U}{\partial q_2}\frac{d^2 q_2}{dq_1{}^2}$$

$$= \left(\frac{\partial^2 U}{\partial q_1 \partial q_2} + \frac{\partial^2 U}{\partial q_2{}^2}\frac{dq_2}{dq_1}\right)\frac{dq_2}{dq_1} + \frac{\partial U}{\partial q_2}\frac{d^2 q_2}{dq_1{}^2}$$

$$= \left(f_{12} + f_{22}\frac{dq_2}{dq_1}\right)\frac{dq_2}{dq_1} + f_2\frac{d^2 q_2}{dq_1{}^2}$$

$$= f_{12}\frac{dq_2}{dq_1} + f_{22}\left(\frac{dq_2}{dq_1}\right)^2 + f_2\frac{d^2 q_2}{dq_1{}^2} \tag{7.43}$$

Thus substituting equations 7.42 and 7.43 in equation 7.41 gives

$$\frac{d^2U}{dq_1^{\,2}} = f_{11} + f_{12}\frac{dq_2}{dq_1} + f_{12}\frac{dq_2}{dq_1} + f_{22}\left(\frac{dq_2}{dq_1}\right)^2 + f_2\frac{d^2q_2}{dq_1^{\,2}}$$

$$= f_{11} + 2f_{12}\frac{dq_2}{dq_1} + f_{22}\left(\frac{dq_2}{dq_1}\right)^2 + f_2\frac{d^2q_2}{dq_1^{\,2}} \qquad (7.44)$$

But from equation 7.34

$$\frac{dq_2}{dq_1} = -\frac{p_1}{p_2}$$

Therefore, since prices p_1 and p_2 are constant,

$$\frac{d^2q_2}{dq_1^{\,2}} = \frac{d}{dq_1}\left(-\frac{p_1}{p_2}\right) = 0$$

and substitution in equation 7.44 gives

$$\frac{d^2U}{dq_1^{\,2}} = f_{11} + 2f_{12}\left(-\frac{p_1}{p_2}\right) + f_{22}\left(-\frac{p_1}{p_2}\right)^2$$

Thus for the utility function to have a maximum we need the condition that

$$f_{11} + 2f_{12}\left(-\frac{p_1}{p_2}\right) + f_{22}\left(-\frac{p_1}{p_2}\right)^2 < 0 \qquad (7.45)$$

Example

So far we have dealt with the general statement that $U = f(q_1, q_2)$ and a budget constraint given by $Y = p_1q_1 + p_2q_2$. We shall now apply the mathematics to a specific numerical example of a two-goods model, and this first involves specifying a particular utility function. Consider the example

$$U = 2q_1q_2 \qquad (7.46)$$

which means that the consumer's utility is twice the product of q_1 and q_2. Suppose also that his income Y is £48 per time period, the price p_1 of commodity 1 is £4, and the price p_2 of commodity 2 is £6. Then, since

$$Y = p_1q_1 + p_2q_2$$

we can substitute the numerical values of Y, p_1, and p_2 to give

$$48 = 4q_1 + 6q_2 \tag{7.47}$$

This can be rearranged to give the equation of the budget line, i.e.

$$q_2 = \frac{48 - 4q_1}{6}$$

or

$$q_2 = 8 - \frac{2}{3}q_1 \tag{7.48}$$

Substitution of equation 7.48 into the utility function (equation 7.46) gives

$$U = 2q_1 \left(8 - \frac{2}{3}q_1 \right)$$

$\therefore$

$$U = 16q_1 - \frac{4}{3}q_1^2 \tag{7.49}$$

Differentiating U with respect to q_1 gives

$$\frac{dU}{dq_1} = 16 - \frac{8}{3}q_1 \tag{7.50}$$

For a maximum or a minimum,

$$\frac{dU}{dq_1} = 0$$

i.e.

$$16 - \frac{8}{3}q_1 = 0$$

$\therefore$

$$q_1 = 6$$

Substituting $q_1 = 6$ into the budget constraint gives

$$q_2 = 8 - \frac{2}{3}(6)$$

$$= 8 - 4$$

$\therefore$

$$q_2 = 4$$

For a maximum we also require that

$$\frac{d^2U}{dq_1^2} < 0$$

Differentiating equation 7.50 with respect to q_1 gives

$$\frac{d^2U}{dq_1^2} = -\frac{8}{3}$$

which is less than zero. Therefore the combination of goods and services that will maximise this consumer's utility, subject to the budget constraint, is 6 units of commodity 1 and 4 units of commodity 2.

FACTOR INPUTS AND OUTPUTS MAXIMISATION

Analogous to the problem of the consumer maximising his utility subject to constraints is the problem of the firm wishing to maximise its output, given a specified level of outlay on factor inputs and given factor prices. Suppose that we have the production function

$$X = f(K, L)$$

and that the firm is assumed to have a fixed amount of money to spend on factors of production. Further, the factors have specified prices and, assuming perfect competition in the factor market, the firm can buy

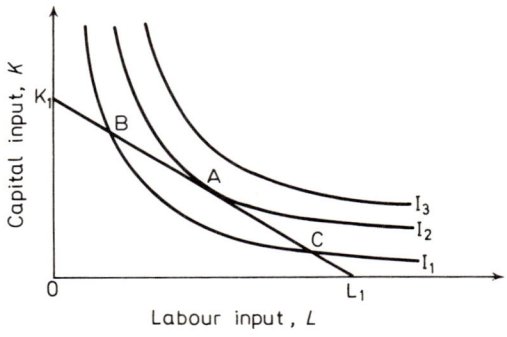

Figure 7.5

any quantity of factor input at a constant price: thus prices are treated as constants. We wish to find the conditions for maximising output, given a specified amount of money to spend on factors and given the factor prices.

The conditions can be shown graphically as in Figure 7.5. The isoquants I_1, I_2, and I_3 represent various levels of output X_1, X_2, and X_3, where $X_1 < X_2 < X_3$. Given the prices of capital and labour, OK_1 is the amount of capital that would be bought if the firm's outlay went entirely on capital, whilst OL_1 is the amount of labour that could be bought if the firm spent its budgeted funds on labour only. (In practice, it is difficult to conceive of a production process involving only capital: even computerised systems require labour.) The line $K_1 L_1$ represents the various combinations of labour and capital inputs that could be bought under the stated conditions and it is called the *isocost curve* (or total-outlay curve). The combinations at the points A, B, and C are each within the firm's range of choices, but B and C are each on I_1 whereas A is on I_2, which represents a higher level of output than that associated with I_1. As the combinations at A, B, and C all cost the same, the firm will choose A, since its aim is assumed to be to maximise output for a given outlay. In principle, the isoquant map has an infinite number of isoquants, so there is always an isoquant to which the isocost curve is tangential. Any point on the isocost curve to the left or right of such a point of tangency must be on an isoquant that represents a lower level of output.

We can now establish more formally the conditions for output maximisation, subject to the stated constraints. Thus we wish to maximise the function

$$X = f(K, L) \tag{7.51}$$

subject to the constraint

$$\phi = p_K K + p_L L \tag{7.52}$$

where ϕ is the total outlay on factors (in money terms), p_K is the price per unit of capital, p_L is the price per unit of labour, and K and L are the units of capital and labour inputs respectively. Given the constraint imposed by specifying a given outlay and prices of factors, K and L are not independent but are related through the total-outlay constraint: more of K means less of L, and vice versa. To see how K and L are related, equation 7.52 can be rearranged to give K as a function of L, i.e.

$$K = \frac{\phi}{p_K} - \frac{p_L}{p_K} L \tag{7.53}$$

To find the rate of change of K with respect to L, we differentiate equation 7.53 to give

$$\frac{dK}{dL} = -\frac{p_L}{p_K} \tag{7.54}$$

or

$$-\frac{dK}{dL} = \frac{p_L}{p_K} \tag{7.55}$$

Returning to the production function, we wish to maximise X subject to the constraint $\phi = p_K K + p_L L$. Since K and L are related, X can be maximised with respect to one of them, say K. For a maximum or minimum,

$$\frac{\mathrm{d}X}{\mathrm{d}K} = 0$$

But, from equations 6.11 and 6.12,

$$\frac{\mathrm{d}X}{\mathrm{d}K} = \frac{\partial X}{\partial K} + \frac{\partial X}{\partial L}\frac{\mathrm{d}L}{\mathrm{d}K}$$

or

$$\frac{\mathrm{d}X}{\mathrm{d}K} = f_K + f_L\frac{\mathrm{d}L}{\mathrm{d}K}$$

Therefore for a maximum or minimum

$$0 = f_K + f_L\frac{\mathrm{d}L}{\mathrm{d}K}$$

i.e.

$$-\frac{\mathrm{d}L}{\mathrm{d}K} = \frac{f_K}{f_L} \tag{7.56}$$

From equations 7.55 and 7.56 it can be seen that the necessary condition for a maximum or minimum is

$$\frac{p_K}{p_L} = \frac{f_K}{f_L} \tag{7.57}$$

In order that X is a maximum, and not a minimum, we require also that

$$\frac{\mathrm{d}^2 X}{\mathrm{d}K^2} < 0$$

We shall not go through the expansion of $\mathrm{d}^2 X/\mathrm{d}K^2$ here but it could be done in the same way as was the utility function in equations 7.41–7.45. Given the usual convex isoquants, the first-order condition (equation 7.57) can be taken to give a maximum. Thus output will be maximised if factors are employed up to the point where the ratio of the factor prices equals the ratio of their marginal products. By rearranging equation 7.57 we get

$$\frac{f_L}{p_L} = \frac{f_K}{p_K} \tag{7.58}$$

which is similar to the result established for consumer maximisation of utility. Hence output is maximised when the marginal pound spent on capital yields the same output as it would if spent on labour. Changes in relative factor prices will change the demand for factors. Suppose initially that a firm is in equilibrium, i.e.

$$\frac{f_L}{p_L} = \frac{f_K}{p_K}$$

If the price of labour were to increase relative to the price of capital, then

$$\frac{f_L}{p_L} < \frac{f_K}{p_K}$$

and so less labour and more capital would be used. The marginal product of labour would increase as less labour is used whilst the marginal product of capital would decline as more capital is used. When once again

$$\frac{f_L}{p_L} = \frac{f_K}{p_K}$$

factor substitution would cease. Remember that the production function $X = f(K, L)$ refers to the *maximum* output produced by factor inputs, i.e. it assumes *technical efficiency*. By considering factor prices and cost outlays, we have introduced the idea of *economic efficiency* — the idea of maximising outputs for a given cost (or we could be minimising costs of a given output). An isoquant is the locus of all technically efficient combinations of K and L that will produce a given output. However, when factor prices and given outlays are introduced, the problem is to choose that particular combination which, given the constraints, will maximise output (or minimise costs).

Equation 7.53, which we derived from the constraint, gave K in terms of L:

$$K = \frac{\phi}{p_K} - \frac{p_L}{p_K} L$$

For those readers who prefer graphical analysis, note that this equation gives the slope of the constraint line in Figure 7.5 as $-p_L/p_K$. Therefore a change in relative factor prices will change the slope of the line and the point of tangency will then be on a different isoquant. Notice also that

ϕ/p_K is the intercept of the constraint line on the vertical axis. It is obvious that an increase in p_K, with ϕ remaining constant, will lower the intercept whilst, if prices and outlay all increase or decrease in the same proportion, the constraint line is unchanged and so is the combination of factors used.

It is worth emphasising that, although there are many similarities between indifference curve analysis and the use of isoquants in production theory, an important difference is that utility cannot be measured: we are concerned with the *ordering* of preferences. In the case of production functions and isoquants, on the other hand, output can in principle be measured.

LAGRANGE MULTIPLIER METHOD

An alternative method of solving constrained optimisation problems will now be examined. Suppose we have a function

$$z = f(x, y) \tag{7.59}$$

and that x and y are related by a constraint

$$\phi(x, y) = 0 \tag{7.60}$$

Since x and y are related, z may be differentiated with respect to x to give (from equation 6.11)

$$\frac{dz}{dx} = \frac{\partial z}{\partial x} + \frac{\partial z}{\partial y}\frac{dy}{dx}$$

For a maximum or minimum value of z,

$$\frac{dz}{dx} = 0$$

i.e.

$$\frac{\partial z}{\partial x} + \frac{\partial z}{\partial y}\frac{dy}{dx} = 0$$

or

$$f_x + f_y \frac{dy}{dx} = 0$$

and so

$$-\frac{dy}{dx} = \frac{f_x}{f_y} \tag{7.61}$$

We can also obtain $-dy/dx$ by differentiating ϕ with respect to x, since

$$\frac{d\phi}{dx} = \frac{\partial \phi}{\partial x} + \frac{\partial \phi}{\partial y}\frac{dy}{dx}$$

But $\phi(x, y) = 0$ for all values of x and y, in other words ϕ is a constant with value zero. Hence $d\phi/dx = 0$ and

$$0 = \frac{\partial\phi}{\partial x} + \frac{\partial\phi}{\partial y}\frac{dy}{dx}$$

or

$$0 = \phi_x + \phi_y \frac{dy}{dx}$$

$\therefore$

$$-\frac{dy}{dx} = \frac{\phi_x}{\phi_y} \qquad (7.62)$$

From equations 7.61 and 7.62, for a maximum or minimum of $f(x, y)$,

$$\frac{f_x}{f_y} = \frac{\phi_x}{\phi_y}$$

or

$$\frac{f_x}{\phi_x} = \frac{f_y}{\phi_y}$$

Now let us write

$$\frac{f_x}{\phi_x} = \frac{f_y}{\phi_y} = -\lambda$$

which can be rewritten as

$$f_x = -\lambda\phi_x \qquad (7.63)$$

and

$$f_y = -\lambda\phi_y \qquad (7.64)$$

or as

$$f_x + \lambda\phi_x = 0 \qquad (7.65)$$

and

$$f_y + \lambda\phi_y = 0 \qquad (7.66)$$

Thus equations 7.65 and 7.66 are the conditions necessary for a maximum or minimum of $f(x, y)$ subject to the constraint $\phi(x, y) = 0$.

If we define a new function

$$u = f(x, y) + \lambda\phi(x, y) \qquad (7.67)$$

then u depends on the three variables x, y and λ. If we partially differentiate u with respect to each variable and set the partial derivatives equal to zero, we obtain

$$\frac{\partial u}{\partial x} = f_x + \lambda\phi_x = 0 \qquad (7.68)$$

$$\frac{\partial u}{\partial y} = f_y + \lambda\phi_y = 0 \qquad (7.69)$$

and

$$\frac{\partial u}{\partial \lambda} = \phi(x, y) = 0 \qquad (7.70)$$

It can be seen that equations 7.68–7.70 are equivalent to equations 7.65, 7.66, and 7.60. Thus, given the function u as defined in equation 7.67, then

$$\frac{\partial u}{\partial x} = 0, \quad \frac{\partial u}{\partial y} = 0, \quad \frac{\partial u}{\partial \lambda} = 0$$

are the conditions necessary for a maximum or minimum of $f(x, y)$ subject to the constraint $\phi(x, y) = 0$. The variable λ is called a Lagrange multiplier.

Note that this method does not indicate whether the stationary point is in fact a maximum or a minimum, and the conditions governing this are beyond the scope of this book. However, the Lagrange multiplier method has the advantage over the previous constrained optimisation method in that it can be applied to functions of more than two variables. The only restriction is that it must be possible to solve equations 7.68–7.70.

Example 1

Suppose we have to find the maximum or minimum value of

$$z = f(x, y) = x^2 + 2xy - 2y \tag{7.71}$$

subject to the constraint

$$2x - y = 1 \tag{7.72}$$

First, equation 7.72 must be written in the form $\phi(x, y) = 0$, i.e. let

$$\phi(x, y) = 2x - y - 1 = 0 \tag{7.73}$$

Then let

$$u = (x^2 + 2xy - 2y) + \lambda(2x - y - 1)$$

Hence

$$\frac{\partial u}{\partial x} = 2x + 2y + 2\lambda$$

$$\frac{\partial u}{\partial y} = 2x - 2 - \lambda$$

and

$$\frac{\partial u}{\partial \lambda} = 2x - y - 1$$

We must therefore solve the simultaneous equations

$$x + y + \lambda = 0 \qquad (7.74)$$
$$2x - 2 - \lambda = 0 \qquad (7.75)$$

and
$$2x - y - 1 = 0 \qquad (7.76)$$

Adding equations 7.74 and 7.75 gives

$$3x + y - 2 = 0 \qquad (7.77)$$

and adding this to equation 7.76 gives

$$5x - 3 = 0$$

∴
$$5x = 3$$

i.e.
$$x = \frac{3}{5}$$

Therefore, by substituting in equation 7.76,

$$2\left(\frac{3}{5}\right) - y - 1 = 0$$

i.e.
$$y = \frac{1}{5}$$

and from equation 7.74

$$\frac{3}{5} + \frac{1}{5} + \lambda = 0$$

∴
$$\lambda = -\frac{4}{5}$$

Therefore the maximum or minimum occurs when

$$x = \frac{3}{5}, \quad y = \frac{1}{5}, \quad \lambda = -\frac{4}{5}$$

Hence the maximum or minimum value of z is given by

$$z = \left(\frac{3}{5}\right)^2 + 2\left(\frac{3}{5}\right)\left(\frac{1}{5}\right) - 2\left(\frac{1}{5}\right)$$

$$= \frac{9}{25} + \frac{6}{25} - \frac{2}{5}$$

$$= \frac{1}{5}$$

Example 2

The Lagrange multiplier method can be applied to the problem of factor input maximisation already discussed. Again we wish to maximise the function

$$X = f(K, L) \tag{7.78}$$

subject to the constraint

$$\phi = p_K K + p_L L \tag{7.79}$$

Therefore, rearranging equation 7.79 to give

$$p_K K + p_L L - \phi = 0$$

we can form the function

$$u = f(K, L) + \lambda(p_K K + p_L L - \phi) \tag{7.80}$$

Then

$$\frac{\partial u}{\partial K} = f_K + \lambda p_K$$

$$\frac{\partial u}{\partial L} = f_L + \lambda p_L$$

and

$$\frac{\partial u}{\partial \lambda} = p_K K + p_L L - \phi$$

We must therefore solve the equations

$$f_K + \lambda p_K = 0 \tag{7.81}$$

$$f_L + \lambda p_L = 0 \tag{7.82}$$

and

$$p_K K + p_L L - \phi = 0 \tag{7.83}$$

From equations 7.81 and 7.82 respectively,

$$\lambda = -\frac{f_K}{p_K}$$

and

$$\lambda = -\frac{f_L}{p_L}$$

Therefore, as we found before, the condition for a maximum or minimum value of x is

$$\frac{f_K}{p_K} = \frac{f_L}{p_L}$$

Chapter 8

MATRIX ALGEBRA

Suppose that a company X manufactures four types of product, A, B, C, and D, and suppose that in a certain month the quantities sold of these were, in thousands, 4, 10, 1, and 5 respectively. The sales of the company could therefore be represented by

$$[4 \text{ of A}, \quad 10 \text{ of B}, \quad 1 \text{ of C}, \quad 5 \text{ of D}]$$

Then suppose that in another month the sales were, again in thousands, 3 A's, 12 B's, 3 C's, and 2 D's. This could be expressed as

$$[3 \text{ of A}, \quad 12 \text{ of B}, \quad 3 \text{ of C}, \quad 2 \text{ of D}]$$

If the first number in the bracket always referred to the sales of A, the second to those of B, the third to those of C, and the fourth to those of D, then the letters A, B, C, and D could be omitted and the sales for the two months would be represented by

$$[4, \quad 10, \quad 1, \quad 5]$$

and

$$[3, \quad 12, \quad 3, \quad 2]$$

The sales for any month could be similarly represented by such an array of numbers, for example

$$[2, \quad 8, \quad 0, \quad 5]$$

would represent a month when 2000 A's, 8000 B's, no C's, and 5000 D's were sold.

Such an array is called in algebra a *vector*. Because we could just as easily have expressed the first month's figures as

$$\begin{bmatrix} 4 \text{ of A} \\ 10 \text{ of B} \\ 1 \text{ of C} \\ 5 \text{ of D} \end{bmatrix} \quad \text{or just} \quad \begin{bmatrix} 4 \\ 10 \\ 1 \\ 5 \end{bmatrix}$$

193

we define two types of vector. In a *row vector* the numbers are written horizontally, for example

$$[4 \quad 10 \quad 1 \quad 5]$$

and in a *column vector* the numbers are written vertically, for example

$$\begin{bmatrix} 4 \\ 10 \\ 1 \\ 5 \end{bmatrix}$$

The numbers in a vector are called *elements*, and the number of elements in a vector is called the *dimension* of the vector. Thus each of the examples given above is of a vector with dimension 4.

MATRICES

Suppose that the three vectors considered above represent the sales figures for the months January, February, and March, i.e.

$$\begin{array}{lcccc} \text{January} & [4, & 10, & 1, & 5] \\ \text{February} & [3, & 12, & 3, & 2] \\ \text{March} & [2, & 8, & 0, & 5] \end{array}$$

The notation already used can be extended to present the sales data for the company for this quarter of the year in one array:

$$\begin{bmatrix} 4 & 10 & 1 & 5 \\ 3 & 12 & 3 & 2 \\ 2 & 8 & 0 & 5 \end{bmatrix}$$

This type of array is called a *matrix*.

A matrix is made up of rows and columns. The element in the ith row and jth column of a matrix **A** is referred to as the (i, j)th element and is often identified as a_{ij}. In the example above, the first row of the matrix is a row vector representing the sales in January and the first column is a column vector representing the sales of product A over the quarter. If a similar matrix is constructed for a second, competing company Y, as follows

$$\begin{bmatrix} 3 & 15 & 0 & 0 \\ 5 & 11 & 3 & 2 \\ 4 & 14 & 6 & 3 \end{bmatrix}$$

This would represent the same data as shown in Table 8.1.

Table 8.1 SALES (IN THOUSANDS) OF FOUR PRODUCTS

Month	*Product*			
	A	B	C	D
January	3	15	0	0
February	5	11	3	2
March	4	14	6	3

The rows of a matrix can be considered as row vectors and the columns can be considered as column vectors. However, it should also be noticed that a vector is merely a special type of matrix: a row vector is a matrix with only one row, and a column vector is a matrix with only one column. A matrix with m rows and n columns is said to be an '$m \times n$' matrix, or a matrix 'of type $m \times n$'. Thus the sales matrices above are each 3×4. Further, the row vector representing sales in January, for example, is a 1×4 matrix and the column vector representing sales of product A is a 3×1 matrix. It is worth noting that a 1×1 matrix (one row and one column) is just a number, for example

$$5$$

can be considered as a 1×1 matrix.

MULTIPLICATION OF A MATRIX BY A CONSTANT

If a second quarter's sales figures for company X were four times those of the first quarter, then the matrix for this second quarter would be

$$\begin{bmatrix} 16 & 40 & 4 & 20 \\ 12 & 48 & 12 & 8 \\ 8 & 32 & 0 & 20 \end{bmatrix}$$

i.e. we have performed the operation

$$4 \times \begin{bmatrix} 4 & 10 & 1 & 5 \\ 3 & 12 & 3 & 2 \\ 2 & 8 & 0 & 5 \end{bmatrix} = \begin{bmatrix} 16 & 40 & 4 & 20 \\ 12 & 48 & 12 & 8 \\ 8 & 32 & 0 & 20 \end{bmatrix}$$

which is an example of multiplying a matrix by a constant. Thus, to multiply a matrix by a constant, each element of the matrix is multiplied by that constant. As further examples,

$$2 \times \begin{bmatrix} 3 & 0 \\ 2 & 1 \\ -3 & 6 \\ 1 & 5 \end{bmatrix} = \begin{bmatrix} 6 & 0 \\ 4 & 2 \\ -6 & 12 \\ 2 & 10 \end{bmatrix}$$

and

$$-3 \times \begin{bmatrix} 4 & -6 \\ 2 & 0 \end{bmatrix} = \begin{bmatrix} -12 & 18 \\ -6 & 0 \end{bmatrix}$$

ADDITION AND SUBTRACTION OF MATRICES

Consider again the sales figures for companies X and Y over the first quarter, i.e. for company X

$$\begin{bmatrix} 4 & 10 & 1 & 5 \\ 3 & 12 & 3 & 2 \\ 2 & 8 & 0 & 5 \end{bmatrix}$$

and for company Y

$$\begin{bmatrix} 3 & 15 & 0 & 0 \\ 5 & 11 & 3 & 2 \\ 4 & 14 & 6 & 3 \end{bmatrix}$$

Suppose that the two companies had amalgamated to form a company Z. Then the sales of company Z of, for example, A's in January would be 7, or C's in February would be 6. It is easy to see that the sales of company Z would be given by the matrix

$$\begin{bmatrix} 4+3 & 10+15 & 1+0 & 5+0 \\ 3+5 & 12+11 & 3+3 & 2+2 \\ 2+4 & 8+14 & 0+6 & 5+3 \end{bmatrix} = \begin{bmatrix} 7 & 25 & 1 & 5 \\ 8 & 23 & 6 & 4 \\ 6 & 22 & 6 & 8 \end{bmatrix}$$

and here we have performed the addition of two matrices.

Thus, to add two matrices together, the corresponding elements of each matrix are added, for example

$$\begin{bmatrix} 3 & 0 \\ 2 & -1 \\ -3 & 4 \end{bmatrix} + \begin{bmatrix} 4 & 2 \\ 5 & 3 \\ 0 & -2 \end{bmatrix} = \begin{bmatrix} 3+4 & 0+2 \\ 2+5 & -1+3 \\ -3+0 & 4-2 \end{bmatrix}$$

$$= \begin{bmatrix} 7 & 2 \\ 7 & 2 \\ -3 & 2 \end{bmatrix}$$

Note that two matrices can be added together *only if they are of the same type:* for instance, the only type of matrix that can be added to a 3 x 4 matrix is another 3 x 4 matrix.

Subtraction of two matrices *of the same type* follows simply in a very similar way. To subtract two matrices of the same type, the corresponding elements of each matrix are subtracted, for example

$$\begin{bmatrix} 5 & 6 \\ 2 & 3 \\ 4 & 7 \\ 5 & 9 \end{bmatrix} - \begin{bmatrix} 4 & 3 \\ 1 & 0 \\ 3 & 1 \\ 2 & 6 \end{bmatrix} = \begin{bmatrix} 5-4 & 6-3 \\ 2-1 & 3-0 \\ 4-3 & 7-1 \\ 5-2 & 9-6 \end{bmatrix}$$

$$= \begin{bmatrix} 1 & 3 \\ 1 & 3 \\ 1 & 6 \\ 3 & 3 \end{bmatrix}$$

and

$$\begin{bmatrix} 2 & -3 & 5 \\ 6 & 0 & 2 \end{bmatrix} - \begin{bmatrix} 1 & 2 & -3 \\ 7 & -1 & 3 \end{bmatrix} = \begin{bmatrix} 2-1 & -3-2 & 5-(-3) \\ 6-7 & 0-(-1) & 2-3 \end{bmatrix}$$

$$= \begin{bmatrix} 1 & -5 & 8 \\ -1 & 1 & -1 \end{bmatrix}$$

MULTIPLICATION OF MATRICES

Consider again the sales figures of company X, given by the matrix

	A	B	C	D
January	4	10	1	5
February	3	12	3	2
March	2	8	0	5

Suppose now that the profit on 1000 A's is £200, the profit on 1000 B's is £100, the profit on 1000 C's is £400, and the profit on 1000 D's is £200. This information could be represented by the following column vector:

	Profit (£)
A	200
B	100
C	400
D	200

For simplicity it is convenient to work with money units of £100, and the profit vector then becomes

$$\begin{bmatrix} 2 \\ 1 \\ 4 \\ 2 \end{bmatrix}$$

If we now wish to find the company's total profit in January, the sales of product A in January must be multiplied by the profits on product A, the sales of B must be multiplied by the profits on B, and so on. Thus the company's total profit in January can be represented by

$$(4 \times 2) + (10 \times 1) + (1 \times 4) + (5 \times 2) = 8 + 10 + 4 + 10$$
$$= 32$$

which denotes £3200 since the money unit was £100. Similarly, the profit in February could be represented by

$$(3 \times 2) + (12 \times 1) + (3 \times 4) + (2 \times 2) = 6 + 12 + 12 + 4$$
$$= 34$$

and the profit in March by

$$(2 \times 2) + (8 \times 1) + (0 \times 4) + (5 \times 2) = 4 + 8 + 0 + 10$$
$$= 22$$

We can therefore produce a 'quarterly total profit' vector

$$
\begin{array}{c}
 \\
\text{January} \\
\text{February} \\
\text{March}
\end{array}
\begin{array}{c}
\text{Total profit} \\
\text{(£100)} \\
\begin{bmatrix} 32 \\ 34 \\ 22 \end{bmatrix}
\end{array}
$$

which has been computed in the following way:

$$
\begin{bmatrix} 4 & 10 & 1 & 5 \\ 3 & 12 & 3 & 2 \\ 2 & 8 & 0 & 5 \end{bmatrix}
\begin{bmatrix} 2 \\ 1 \\ 4 \\ 2 \end{bmatrix}
=
\begin{bmatrix}
\begin{bmatrix} 4 & 10 & 1 & 5 \end{bmatrix} \begin{bmatrix} 2 \\ 1 \\ 4 \\ 2 \end{bmatrix} \\
\begin{bmatrix} 3 & 12 & 3 & 2 \end{bmatrix} \begin{bmatrix} 2 \\ 1 \\ 4 \\ 2 \end{bmatrix} \\
\begin{bmatrix} 2 & 8 & 0 & 5 \end{bmatrix} \begin{bmatrix} 2 \\ 1 \\ 4 \\ 2 \end{bmatrix}
\end{bmatrix}
$$

$$= \begin{bmatrix} (4 \times 2) + (10 \times 1) + (1 \times 4) + (5 \times 2) \\ (3 \times 2) + (12 \times 1) + (3 \times 4) + (2 \times 2) \\ (2 \times 2) + (8 \times 1) + (0 \times 4) + (5 \times 2) \end{bmatrix}$$

$$= \begin{bmatrix} 32 \\ 34 \\ 22 \end{bmatrix}$$

Suppose, further, that the tax payable on 1000 sold of each of A, B, C, and D is £10, £20, £50, and £30, respectively. Then, if we work in tax units of £10, we can produce a tax vector:

Tax
(£10)

$$\begin{matrix} A \\ B \\ C \\ D \end{matrix} \begin{bmatrix} 1 \\ 2 \\ 5 \\ 3 \end{bmatrix}$$

In the same way as before, a quarterly tax vector can be constructed

$$\begin{bmatrix} 4 & 10 & 1 & 5 \\ 3 & 12 & 3 & 2 \\ 2 & 8 & 0 & 5 \end{bmatrix} \begin{bmatrix} 1 \\ 2 \\ 5 \\ 3 \end{bmatrix} = \begin{bmatrix} \begin{bmatrix} 4 & 10 & 1 & 5 \end{bmatrix} \begin{bmatrix} 1 \\ 2 \\ 5 \\ 3 \end{bmatrix} \\ \begin{bmatrix} 3 & 12 & 3 & 2 \end{bmatrix} \begin{bmatrix} 1 \\ 2 \\ 5 \\ 3 \end{bmatrix} \\ \begin{bmatrix} 2 & 8 & 0 & 5 \end{bmatrix} \begin{bmatrix} 1 \\ 2 \\ 5 \\ 3 \end{bmatrix} \end{bmatrix}$$

$$= \begin{bmatrix} (4 \times 1) + (10 \times 2) + (1 \times 5) + (5 \times 3) \\ (3 \times 1) + (12 \times 2) + (3 \times 5) + (2 \times 3) \\ (2 \times 1) + (8 \times 2) + (0 \times 5) + (5 \times 3) \end{bmatrix}$$

$$= \begin{bmatrix} 4 + 20 + 5 + 15 \\ 3 + 24 + 15 + 6 \\ 2 + 16 + 0 + 15 \end{bmatrix}$$

$$= \begin{bmatrix} 44 \\ 48 \\ 33 \end{bmatrix}$$

i.e. £440 tax was paid in January, £480 in February, and £330 in March.

Next, suppose we combine the profit and tax vectors to form a finance matrix, thus

	Profit (£100)	Tax (£10)
A	2	1
B	1	2
C	4	5
D	2	3

The total profit and the total tax for the quarter could then be calculated in one operation:

$$\begin{bmatrix} 4 & 10 & 1 & 5 \\ 3 & 12 & 3 & 2 \\ 2 & 8 & 0 & 5 \end{bmatrix} \begin{bmatrix} 2 & 1 \\ 1 & 2 \\ 4 & 5 \\ 2 & 3 \end{bmatrix}$$

$$= \begin{bmatrix} (4 \times 2) + (10 \times 1) + (1 \times 4) + (5 \times 2) & (4 \times 1) + (10 \times 2) + (1 \times 5) + (5 \times 3) \\ (3 \times 2) + (12 \times 1) + (3 \times 4) + (2 \times 2) & (3 \times 1) + (12 \times 2) + (3 \times 5) + (2 \times 3) \\ (2 \times 2) + (8 \times 1) + (0 \times 4) + (5 \times 2) & (2 \times 1) + (8 \times 2) + (0 \times 5) + (5 \times 3) \end{bmatrix}$$

$$= \begin{bmatrix} 32 & 44 \\ 34 & 48 \\ 22 & 33 \end{bmatrix}$$

Here, we have performed matrix multiplication. Notice that the first column of the product is formed by taking each element of the first row of the first matrix and multiplying it by the corresponding element of the first column of the second matrix and adding. Each other row or column is formed in a similar way. More formally, to multiply a matrix **X** by a matrix **Y,** the element in the *i*th row and *j*th column of the product matrix **XY** is formed by multiplying each element of the *i*th row of **X** by the corresponding element of the *j*th column of **Y** and adding these together.

Note that the product **XY** of two matrices **X** and **Y** can be formed only if the *number of columns of* **X** *equals the number of rows of* **Y.** Only in this way can there be, for every element in the *i*th row of **X,** a corresponding element in the *j*th column of **Y.** Thus, if **X** is of type *m* x *p* and **Y** is of type *p* x *n*, then the product matrix **XY** will be of type *m* x *n* (*m* rows and *n* columns). For example, suppose we wish to carry out the following multiplication:

$$\begin{bmatrix} 2 & 0 \\ -3 & 1 \\ 4 & -2 \end{bmatrix} \begin{bmatrix} 6 & 0 & 1 & 5 \\ -3 & 1 & 4 & 0 \end{bmatrix}$$

$$= \begin{bmatrix} [2 \ \ 0]\begin{bmatrix}6\\-3\end{bmatrix} & [2 \ \ 0]\begin{bmatrix}0\\1\end{bmatrix} & [2 \ \ 0]\begin{bmatrix}1\\4\end{bmatrix} & [2 \ \ 0]\begin{bmatrix}5\\0\end{bmatrix} \\ [-3 \ \ 1]\begin{bmatrix}6\\-3\end{bmatrix} & [-3 \ \ 1]\begin{bmatrix}0\\1\end{bmatrix} & [-3 \ \ 1]\begin{bmatrix}1\\4\end{bmatrix} & [-3 \ \ 1]\begin{bmatrix}5\\0\end{bmatrix} \\ [4 \ \ -2]\begin{bmatrix}6\\-3\end{bmatrix} & [4 \ \ -2]\begin{bmatrix}0\\1\end{bmatrix} & [4 \ \ -2]\begin{bmatrix}1\\4\end{bmatrix} & [4 \ \ -2]\begin{bmatrix}5\\0\end{bmatrix} \end{bmatrix}$$

$$= \begin{bmatrix} (2 \times 6) + (0 \times (-3)) & (2 \times 0) + (0 \times 1) \\ ((-3) \times 6) + (1 \times (-3)) & ((-3) \times 0) + (1 \times 1) \\ (4 \times 6) + ((-2) \times (-3)) & (4 \times 0) + ((-2) \times 1) \end{bmatrix}$$

$$\begin{bmatrix} (2 \times 1) + (0 \times 4) & (2 \times 5) + (0 \times 0) \\ ((-3) \times 1) + (1 \times 4) & ((-3) \times 5) + (1 \times 0) \\ (4 \times 1) + ((-2) \times 4) & (4 \times 5) + ((-2) \times 0) \end{bmatrix}$$

$$= \begin{bmatrix} 12+0 & 0+0 & 2+0 & 10+0 \\ -18-3 & 0+1 & -3+4 & -15+0 \\ 24+6 & 0-2 & 4-8 & 20+0 \end{bmatrix}$$

$$= \begin{bmatrix} 12 & 0 & 2 & 10 \\ -21 & 1 & 1 & -15 \\ 30 & -2 & -4 & 20 \end{bmatrix}$$

This is an example of a 3 × 2 matrix multiplied by a 2 × 4 matrix, giving a 3 × 4 matrix as the product.

Care must be taken in writing the product of matrices **X** and **Y**. In the example above, where

$$\mathbf{X} = \begin{bmatrix} 2 & 0 \\ -3 & 1 \\ 4 & -2 \end{bmatrix} \quad \text{and} \quad \mathbf{Y} = \begin{bmatrix} 6 & 0 & 1 & 5 \\ -3 & 1 & 4 & 0 \end{bmatrix}$$

then we can form the product **XY** (a 3 × 2 matrix multiplied by a 2 × 4 matrix) but not the product **YX** (a 2 × 4 matrix cannot be multiplied by a 3 × 2 matrix). Even if the product can be formed either way, the matrices produced are rarely equal. For example, if

$$\mathbf{X} = \begin{bmatrix} 2 & 0 & -3 \end{bmatrix} \quad \text{and} \quad \mathbf{Y} = \begin{bmatrix} -1 \\ 2 \\ 4 \end{bmatrix}$$

then

$$\mathbf{XY} = [(2 \times (-1)) + (0 \times 2) + ((-3) \times 4)]$$
$$= [-2 + 0 - 12]$$
$$= [-14]$$

i.e. a 1 × 3 matrix multiplied by a 3 × 1 matrix gives a 1 × 1 matrix; but

$$\mathbf{YX} = \begin{bmatrix} (-1) \times 2 & (-1) \times 0 & (-1) \times (-3) \\ 2 \times 2 & 2 \times 0 & 2 \times (-3) \\ 4 \times 2 & 4 \times 0 & 4 \times (-3) \end{bmatrix}$$

$$= \begin{bmatrix} -2 & 0 & 3 \\ 4 & 0 & -6 \\ 8 & 0 & -12 \end{bmatrix}$$

i.e. a 3 x 1 matrix multiplied by a 1 x 3 matrix gives a 3 x 3 matrix.
Thus **XY** and **YX** here are matrices of different types.

As another example, if

$$X = \begin{bmatrix} 2 & 0 \\ -1 & 3 \end{bmatrix} \quad \text{and} \quad Y = \begin{bmatrix} -1 & 2 \\ 3 & 2 \end{bmatrix}$$

then

$$XY = \begin{bmatrix} \begin{bmatrix} 2 & 0 \end{bmatrix} \begin{bmatrix} -1 \\ 3 \end{bmatrix} & \begin{bmatrix} 2 & 0 \end{bmatrix} \begin{bmatrix} 2 \\ 2 \end{bmatrix} \\ \begin{bmatrix} -1 & 3 \end{bmatrix} \begin{bmatrix} -1 \\ 3 \end{bmatrix} & \begin{bmatrix} -1 & 3 \end{bmatrix} \begin{bmatrix} 2 \\ 2 \end{bmatrix} \end{bmatrix}$$

$$\begin{bmatrix} (2 \times (-1)) + (0 \times 3) & (2 \times 2) + (0 \times 2) \\ ((-1) \times (-1)) + (3 \times 3) & ((-1) \times 2) + (3 \times 2) \end{bmatrix}$$

$$= \begin{bmatrix} -2 + 0 & 4 + 0 \\ 1 + 9 & -2 + 6 \end{bmatrix}$$

$$= \begin{bmatrix} -2 & 4 \\ 10 & 4 \end{bmatrix}$$

but

$$YX = \begin{bmatrix} \begin{bmatrix} -1 & 2 \end{bmatrix} \begin{bmatrix} 2 \\ -1 \end{bmatrix} & \begin{bmatrix} -1 & 2 \end{bmatrix} \begin{bmatrix} 0 \\ 3 \end{bmatrix} \\ \begin{bmatrix} 3 & 2 \end{bmatrix} \begin{bmatrix} 2 \\ -1 \end{bmatrix} & \begin{bmatrix} 3 & 2 \end{bmatrix} \begin{bmatrix} 0 \\ 3 \end{bmatrix} \end{bmatrix}$$

$$= \begin{bmatrix} ((-1) \times 2) + (2 \times (-1)) & ((-1) \times 0) + (2 \times 3) \\ (3 \times 2) + (2 \times (-1)) & (3 \times 0) + (2 \times 3) \end{bmatrix}$$

$$= \begin{bmatrix} -2 - 2 & 0 + 6 \\ 6 - 2 & 0 + 6 \end{bmatrix}$$

$$= \begin{bmatrix} -4 & 6 \\ 4 & 6 \end{bmatrix}$$

So here **XY** and **YX** are of the same type but have different elements.

In general, matrices *do not commute* (i.e. **XY** does not equal **YX**). A few exceptions to this (i.e. matrices that do commute) will be seen later.

THE ZERO MATRIX

An $m \times n$ matrix with all its elements zero is called the $m \times n$ zero matrix. It is denoted by $\boldsymbol{0}_{m \times n}$ (or just by $\boldsymbol{0}$ if its type is obvious). These matrices behave with respect to other matrices in the same way as the number zero behaves with respect to other numbers: thus, a zero matrix has no effect when added to another matrix of the same type, and when a zero matrix is multiplied by any other matrix the product is another zero matrix.

As an example of adding a zero matrix:

$$\begin{bmatrix} 3 & -2 \\ 4 & 1 \\ -5 & 2 \end{bmatrix} + \begin{bmatrix} 0 & 0 \\ 0 & 0 \\ 0 & 0 \end{bmatrix} = \begin{bmatrix} 3+0 & -2+0 \\ 4+0 & 1+0 \\ -5+0 & 2+0 \end{bmatrix} = \begin{bmatrix} 3 & -2 \\ 4 & 1 \\ -5 & 2 \end{bmatrix}$$

In general,

$$\boldsymbol{X}_{m \times n} + \boldsymbol{0}_{m \times n} = \boldsymbol{X}_{m \times n}$$

Similarly, as an example of multiplying by a zero matrix:

$$\begin{bmatrix} 1 & 3 \\ -2 & -1 \\ 4 & -4 \end{bmatrix} \begin{bmatrix} 0 & 0 & 0 \\ 0 & 0 & 0 \end{bmatrix}$$

$$= \begin{bmatrix} (1 \times 0) + (3 \times 0) & (1 \times 0) + (3 \times 0) \\ ((-2) \times 0) + ((-1) \times 0) & ((-2) \times 0) + ((-1) \times 0) \\ (4 \times 0) + ((-4) \times 0) & (4 \times 0) + ((-4) \times 0) \end{bmatrix}$$

$$\begin{matrix} (1 \times 0) + (3 \times 0) \\ ((-2) \times 0) + ((-1) \times 0) \\ (4 \times 0) + ((-4) \times 0) \end{matrix}$$

$$= \begin{bmatrix} 0 & 0 & 0 \\ 0 & 0 & 0 \\ 0 & 0 & 0 \end{bmatrix}$$

In general,

$$\mathbf{X}_{m \times p} \times \mathbf{0}_{p \times n} = \mathbf{0}_{m \times n} \tag{8.1}$$

The reader should also satisfy himself here that

$$\mathbf{0}_{m \times p} \times \mathbf{X}_{p \times n} = \mathbf{0}_{m \times n} \tag{8.2}$$

SQUARE MATRICES

We shall now examine more closely the properties of a matrix with the same number of rows as columns, i.e. it is of type $n \times n$. This kind of matrix is called a *square matrix*.

THE IDENTITY MATRIX

An $n \times n$ matrix with all elements 0 except those lying on the diagonal from the top left to the bottom right corners, which are 1, is called the $n \times n$ *identity matrix*. This is denoted by $\mathbf{I}_{n \times n}$ or simply by $\mathbf{I}$ if the type is obvious. For example,

$$\mathbf{I}_{3 \times 3} = \begin{bmatrix} 1 & 0 & 0 \\ 0 & 1 & 0 \\ 0 & 0 & 1 \end{bmatrix}$$

The $n \times n$ identity matrix behaves with respect to other $n \times n$ matrices in the same way as the number 1 does with respect to other numbers, i.e. if an $n \times n$ matrix is multiplied by $\mathbf{I}_{n \times n}$ it is unchanged. Thus

$$\mathbf{XI} = \mathbf{X} \tag{8.3}$$

For example,

$$\begin{bmatrix} 2 & 3 \\ -1 & 4 \end{bmatrix} \begin{bmatrix} 1 & 0 \\ 0 & 1 \end{bmatrix} = \begin{bmatrix} (2 \times 1) + (3 \times 0) & (2 \times 0) + (3 \times 1) \\ ((-1) \times 1) + (4 \times 0) & ((-1) \times 0) + (4 \times 1) \end{bmatrix}$$

$$= \begin{bmatrix} 2 + 0 & 0 + 3 \\ -1 + 0 & 0 + 4 \end{bmatrix}$$

$$= \begin{bmatrix} 2 & 3 \\ -1 & 4 \end{bmatrix}$$

Also, $$IX = X$$

For example,

$$\begin{bmatrix} 1 & 0 \\ 0 & 1 \end{bmatrix} \begin{bmatrix} 2 & 3 \\ -1 & 4 \end{bmatrix} = \begin{bmatrix} (1 \times 2) + (0 \times (-1)) & (1 \times 3) + (0 \times 4) \\ (0 \times 2) + (1 \times (-1)) & (0 \times 3) + (1 \times 4) \end{bmatrix}$$

$$= \begin{bmatrix} 2 & 3 \\ -1 & 4 \end{bmatrix}$$

We can see that $I_{n \times n}$ *commutes* with any other $n \times n$ matrix, i.e.

$$IX = XI \qquad (8.4)$$

THE INVERSE MATRIX

Suppose A is an $n \times n$ matrix. If another $n \times n$ matrix, C, exists such that

$$CA = I$$

then C is called an *inverse* of A and we write

$$C = A^{-1}$$

Thus A^{-1} is a matrix such that

$$A^{-1}A = I$$

It can also be shown that

$$AA^{-1} = I \qquad (8.5)$$

and so A and A^{-1} commute.

A matrix can have only one inverse, if it has one at all. To show this suppose B and C are both inverses of A. Then we have, from equation 8.5,

$$BA = AB = I$$

and

$$CA = AC = I$$

But from equation 8.3

$$B = BI$$

Therefore, since $I = AC$,

$$B = B(AC)$$
$$= (BA)C$$
$$= IC$$
$$= C$$

Therefore, B and C are the same matrix.

As an example, if

$$A = \begin{bmatrix} 4 & 3 \\ 1 & 2 \end{bmatrix} \quad \text{then} \quad A^{-1} = \begin{bmatrix} \frac{2}{5} & -\frac{3}{5} \\ -\frac{1}{5} & \frac{4}{5} \end{bmatrix}$$

because

$$AA^{-1} = \begin{bmatrix} \frac{8}{5} - \frac{3}{5} & -\frac{12}{5} + \frac{12}{5} \\ \frac{2}{5} - \frac{2}{5} & -\frac{3}{5} + \frac{8}{5} \end{bmatrix}$$

$$= \begin{bmatrix} 1 & 0 \\ 0 & 1 \end{bmatrix}$$

The use of the inverse matrix and methods of finding it will be shown later in this chapter.

SYSTEMS OF LINEAR SIMULTANEOUS EQUATIONS

Consider the set of linear simultaneous equations

$$x + 2y - z = 2 \tag{8.6a}$$
$$-x + y = 4 \tag{8.6b}$$

and
$$2x + 3z = 6 \tag{8.6c}$$

It is possible to form a matrix A and vectors X and B as follows:

$$A = \begin{bmatrix} 1 & 2 & -1 \\ -1 & 1 & 0 \\ 2 & 0 & 3 \end{bmatrix} \tag{8.7}$$

is called the *coefficient matrix* (the first column of A is made up of the coefficients of x in the three equations, and the second column is the coefficients of y, and the third column is the coefficients of z);

$$\mathbf{X} = \begin{bmatrix} x \\ y \\ z \end{bmatrix} \tag{8.8}$$

is called the *vector of unknowns* (x, y, and z being the variables whose values we have to find); and

$$\mathbf{B} = \begin{bmatrix} 2 \\ 4 \\ 6 \end{bmatrix} \tag{8.9}$$

is called the *requirement vector* (formed from the values of the equations).

Consider now what happens when $\mathbf{A}$ is multiplied by $\mathbf{X}$:

$$\mathbf{AX} = \begin{bmatrix} 1 & 2 & -1 \\ -1 & 1 & 0 \\ 2 & 0 & 3 \end{bmatrix} \begin{bmatrix} x \\ y \\ z \end{bmatrix}$$

$$= \begin{bmatrix} (1 \times x) + (2 \times y) + (-1 \times z) \\ (-1 \times x) + (1 \times y) + (0 \times z) \\ (2 \times x) + (0 \times y) + (3 \times z) \end{bmatrix}$$

$$= \begin{bmatrix} x + 2y - z \\ -x + y \\ 2x + 3z \end{bmatrix}$$

But from equations 8.6, $x + 2y - z = 2$, $-x + y = 4$, and $2x + 3z = 6$, and so

$$\mathbf{AX} = \begin{bmatrix} 2 \\ 4 \\ 6 \end{bmatrix} = \mathbf{B}$$

Hence the system of equations 8.6 can be represented by the matrix equation

$$\mathbf{AX} = \mathbf{B} \tag{8.10}$$

Any system of simultaneous linear equations can be represented in this form. Consider the n equations in the n unknowns $x_1, x_2, \ldots, x_n$:

$$a_{11}x_1 + a_{12}x_2 + \ldots + a_{1n}x_n = b_1 \qquad (8.11\text{a})$$

$$a_{21}x_1 + a_{22}x_2 + \ldots + a_{2n}x_n = b_2 \qquad (8.11\text{b})$$

and
$$a_{n1}x_1 + a_{n2}x_2 + \ldots + a_{nn}x_n = b_n \qquad (8.11\text{n})$$

If we let

$$A = \begin{bmatrix} a_{11} & a_{12} & \ldots & a_{1n} \\ a_{21} & a_{22} & \ldots & a_{2n} \\ \cdot & \cdot & & \cdot \\ \cdot & \cdot & & \cdot \\ \cdot & \cdot & & \cdot \\ a_{n1} & a_{n2} & \ldots & a_{nn} \end{bmatrix}$$

$$X = \begin{bmatrix} x_1 \\ x_2 \\ \cdot \\ \cdot \\ \cdot \\ x_n \end{bmatrix} \quad \text{and} \quad B = \begin{bmatrix} b_1 \\ b_2 \\ \cdot \\ \cdot \\ \cdot \\ b_n \end{bmatrix}$$

then the system of equations 8.11 can be represented by

$$AX = B \qquad (8.12)$$

Note that A is an $n \times n$ matrix and that X and B are $n \times 1$ matrices: an $n \times n$ matrix multiplied by an $n \times 1$ matrix gives an $n \times 1$ matrix.

Suppose we find the inverse (A^{-1}) of A and then multiply A^{-1} by each side of equation 8.12 to give

$$A^{-1}AX = A^{-1}B$$

Then, since $A^{-1}A = I$,

$$IX = A^{-1}B$$

and, since $IX = X$,

$$X = A^{-1}B$$

Therefore the system of equations is solved by multiplying A^{-1} by B.

Example

The system of equations

$$4x_1 + 3x_2 = 10 \qquad\qquad (8.13a)$$

and

$$x_1 + 2x_2 = 5 \qquad\qquad (8.13b)$$

can be represented by

$$AX = B$$

where $A = \begin{bmatrix} 4 & 3 \\ 1 & 2 \end{bmatrix}$, $X = \begin{bmatrix} x_1 \\ x_2 \end{bmatrix}$,   and $B = \begin{bmatrix} 10 \\ 5 \end{bmatrix}$

Now, we have already seen (page 208) that, for this matrix A,

$$A^{-1} = \begin{bmatrix} \frac{2}{5} & -\frac{3}{5} \\ -\frac{1}{5} & \frac{4}{5} \end{bmatrix}$$

and so $X = A^{-1}B$ becomes

$$\begin{bmatrix} x_1 \\ x_2 \end{bmatrix} = \begin{bmatrix} \frac{2}{5} & -\frac{3}{5} \\ -\frac{1}{5} & \frac{4}{5} \end{bmatrix} \begin{bmatrix} 10 \\ 5 \end{bmatrix}$$

$$= \begin{bmatrix} \frac{20}{5} - \frac{15}{5} \\ -\frac{10}{5} + \frac{20}{5} \end{bmatrix}$$

$$= \begin{bmatrix} 1 \\ 2 \end{bmatrix}$$

Hence, $x_1 = 1$ and $x_2 = 2$.

This example shows how useful the inverse matrix can be, and we shall now examine methods of finding inverse matrices.

ELEMENTARY ROW OPERATIONS

Consider the set of simultaneous linear equations

$$x - 2y = 6 \qquad\qquad (8.14a)$$
$$2x + y = 2 \qquad\qquad (8.14b)$$

It can easily be seen by substitution that this system has the solution $x = 2, y = -2$. One way of solving the equations is to perform certain operations that should be well known. These operations simply change the system into other systems *with the same solution.*

The following are examples of operations which can be carried out without changing the solution of the system of equations:

(1) Changing the order of the equations: it is obvious that

$$2x + y = 2 \qquad\qquad (8.15a)$$
$$x - 2y = 6 \qquad\qquad (8.15b)$$

still has the solution $x = 2, y = -2$.

(2) Multiplying an equation by any non-zero constant: for example, if equation 8.14b is multiplied by 2, the system becomes

$$x - 2y = 6 \qquad\qquad (8.16a)$$
$$4x + 2y = 4 \qquad\qquad (8.16b)$$

which still has the solution $x = 2, y = -2$.

(3) Adding a multiple of one equation to the other equation: for example, if equation 8.16b is added to equation 8.14a, we obtain

$$5x = 10 \qquad\qquad (8.17a)$$
$$2x + y = 2 \qquad\qquad (8.17b)$$

The solution is still $x = 2, y = -2$, and this of course is one way we could solve the equations to obtain the value of x ($5x = 10$ gives $x = 2$).

The elementary row operations are very similar to these permissible operations on equations, and they can be justified by noting the correspondence between the rows of a matrix and the coefficients of a system of equations. The elementary row operations are:

(1) Changing the order of the rows of a matrix.
(2) Multiplying a row of a matrix by a non-zero constant.
(3) Adding a multiple of one row of a matrix to another row of
   that matrix.

If row operations are performed on a matrix **A** to obtain matrix **B**,
then **B** is said to be *row equivalent* to **A** and we write

$$B \sim A$$

Because it would be possible to start with **B** and return to **A** by
reversing the previous row operations, it must also follow that **A** is row
equivalent to **B**, i.e.

$$A \sim B$$

Example

Let

$$A = \begin{bmatrix} 1 & -2 & 3 & 4 \\ 2 & 0 & -1 & 6 \\ -3 & 4 & 2 & 0 \end{bmatrix}$$

Interchanging the first and third rows gives

$$\begin{bmatrix} 1 & -2 & 3 & 4 \\ 2 & 0 & -1 & 6 \\ -3 & 4 & 2 & 0 \end{bmatrix} \sim \begin{bmatrix} -3 & 4 & 2 & 0 \\ 2 & 0 & -1 & 6 \\ 1 & -2 & 3 & 4 \end{bmatrix}$$

Multiplying the second row by 2 gives

$$\begin{bmatrix} 1 & -2 & 3 & 4 \\ 2 & 0 & -1 & 6 \\ -3 & 4 & 2 & 0 \end{bmatrix} \sim \begin{bmatrix} 1 & -2 & 3 & 4 \\ 4 & 0 & -2 & 12 \\ -3 & 4 & 2 & 0 \end{bmatrix}$$

Adding, to the third row, the first row multiplied by 3 gives

$$\begin{bmatrix} 1 & -2 & 3 & 4 \\ 2 & 0 & -1 & 6 \\ -3 & 4 & 2 & 0 \end{bmatrix} \sim \begin{bmatrix} 1 & -2 & 3 & 4 \\ 2 & 0 & -1 & 6 \\ 0 & -2 & 11 & 12 \end{bmatrix}$$

FINDING THE INVERSE MATRIX

It can be shown that, if we form the $n \times 2n$ matrix $[A I]$, i.e. if the $n \times n$ identity matrix is put alongside A, then

$$[AI] \sim [I A^{-1}] \qquad (8.18)$$

and this gives a way of finding A^{-1}.

As an example, let us show that the inverse of

$$\begin{bmatrix} 4 & 3 \\ 1 & 2 \end{bmatrix}$$

is

$$\begin{bmatrix} \frac{2}{5} & -\frac{3}{5} \\ -\frac{1}{5} & \frac{4}{5} \end{bmatrix}$$

Starting with

$$[AI] = \begin{bmatrix} 4 & 3 & 1 & 0 \\ 1 & 2 & 0 & 1 \end{bmatrix}$$

the first and second rows can be interchanged to give

$$\begin{bmatrix} 1 & 2 & 0 & 1 \\ 4 & 3 & 1 & 0 \end{bmatrix}$$

Then adding, to the second row, -4 times the first row, i.e. adding $(-4, -8, 0, -4)$, gives

$$\begin{bmatrix} 1 & 2 & 0 & 1 \\ 0 & -5 & 1 & -4 \end{bmatrix}$$

and multiplying the second row by $-\frac{1}{5}$ gives

$$\begin{bmatrix} 1 & 2 & 0 & 1 \\ 0 & 1 & -\frac{1}{5} & \frac{4}{5} \end{bmatrix}$$

As the last stage, the second row is multiplied by -2 to give $(0, -2, \frac{2}{5}, -\frac{8}{5})$, which is added to the first row, thus

$$\begin{bmatrix} 1 & 0 & \frac{2}{5} & -\frac{3}{5} \\ 0 & 1 & -\frac{1}{5} & \frac{4}{5} \end{bmatrix} = [I A^{-1}]$$

Hence

$$A^{-1} = \begin{bmatrix} \frac{2}{5} & -\frac{3}{5} \\ -\frac{1}{5} & \frac{4}{5} \end{bmatrix}$$

DETERMINANTS

Every *square* matrix **A** has a number associated with it called its *determinant*, denoted by det **A**. For example, if

$$A = \begin{bmatrix} 1 & 2 & 3 \\ 3 & 2 & 1 \\ 2 & 3 & 1 \end{bmatrix}$$

then det **A** can be written as

$$\det A = \begin{vmatrix} 1 & 2 & 3 \\ 3 & 2 & 1 \\ 2 & 3 & 1 \end{vmatrix}$$

The value of a determinant is calculated in the following way. Consider first the 2 x 2 matrix

$$A = \begin{bmatrix} a & b \\ c & d \end{bmatrix}$$

then

$$\det A = \begin{vmatrix} a & b \\ c & d \end{vmatrix} = ad - bc$$

For example,

$$\begin{vmatrix} 3 & 2 \\ 1 & 4 \end{vmatrix} = (3 \times 4) - (2 \times 1)$$

$$= 12 - 2$$

$$= 10$$

and
$$\begin{vmatrix} 4 & -2 \\ 5 & -7 \end{vmatrix} = (4 \times (-7)) - ((-2) \times 5)$$

$$= -28 - (-10)$$

$$= -18$$

For a 3 x 3 matrix, let

$$\mathbf{A} = \begin{bmatrix} a_{11} & a_{12} & a_{13} \\ a_{21} & a_{22} & a_{23} \\ a_{31} & a_{32} & a_{33} \end{bmatrix}$$

Then

$$\det \mathbf{A} = \begin{vmatrix} a_{11} & a_{12} & a_{13} \\ a_{21} & a_{22} & a_{23} \\ a_{31} & a_{32} & a_{33} \end{vmatrix}$$

The value of det **A** can be calculated in six different ways (one for each row and one for each column). The most common is expansion by the first row, as follows

$$\det \mathbf{A} = a_{11} \begin{vmatrix} a_{11} & a_{12} & a_{13} \\ a_{21} & a_{22} & a_{23} \\ a_{31} & a_{32} & a_{33} \end{vmatrix} - a_{12} \begin{vmatrix} a_{11} & a_{12} & a_{13} \\ a_{21} & a_{22} & a_{23} \\ a_{31} & a_{32} & a_{33} \end{vmatrix} + a_{13} \begin{vmatrix} a_{11} & a_{12} & a_{13} \\ a_{21} & a_{22} & a_{23} \\ a_{31} & a_{32} & a_{33} \end{vmatrix}$$

$$= a_{11} \begin{vmatrix} a_{22} & a_{23} \\ a_{32} & a_{33} \end{vmatrix} - a_{12} \begin{vmatrix} a_{21} & a_{23} \\ a_{31} & a_{33} \end{vmatrix} + a_{13} \begin{vmatrix} a_{21} & a_{22} \\ a_{31} & a_{32} \end{vmatrix}$$

$$= a_{11}(a_{22}a_{33} - a_{23}a_{32}) - a_{12}(a_{21}a_{33} - a_{23}a_{31})$$
$$+ a_{13}(a_{21}a_{32} - a_{22}a_{31})$$

For example,

$$\begin{vmatrix} 1 & -2 & -1 \\ 0 & 3 & 4 \\ 2 & 1 & 5 \end{vmatrix} = 1 \begin{vmatrix} 3 & 4 \\ 1 & 5 \end{vmatrix} - (-2) \begin{vmatrix} 0 & 4 \\ 2 & 5 \end{vmatrix} + (-1) \begin{vmatrix} 0 & 3 \\ 2 & 1 \end{vmatrix}$$

$$= 1 [(3 \times 5) - (4 \times 1)] - (-2) [(0 \times 5) - (4 \times 2)]$$
$$+ (-1) [(0 \times 1) - (3 \times 2)]$$

$$= 1(15 - 4) - (-2)(0 - 8) + (-1)(0 - 6)$$
$$= 1(11) - (-2)(-8) + (-1)(-6)$$
$$= 11 - 16 + 6$$
$$= 1$$

A determinant can be evaluated by expanding along any row or column. For each element in a particular row (or column), the row and the column of the element is eliminated, leaving a 2 x 2 determinant which can be evaluated. This 2 x 2 determinant is multiplied by

$$(-1)^{\text{row number + column number}}$$

This procedure gives the *cofactor* of the original element. The determinant is found by multiplying each element of a row (or column) by its cofactor, and adding. This applies to the determinant of a matrix of any size. For example, if we expand the above example by the second column, then

$$\begin{vmatrix} 1 & -2 & -1 \\ 0 & 3 & 4 \\ 2 & 1 & 5 \end{vmatrix}$$

$$= (-2)(-1)^{1+2} \begin{vmatrix} 0 & 4 \\ 2 & 5 \end{vmatrix} + 3(-1)^{2+2} \begin{vmatrix} 1 & -1 \\ 2 & 5 \end{vmatrix} + 1(-1)^{3+2} \begin{vmatrix} 1 & -1 \\ 0 & 4 \end{vmatrix}$$

$$= (-2)(-1)\,[(0 \times 5) - (4 \times 2)] + 3(+1)\,[(1 \times 5) - ((-1) \times 2)]$$
$$+ 1(-1)\,[(1 \times 4) - ((-1) \times 0)]$$

$$= 2(0 - 8) + 3[5 - (-2)] + (-1)(4 - 0)$$
$$= 2(-8) + (3 \times 7) - 4$$
$$= -16 + 21 - 4$$
$$= 1$$

THE TRANSPOSE MATRIX

If

$$\mathbf{A} = \begin{bmatrix} a_{11} & a_{12} & \cdots & a_{1n} \\ a_{21} & a_{22} & \cdots & a_{2n} \\ \cdot & \cdot & & \cdot \\ \cdot & \cdot & & \cdot \\ \cdot & \cdot & & \cdot \\ a_{m1} & a_{m2} & \cdots & a_{mn} \end{bmatrix}$$

Then the transpose of **A**, written $\mathbf{A}^T$, is defined by

$$\mathbf{A}^T = \begin{bmatrix} a_{11} & a_{21} & \cdot & \cdot & a_{m1} \\ a_{12} & a_{22} & \cdot & \cdot & a_{m2} \\ \cdot & \cdot & & & \cdot \\ \cdot & \cdot & & & \cdot \\ \cdot & \cdot & & & \cdot \\ a_{1n} & a_{2n} & \cdot & \cdot & a_{mn} \end{bmatrix}$$

i.e. rows become columns and columns become rows. For example,

$$\begin{bmatrix} 2 & 0 & 1 & 3 \\ 4 & 5 & -1 & -2 \end{bmatrix}^T = \begin{bmatrix} 2 & 4 \\ 0 & 5 \\ 1 & -1 \\ 3 & -2 \end{bmatrix}$$

and

$$\begin{bmatrix} 3 & 5 & 8 \\ -1 & 2 & 4 \\ -3 & 1 & -1 \end{bmatrix}^T = \begin{bmatrix} 3 & -1 & -3 \\ 5 & 2 & 1 \\ 8 & 4 & -1 \end{bmatrix}$$

THE ADJOINT MATRIX

The adjoint matrix is the transpose of the matrix of cofactors. For example, if

$$\mathbf{A} = \begin{bmatrix} 2 & 0 & 1 \\ -3 & 1 & 2 \\ -2 & 3 & -1 \end{bmatrix}$$

then

$$\text{adj } \mathbf{A} = \begin{bmatrix} \begin{vmatrix} 1 & 2 \\ 3 & -1 \end{vmatrix} & -\begin{vmatrix} -3 & 2 \\ -2 & -1 \end{vmatrix} & \begin{vmatrix} -3 & 1 \\ -2 & 3 \end{vmatrix} \\ -\begin{vmatrix} 0 & 1 \\ 3 & -1 \end{vmatrix} & \begin{vmatrix} 2 & 1 \\ -2 & -1 \end{vmatrix} & -\begin{vmatrix} 2 & 0 \\ -2 & 3 \end{vmatrix} \\ \begin{vmatrix} 0 & 1 \\ 1 & 2 \end{vmatrix} & -\begin{vmatrix} 2 & 1 \\ -3 & 2 \end{vmatrix} & \begin{vmatrix} 2 & 0 \\ -3 & 1 \end{vmatrix} \end{bmatrix}^T$$

$$= \begin{bmatrix} (-1-6) & -(3+4) & (-9+2) \\ -(0-3) & (-2+2) & -(6-0) \\ (0-1) & -(4+3) & (2-0) \end{bmatrix}^T$$

$$= \begin{bmatrix} -7 & -7 & -7 \\ 3 & 0 & -6 \\ -1 & -7 & 2 \end{bmatrix}^T$$

$$= \begin{bmatrix} -7 & 3 & -1 \\ -7 & 0 & -7 \\ -7 & -6 & 2 \end{bmatrix}$$

ANOTHER METHOD OF FINDING THE INVERSE MATRIX

The inverse matrix can be found by means of the equation

$$A^{-1} = \left(\frac{1}{\det A} \right) \text{adj } A$$

Therefore a matrix A can only have an inverse if $\det A \neq 0$. In the above example

$$\det A = \begin{vmatrix} 2 & 0 & 1 \\ -3 & 1 & 2 \\ -2 & 3 & -1 \end{vmatrix}$$

$$= 2 \begin{vmatrix} 1 & 2 \\ 3 & -1 \end{vmatrix} - 0 + 1 \begin{vmatrix} -3 & 1 \\ -2 & 3 \end{vmatrix}$$

$$= 2(-1-6) + 1(-9+2)$$

$$= 2(-7) + (-7)$$

$$= -21$$

Therefore

$$A^{-1} = -\tfrac{1}{21} \begin{bmatrix} -7 & 3 & -1 \\ -7 & 0 & -7 \\ -7 & -6 & 2 \end{bmatrix}$$

In order to check that this inverse is correct, we can multiply A^{-1} by A:

$$A^{-1}A = -\frac{1}{21}\begin{bmatrix} -7 & 3 & -1 \\ -7 & 0 & -7 \\ -7 & -6 & 2 \end{bmatrix}\begin{bmatrix} 2 & 0 & 1 \\ -3 & 1 & 2 \\ -2 & 3 & -1 \end{bmatrix}$$

$$= -\frac{1}{21}\begin{bmatrix} -14-9+2 & 0+3-3 & -7+6+1 \\ -14+0+14 & 0+0-21 & -7+0+7 \\ -14+18-4 & 0-6+6 & -7-12-2 \end{bmatrix}$$

$$= -\frac{1}{21}\begin{bmatrix} -21 & 0 & 0 \\ 0 & -21 & 0 \\ 0 & 0 & -21 \end{bmatrix}$$

$$= \begin{bmatrix} 1 & 0 & 0 \\ 0 & 1 & 0 \\ 0 & 0 & 1 \end{bmatrix}$$

$$= I$$

Thus A^{-1} found by this method is correct.

MACRO-ECONOMIC MODELS

Macro-economic models are used by governments in their attempts to 'manage' the economy. Such models are quite complicated in that they contain a large number of variables and equations. One consequence of this is that matrix algebra is used to handle the systems of equations. The macro model that most students of economics have come across is often presented diagrammatically as in Figure 8.1. This model was discussed in detail in Chapter 1 (see pages 33—35).

The endogenous variables in this model are income Y and consumption expenditure C. Investment is treated as an exogenous variable and is therefore not related to income (or saving). At any level of current income, investment equals I_0 (a *particular* value of I). Consumption is related to income by the function $C = a + bY$, where a represents autonomous consumption (i.e. consumption unrelated to income) and b, the slope of the consumption function, is the marginal propensity to consume. Remember that this consumption function shows what consumers *plan* to spend at any income level, whilst the investment level I_0 is a particular value of the exogenous variable which shows the amount that entrepreneurs *plan* to invest per time period.

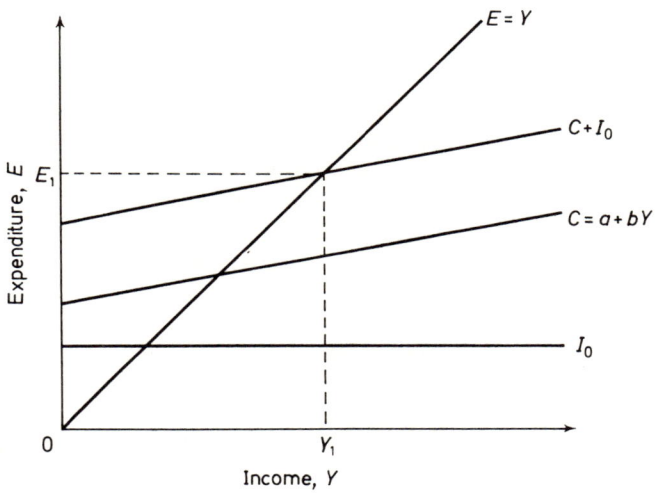

Figure 8.1

Thus, the line $C + I_0$ shows the total expenditure, or planned aggregate expenditure, E. The $E = Y$ line (sometimes loosely called the 45° line) from the origin is simply a guide line, being the locus of all points showing the value of current output (and hence current income) and spending needed to maintain that value of Y. At an income level Y_1, planned expenditure E_1 equals the current output and planned investment equals actual investment. At any income level *below* Y_1, the system cannot be in equilibrium because planned investment is greater than actual investment; at any income level *above* Y_1, planned investment is less than actual investment. Lastly, changes in autonomous consumption a, in planned investment I_0, or in the marginal propensity to consume b will change the equilibrium level of income. We could treat a and b as constants and examine the effects on Y and C of changes in I_0.

AN ALGEBRAIC FORMULATION OF THE MODEL

The functions in Figure 8.1 can be expressed algebraically, thus the
model can be written:

$$Y \equiv C + I \qquad (8.19)$$

$$C = a + bY \quad (0 < b < 1) \qquad (8.20)$$

and $$I = I_0 \qquad (8.21)$$

Identity 8.19 is an accounting expression indicating that consumption
expenditure plus investment expenditure defines current income.
Equation 8.20 is a hypothesis about economic behaviour: namely, as
income increases so will consumer expenditure, but not all of the
increased income will be spent on consumption (because $0 < b < 1$).
Equation 8.21 states that planned investment expenditure is equal to
an amount I_0 which, when substituted into identity 8.19, gives

$$Y = C + I_0 \qquad (8.22)$$

(an equality and not an identity). Equation 8.22 is the equilibrium
condition for the model. There are endogenous variables Y and C on
both sides of equations 8.20 and 8.22 and, although I has a given value
I_0, Y and C can take on a number of possible values. However, only *one*
pair of values of Y and C will simultaneously solve the system and give
an equilibrium solution. By substituting equation 8.20 into equation
8.22, we can obtain

$$Y = \frac{a + I_0}{1 - b} \qquad (8.23)$$

which, when substituted back into equation 8.20, gives

$$C = \frac{a + bI_0}{1 - b} \qquad (8.24)$$

These values of Y and C are equilibrium values, and equations 8.23 and
8.24 are called solution equations, or reduced-form equations.

The purpose of econometrics is to estimate the values of parameters
such as a and b. It will now be useful to introduce the student to
matrix methods of achieving the solution equations in macro-economic
models. This is *not* because matrix methods are necessary in such
elementary models as that used above, but in order to give confidence
in using matrix algebra as a preparation for handling more complex

models and for reading economics journals in which such mathematics appears.

MATRIX FORMULATION

Let us assume that b is a constant and that I_0 and a are exogenous variables. The above model could be set out in the following way:

$$Y - C = I_0 \tag{8.25}$$

and

$$-bY + C = a \tag{8.26}$$

These two equations can be written in matrix notation to show how the rules and operations developed earlier in this chapter apply. Notice that in equation 8.25 the coefficient of Y is 1 and of C is -1. In equation 8.26, the coefficients are $-b$ and 1 respectively. Thus we can write

$$\begin{bmatrix} I_0 \\ a \end{bmatrix} = \begin{bmatrix} 1 & -1 \\ -b & 1 \end{bmatrix} \begin{bmatrix} Y \\ C \end{bmatrix} \tag{8.27}$$

The vector of the exogenous variables I_0 and a is a 2 x 1 matrix, the matrix of coefficients is a 2 x 2 matrix, and the vector of the endogenous variables Y and C is a 2 x 1 matrix. Thus on the right-hand side we have a 2 x 2 matrix multiplied by a 2 x 1 matrix, which will give a 2 x 1 matrix, i.e.

$$\begin{bmatrix} 1 & -1 \\ -b & 1 \end{bmatrix} \begin{bmatrix} Y \\ C \end{bmatrix} = \begin{bmatrix} Y - C \\ -bY + C \end{bmatrix} \tag{8.28}$$

Equations 8.27 and 8.28 lead readily to the original equations 8.25 and 8.26, namely

$$I_0 = Y - C$$

and

$$a = -bY + C$$

Although this procedure provides a reminder of matrix operations, we are here treating I_0 and a as exogenous variables and Y and C as endogenous variables and therefore really need Y and C each as a function of I_0 and a.

To obtain this result a few more of the rules of matrix operations must be applied. We have already seen that, given a square matrix **A**, then $AA^{-1} = I$ (i.e. a matrix A multiplied by its inverse will give an identity matrix). Also, we have seen that $AI = A$. Now suppose

$$A = \begin{bmatrix} 1 & -1 \\ -b & 1 \end{bmatrix}$$

and that we can find the inverse (A^{-1}) of this. Then, multiplying each side of equation 8.27 by A^{-1} gives

$$A^{-1} \begin{bmatrix} I_0 \\ a \end{bmatrix} = A^{-1} \begin{bmatrix} 1 & -1 \\ -b & 1 \end{bmatrix} \begin{bmatrix} Y \\ C \end{bmatrix}$$

i.e.

$$A^{-1} \begin{bmatrix} I_0 \\ a \end{bmatrix} = A^{-1}A \begin{bmatrix} Y \\ C \end{bmatrix}$$

∴

$$A^{-1} \begin{bmatrix} I_0 \\ a \end{bmatrix} = \begin{bmatrix} Y \\ C \end{bmatrix}$$

i.e.

$$\begin{bmatrix} Y \\ C \end{bmatrix} = A^{-1} \begin{bmatrix} I_0 \\ a \end{bmatrix} \qquad (8.29)$$

Therefore, having found A^{-1}, we can express Y and C in terms of I_0 and a.

In order to find A^{-1}, first form the matrix $[AI]$:

$$[AI] = \begin{bmatrix} 1 & -1 & 1 & 0 \\ -b & 1 & 0 & 1 \end{bmatrix}$$

$$\sim \begin{bmatrix} 1 & -1 & 1 & 0 \\ 0 & 1-b & b & 1 \end{bmatrix} \qquad \text{(Row 2 + }b\text{ x Row 1)}$$

$$\sim \begin{bmatrix} 1 & -1 & 1 & 0 \\ 0 & 1 & \dfrac{b}{1-b} & \dfrac{1}{1-b} \end{bmatrix} \quad \left(\dfrac{1}{1-b} \text{ x Row 2}\right)$$

$$\sim \begin{bmatrix} 1 & 0 & 1+\dfrac{b}{1-b} & \dfrac{1}{1-b} \\ 0 & 1 & \dfrac{b}{1-b} & \dfrac{1}{1-b} \end{bmatrix} \quad \text{(Row 1 + Row 2)}$$

$$= [I\,A^{-1}]$$

Hence

$$A^{-1} = \begin{bmatrix} 1 + \dfrac{b}{1-b} & \dfrac{b}{1-b} \\[2mm] \dfrac{b}{1-b} & \dfrac{1}{1-b} \end{bmatrix}$$

$$= \begin{bmatrix} \dfrac{1}{1-b} & \dfrac{1}{1-b} \\[2mm] \dfrac{b}{1-b} & \dfrac{1}{1-b} \end{bmatrix}$$

Then, from equation 8.29,

$$\begin{bmatrix} Y \\ C \end{bmatrix} = \begin{bmatrix} \dfrac{1}{1-b} & \dfrac{1}{1-b} \\[2mm] \dfrac{b}{1-b} & \dfrac{1}{1-b} \end{bmatrix} \begin{bmatrix} I_0 \\ a \end{bmatrix}$$

$$= \begin{bmatrix} \dfrac{I_0}{1-b} + \dfrac{a}{1-b} \\[2mm] \dfrac{bI_0}{1-b} + \dfrac{a}{1-b} \end{bmatrix}$$

Hence
$$Y = \frac{I_0 + a}{1-b}$$

and
$$C = \frac{bI_0 + a}{1-b}$$

Although matrix methods are not necessary for the solution of such a simple system, as soon as more complex macro models have to be dealt with, such methods are extremely useful. The student who progresses this far will be well equipped to move on to more realistic models. For example, in the above model we are looking at the equilibrium condition in the goods and services sector. If investment I were assumed to be a function of the rate of interest, then the level of I would depend on equilibrium in the monetary sector. Thus we would have more equations. If we were also to introduce a production sector with the demand and supply of labour as a function of real wages, then the money supply would be related to real wages via the price level and so the simultaneous equation system would become more complex.

INPUT–OUTPUT ANALYSIS

The student who has undertaken a course in macro-economics will be familiar with such concepts as final aggregate demand, national income, and aggregate investment. It ought to be obvious that the amount of economic activity in a system is much greater than that associated with transactions concerning the sale of goods and services to the final user. A hint of this appears in macro-economics when we refer to the problem of double counting in calculating national income. To be more explicit, the output of many firms is sold to other firms for whom such purchases are inputs into their particular production process. For example, mining companies sell ore to steel companies, which produce steel that is sold to firms producing cars, washing machines, tools, etc. Additionally, the steel-producing firms sell steel to can-producing firms, which then sell cans to companies making paint, processed foods, pet-foods, etc., which are then sold to wholesalers and retailers. For our purposes, we wish to know something of the flow of inputs and outputs between the various sectors of the economy. The kind of questions that might be of interest are:

(1) For a given increase in the demand for final output, what will have to be the increase in inputs in various sectors of the economy?
(2) Where are bottlenecks in production likely to occur?
(3) How much of the output of each sector is used as intermediate output in the production process (for example, as inputs of other sectors)?

Input–output analysis provides an analytical framework and technique for coping with such problems.

A SIMPLE INPUT–OUTPUT MODEL

We shall ignore most of the practical difficulties involved in actually constructing input–output models and obtaining data and shall concentrate on the basic concepts of an input–output model. A point worth stressing is that the definition of a sector is arbitrary, as are the decisions to include a particular firm within a particular industry and to include that industry within a particular sector. The main point is that, such decisions having been made, then it is crucial to be consistent. For example, if a small firm makes springs for car seats, do we include it in the engineering industry or in the car industry? Is the car industry to be treated as part of the engineering, wholesale, or retail businesses? The first point to grasp is that the output of each sector can be disposed of in any one, or all, of the following ways:

(1) A sector buys some of its own output (machine-tool firms need machine tools, insurance companies need insurance, and so on).
(2) A sector will sell output to other firms who use it as an input in their own productive process (machine-tool firms sell machine tools to textile firms, who use these tools in the process of producing textiles). Such sales are known as intermediate output.
(3) A sector will also sell some of its output as final demand (final demand means the demand of the final consumer).

The total of a sector's sales to itself, to other firms as intermediate output, and to final consumers adds up to the total output of the sector.

The principle of intersectoral flow is illustrated in Table 8.2, where the outputs are measured in money units so that they may be equated. Immediately, one can see that matrix notation will be useful in handling the data contained in Table 8.2. The first row of figures shows

Table 8.2 INTERSECTORAL FLOW

Output from	Intermediate output			Final demand	Total output
	Primary	*Manufacturing*	*Services*		
Primary	30	100	70	100	300
Manufacturing	10	20	49	321	400
Services	10	40	10	360	420

what happens to the total output of the primary sector (note all the money units of output in the row are the same and can be added). The businesses in the primary sector use 30 units of output from the sector itself, whilst 100 units are sold to firms in the manufacturing sector and 70 units to the services sector. The total of 30 + 100 + 70 is the amount of the primary sector's output used as intermediate input by all sectors. Additionally, 100 units of output are sold to the final consumer, so the total output of the sector is 300 units.

In order to identify the uses to which the output of each sector is put, the following notation can be used: for the primary sector we shall use the subscript 1, for the manufacturing sector 2, and for the services sector 3. We can also define X_i as the output of sector i. Thus in the model of intersectoral flow,

X_1 = 300 units (primary sector),
X_2 = 400 units (manufacturing sector),
and X_3 = 420 units (services sector).

These data are from the last column of Table 8.2 and give the total-output vector **X** as

$$X = \begin{bmatrix} 300 \\ 400 \\ 420 \end{bmatrix} \tag{8.30}$$

The next step is to identify that part of the total output of a particular sector that is supplied to sectors (including itself) as inputs. To do this we define X_{ij} as the value of output from sector i sold to sector j. Thus the sales of output from the primary sector to the manufacturing sector are 100 units, which could be written as

$$X_{ij} = 100$$

where $i = 1, j = 2$. In fact, X_{ij} identifies an element in a particular row and column in Table 8.2. The data referring to intersectoral transactions can be set out in the form of an *intersectoral-flow matrix*, which we shall, for convenience, call **T**:

$$T = \begin{bmatrix} 30 & 100 & 70 \\ 10 & 20 & 49 \\ 10 & 40 & 10 \end{bmatrix} = \begin{bmatrix} X_{11} & X_{12} & X_{13} \\ X_{21} & X_{22} & X_{23} \\ X_{31} & X_{32} & X_{33} \end{bmatrix} \tag{8.31}$$

(a 3 x 3 matrix). Every element in **T** represents the output of one sector used by itself, or by another sector, in further production. For example, X_{23} is the element in the second row, third column, and (given our notation and definitions) is the sale of 49 units of output by the manufacturing sector to the services sector. Thus the summation of the output of a sector which is used as intermediate output is obtained by adding the elements in a row. For example,

$$\sum_{j=1}^{3} X_{1j}$$

means add the elements in the first row, i.e. find $X_{11} + X_{12} + X_{13}$.

Referring back to Table 8.2, we see that the elements in the first *column* show the values of inputs purchased by the primary sector in order to produce its total output of 300 units. These purchases are:

30 units from itself (X_{11}),
10 units from the manufacturing sector (X_{21}),
and 10 units from the services sector (X_{31}).

These are the elements in the first column of matrix T. If we treat each column of T as a vector, we can write

$$T_1 = \begin{bmatrix} 30 \\ 10 \\ 10 \end{bmatrix}, \quad T_2 = \begin{bmatrix} 100 \\ 20 \\ 40 \end{bmatrix}, \quad \text{and} \quad T_3 = \begin{bmatrix} 70 \\ 49 \\ 10 \end{bmatrix}$$

where T_1 is the purchases of inputs by the primary sector, T_2 is the purchases of inputs by the manufacturing sector, and T_3 is the purchases of inputs by the services sector. The column in Table 8.2 headed 'Final demand' contains the sales of output from each sector in the form of final demand. This can be written as a vector D:

$$D = \begin{bmatrix} 100 \\ 321 \\ 360 \end{bmatrix}$$

Using matrix notation, we can thus set out the model in the following way:

$$X = T_1 + T_2 + T_3 + D \tag{8.32}$$

Total output of the system is equal to the purchases of intermediate output by sectors, plus output sold to final users. (The student should write these vectors out in full in order to be satisfied that this system is in fact the original input—output table.) As things stand at the moment, we have simply set out the model in matrix notation, which enables certain magnitudes to be identified, as follows:

X_i identifies the total output of sector i,

$\sum_{j=1}^{3} X_{ij}$ identifies the sales of sector i to other sectors including itself (intermediate output), and $\sum\limits_{i=1}^{3} X_i$ identifies the total output of the system.

Consider, now, the following problem. There exists a final demand for the output of each sector, and from Table 8.2 it can be seen that the manufacturing sector sold 321 units as final demand. If the final demand increases, there will be a chain reaction throughout the system because, in order to produce 321 units of final demand, the manufacturing sector used 10 units of inputs from the primary sector and 49 units from the services sector, as well as 20 units from its own sector. To meet an increased final demand, the manufacturing sector would have to increase its purchases of inputs from all sectors, and these in turn will have to increase *their* purchases of inputs. Suppose we wish to find what increases there will have to be in the output of the sectors if there is an increase in the final demand for the output of the manufacturing sector. The answer cannot easily be obtained by simply setting the model in matrix form, as we have done so far. We shall need another matrix containing further information, and some of the matrix operations demonstrated earlier will have to be performed.

TECHNICAL COEFFICIENTS

In order to solve such problems as that posed above, we start by considering what inputs are needed to produce one unit of output in any particular sector. Consider the total output of the manufacturing sector, namely 400 units. The inputs used were 100 units from the primary sector, 20 units from the manufacturing sector itself, and 40 units from the services sector. Consider also the sales of the primary sector to the manufacturing sector: the input of primary output in manufacturing was 100 units. The total output of the manufacturing sector is 400 units, so the ratio of primary inputs to manufacturing output is $\frac{100}{400}$ or $\frac{1}{4}$. Using matrix notation, we can state that the demand of sector j for the output of sector i is proportional to the total output of industry j. If we use a_{ij} to denote this proportion, then

$$a_{ij} = \frac{X_{ij}}{X_j} \tag{8.33}$$

In the example quoted above,

$$a_{ij} = \frac{100}{400} = \frac{1}{4}$$

This is known as the *input–output coefficient*. The crucial assumption made in input–output analysis is that *this ratio stays constant over different levels of output*. Also, it is assumed that

$$0 \leqslant a_{ij} \leqslant 1$$

It is now possible to set up the model in matrix form, but this time incorporating the input–output coefficients (which from now on we shall simply refer to as *technical coefficients*) into the model. There are three sectors, and the following statement is true for each of them:

$$X_i = \sum_{j=1}^{3} X_{ij} + D_i \qquad (8.34)$$

where $i = 1, 2, 3$. But from equation 8.33

$$a_{ij} = \frac{X_{ij}}{X_j}$$

$$\therefore \qquad a_{ij}X_j = X_{ij} \qquad (8.35)$$

We can substitute equation 8.35 into equation 8.34 to give

$$X_i = \sum_{j=1}^{3} a_{ij}X_j + D_i \qquad (8.36)$$

where $i = 1, 2, 3$. This can be written out in full as:

$$X_1 = a_{11}X_1 + a_{12}X_2 + a_{13}X_3 + D_1 \qquad (8.37a)$$
$$X_2 = a_{21}X_1 + a_{22}X_2 + a_{23}X_3 + D_2 \qquad (8.37b)$$
$$X_3 = a_{31}X_1 + a_{32}X_2 + a_{33}X_3 + D_3 \qquad (8.37c)$$

Note that we have defined a_{12}, for example, as X_{12}/X_2, i.e. the sales of sector 1 to sector 2 as a proportion of the output of sector 2. Thus

$$a_{12}X_2 = \frac{X_{12}}{X_2} X_2 = X_{12}$$

As $a_{12}X_2$ is the same as X_{12}, the set of equations 8.37 is the same as the original model. The important difference is that the reformulation, involving a_{ij}, enables certain operations to be carried out to yield answers to important questions.

Equations 8.37 can be rearranged as:

$$X_1 - a_{11}X_1 - a_{12}X_2 - a_{13}X_3 = D_1 \tag{8.38a}$$

$$X_2 - a_{21}X_1 - a_{22}X_2 - a_{23}X_3 = D_2 \tag{8.38b}$$

$$X_3 - a_{31}X_1 - a_{32}X_2 - a_{33}X_3 = D_3 \tag{8.38c}$$

and these equations can be written in matrix notation as:

$$\begin{bmatrix} 1 - a_{11} & -a_{12} & -a_{13} \\ -a_{21} & 1 - a_{22} & -a_{23} \\ -a_{31} & -a_{32} & 1 - a_{33} \end{bmatrix} \begin{bmatrix} X_1 \\ X_2 \\ X_3 \end{bmatrix} = \begin{bmatrix} D_1 \\ D_2 \\ D_3 \end{bmatrix}$$

Note that

$$\begin{bmatrix} 1 - a_{11} & -a_{12} & -a_{13} \\ -a_{21} & 1 - a_{22} & -a_{23} \\ -a_{31} & -a_{32} & 1 - a_{33} \end{bmatrix} = \begin{bmatrix} 1 & 0 & 0 \\ 0 & 1 & 0 \\ 0 & 0 & 1 \end{bmatrix} - \begin{bmatrix} a_{11} & a_{12} & a_{13} \\ a_{21} & a_{22} & a_{23} \\ a_{31} & a_{32} & a_{33} \end{bmatrix}$$

The 3 × 3 matrix containing the elements a_{11}, a_{12}, etc., is the *matrix of the technical input–output coefficients*, which we shall call matrix **A**, and, as is conventional, the identity matrix is designated **I**. Therefore

$$\begin{bmatrix} 1 - a_{11} & -a_{12} & -a_{13} \\ -a_{21} & 1 - a_{22} & -a_{23} \\ -a_{31} & -a_{32} & 1 - a_{33} \end{bmatrix} = I - A$$

Thus

$$(I - A)\,X = D \tag{8.39}$$

where **X** is the total output vector and **D** is the final demand vector.

In order to see what changes are needed in each sector if final demand changes, we need to obtain total output as a function of final demand. To achieve this, we proceed as follows. Multiplying both sides of equation 8.39 by $(I - A)^{-1}$ gives

$$(I - A)^{-1}(I - A)\,X = (I - A)^{-1}D$$

But

$$(I - A)^{-1}(I - A) = I$$

and so

$$IX = (I - A)^{-1}D$$

Also, since $IX = X$,

$$X = (I - A)^{-1}D$$

Thus the output of each sector is equal to the sum of the elements of the final vector times the elements in the relevant row of the inverse of the matrix $(I - A)$. From this we can go on to obtain changes in the output of each sector given changes in final demand. To demonstrate these methods, let us work through the particular case of the data in Table 8.2.

NUMERICAL EXAMPLE OF INPUT–OUTPUT MODEL

We need to obtain

$$X = (I - A)^{-1}D$$

The data in Table 8.2 provide A, the matrix of technical coefficients:

$$A = \begin{bmatrix} \dfrac{X_{11}}{X_1} & \dfrac{X_{12}}{X_2} & \dfrac{X_{13}}{X_3} \\[2mm] \dfrac{X_{21}}{X_1} & \dfrac{X_{22}}{X_2} & \dfrac{X_{23}}{X_3} \\[2mm] \dfrac{X_{31}}{X_1} & \dfrac{X_{32}}{X_2} & \dfrac{X_{33}}{X_3} \end{bmatrix} = \begin{bmatrix} \dfrac{30}{300} & \dfrac{100}{400} & \dfrac{70}{420} \\[2mm] \dfrac{10}{300} & \dfrac{20}{400} & \dfrac{49}{420} \\[2mm] \dfrac{10}{300} & \dfrac{40}{400} & \dfrac{10}{420} \end{bmatrix} = \begin{bmatrix} \dfrac{1}{10} & \dfrac{1}{4} & \dfrac{1}{6} \\[2mm] \dfrac{1}{30} & \dfrac{1}{20} & \dfrac{7}{60} \\[2mm] \dfrac{1}{30} & \dfrac{1}{10} & \dfrac{1}{42} \end{bmatrix}$$

Therefore

$$I - A = \begin{bmatrix} 1 & 0 & 0 \\ 0 & 1 & 0 \\ 0 & 0 & 1 \end{bmatrix} - \begin{bmatrix} \dfrac{1}{10} & \dfrac{1}{4} & \dfrac{1}{6} \\[2mm] \dfrac{1}{30} & \dfrac{1}{20} & \dfrac{7}{60} \\[2mm] \dfrac{1}{30} & \dfrac{1}{10} & \dfrac{1}{42} \end{bmatrix}$$

$$= \begin{bmatrix} \dfrac{9}{10} & -\dfrac{1}{4} & -\dfrac{1}{6} \\[2mm] -\dfrac{1}{30} & \dfrac{19}{20} & -\dfrac{7}{60} \\[2mm] -\dfrac{1}{30} & -\dfrac{1}{10} & \dfrac{41}{42} \end{bmatrix}$$

$$= \begin{bmatrix} 0.90 & -0.25 & -0.17 \\ -0.03 & 0.95 & -0.12 \\ -0.03 & -0.10 & 0.98 \end{bmatrix}$$

In order to find $(I - A)^{-1}$ we therefore write

$$\begin{bmatrix} 0.90 & -0.25 & -0.17 & 1 & 0 & 0 \\ -0.03 & 0.95 & -0.12 & 0 & 1 & 0 \\ -0.03 & -0.10 & 0.98 & 0 & 0 & 1 \end{bmatrix}$$

$$\begin{bmatrix} 1 & -0.28 & -0.19 & 1.11 & 0 & 0 \\ -0.03 & 0.95 & -0.12 & 0 & 1 & 0 \\ 0 & -1.05 & 1.10 & 0 & -1 & 1 \end{bmatrix} \quad \begin{array}{l} \left(\dfrac{1}{0.90} \times \text{Row 1} \right) \\ (\text{Row 3} + (-1) \\ \qquad \times \text{Row 2}) \end{array}$$

$$\sim \begin{bmatrix} 1 & -0.28 & -0.19 & 1.11 & 0 & 0 \\ 0 & 0.94 & -0.13 & 0.03 & 1 & 0 \\ 0 & -1.05 & 1.10 & 0 & -1 & 1 \end{bmatrix} \quad \begin{array}{l} (\text{Row 2} + 0.03 \\ \qquad \times \text{Row 1}) \end{array}$$

$$\sim \begin{bmatrix} 1 & -0.28 & -0.19 & 1.11 & 0 & 0 \\ 0 & 1 & -0.14 & 0.03 & 1.06 & 0 \\ 0 & -1.05 & 1.10 & 0 & -1 & 1 \end{bmatrix} \quad \left(\dfrac{1}{0.94} \times \text{Row 2} \right)$$

$$\sim \begin{bmatrix} 1 & 0 & -0.23 & 1.12 & 0.30 & 0 \\ 0 & 1 & -0.14 & 0.03 & 1.06 & 0 \\ 0 & 0 & 0.95 & 0.03 & 0.11 & 1 \end{bmatrix} \quad \begin{array}{l} (\text{Row 1} + 0.28 \\ \qquad \times \text{Row 2}) \\ (\text{Row 3} + 1.05 \\ \qquad \times \text{Row 2}) \end{array}$$

$$\sim \begin{bmatrix} 1 & 0 & -0.23 & 1.12 & 0.30 & 0 \\ 0 & 1 & -0.14 & 0.03 & 1.06 & 0 \\ 0 & 0 & 1 & 0.03 & 0.12 & 1.05 \end{bmatrix} \quad \left(\dfrac{1}{0.95} \times \text{Row 3} \right)$$

$$\sim \begin{bmatrix} 1 & 0 & 0 & 1.13 & 0.33 & 0.24 \\ 0 & 1 & 0 & 0.03 & 1.08 & 0.15 \\ 0 & 0 & 1 & 0.03 & 0.12 & 1.05 \end{bmatrix} \quad \begin{array}{l} (\text{Row 1} + 0.23 \\ \qquad \times \text{Row 3}) \\ (\text{Row 2} + 0.14 \\ \qquad \times \text{Row 3}) \end{array}$$

Hence

$$(I - A)^{-1} = \begin{bmatrix} 1.13 & 0.33 & 0.24 \\ 0.03 & 1.08 & 0.15 \\ 0.03 & 0.12 & 1.05 \end{bmatrix}$$

We can now set up the full input—output model:

$$X = (I - A)^{-1}D$$

i.e.

$$\begin{bmatrix} 300 \\ 400 \\ 420 \end{bmatrix} = \begin{bmatrix} 1.13 & 0.33 & 0.24 \\ 0.03 & 1.08 & 0.15 \\ 0.03 & 0.12 & 1.05 \end{bmatrix} \begin{bmatrix} 100 \\ 321 \\ 360 \end{bmatrix}$$

Thus X_1, which is 300 units of output of sector 1, is the summation of the elements of the first *row* of $(I - A)^{-1}$ times the elements of the final demand vector **D**, i.e.

$$300 = (1.13 \times 100) + (0.33 \times 321) + (0.24 \times 360)$$

(*N.B.* The reader who checks this will realise that rounding errors result in slight inaccuracy.) Similarly, X_2 and X_3 can be related to final demand.

We can now deal with the question of what will be the increase in the total output of each sector if the final demand for the products of one or more sectors increases. If the change in total output is given by ΔX and the change in final demand by ΔD, we can write

$$\Delta X = (I - A)^{-1}\Delta D$$

which means that the sum of the elements in row i of $(I - A)^{-1}$ times the vector giving changes in final demand for sector output gives the change in the total output of X_i. Suppose that the final demand for the output of the manufacturing sector increased by 32 units (a 10% increase). The new final demand vector would be

$$\begin{bmatrix} 100 \\ 353 \\ 360 \end{bmatrix}$$

and so

$$\Delta D = \begin{bmatrix} 100 \\ 353 \\ 360 \end{bmatrix} - \begin{bmatrix} 100 \\ 321 \\ 360 \end{bmatrix} = \begin{bmatrix} 0 \\ 32 \\ 0 \end{bmatrix}$$

The increase in final output in *each* sector to sustain this increased demand for the output of the manufacturing sector is given by

$$\Delta X = (I - A)^{-1}\Delta D$$

$$= \begin{bmatrix} 1.13 & 0.33 & 0.24 \\ 0.03 & 1.08 & 0.15 \\ 0.03 & 0.12 & 1.05 \end{bmatrix} \begin{bmatrix} 0 \\ 32 \\ 0 \end{bmatrix}$$

$$= \begin{bmatrix} 11 \\ 35 \\ 4 \end{bmatrix}$$

Thus the change in total output needed in *each* sector to support the increase in final demand of 10% in manufacturing output is 11 units in the primary sector, 35 units in the manufacturing sector itself, and 4 units in the services sector, i.e.

$$\Delta X_1 = 11$$
$$\Delta X_2 = 35$$
$$\Delta X_3 = 4$$

We shall proceed no further with input–output analysis, for the use of matrix methods should now be obvious. Those students who wish to pursue input–output analysis further should refer to the basic texts on the subject (many more economics problems can be handled by input–output methods).

Chapter 9

LINEAR PROGRAMMING

A certain type of constrained optimisation problem is called a 'linear programming' (abbreviated to LP) problem. One method of solving certain linear programming problems is presented here, but first an example of this type of problem will be considered.

Suppose a company manufactures two products, X and Y. In a given month advance orders have already been placed for 100 of X and 200 of Y, and it is company policy to produce a total of at least 500 items per month. Each X requires 6 hours on the company's machines and each Y requires 5 hours, and there is a maximum of 6000 machine hours available each month. There are two basic raw materials, A and B, used in the manufacture of both X and Y. To make each X, 3 lb of A and 1 lb of B are used, and to make each Y, 1 lb of A and 2 lb of B are used. In this particular month, the company has available only 2400 lb of A and 2000 lb of B. If the profit on each X is £3 and the profit on each Y is £2, the problem is to find how many of each of X and Y should be made in this month to maximise the company's total profit.

As before, we have an optimisation problem — but this time it is profit which has to be maximised. Suppose that the number of X's made by the company is x and the number of Y's made is y. Then the total profit P_T is given by

$$P_T = 3x + 2y$$

since x number of X's at £3 profit each and y number of Y's at £2 profit each are being made. This function

$$f \equiv 3x + 2y$$

which has to be optimised is called the *objective function*.

However, there are now far more constraints than in the problems considered earlier in the book. First, there are the advance orders on X and Y that must be met. In the case of X this is an order of 100, and therefore the number of X's made must be at least 100: more than

237

100 could be made, but not less, otherwise the order could not be met. Since x is the number of X's to be made,

$$x \geqslant 100$$

Similarly, since the advance order on Y is 200 and y is the number of Y's to be made,

$$y \geqslant 200$$

Next, there is the company policy that a total of at least 500 items is to be made. The total number of items to be made is $x + y$, and therefore

$$x + y \geqslant 500$$

Each X requires 6 hours and each Y requires 5 hours on the company's machines, and the total production time is therefore $6x + 5y$. This must not exceed 6000 hours, although it could be less than 6000 hours, implying that the machinery would not be used to full capacity. Hence

$$6x + 5y \leqslant 6000$$

Then there are the raw material constraints: 3 lb of A are used in the manufacture of each X and 1 lb of A is used in the manufacture of each Y. Therefore the total amount of A used is $3x + y$ and this cannot be greater than 2400 lb, i.e.

$$3x + y \leqslant 2400$$

Similarly, the total amount of B used is $x + 2y$ and this cannot be greater than 2000 lb, i.e.

$$x + 2y \leqslant 2000$$

In each of these last two formulae, allowance is made for the fact that not all of a particular raw material may be used up, but obviously more cannot be used than the company possesses.

These are all the main constraints, but for completeness we include the *non-negativity constraints:*

$$x \geqslant 0$$

$$y \geqslant 0$$

Non-negativity constraints are included in most linear programming problems. Here they imply the common-sense restriction that negative quantities of the products X and Y cannot be made. Note, however, that they are redundant in this particular problem because they are implied by the more powerful constraints $x \geqslant 100$ and $y \geqslant 200$.

Summarising, then, the problem is to find the values of x and y which maximise the function

$$f \equiv 3x + 2y \tag{9.1}$$

subject to the constraints

$$x \geqslant 100 \tag{9.2}$$

$$y \geqslant 200 \tag{9.3}$$

$$x + y \geqslant 500 \tag{9.4}$$

$$6x + 5y \leqslant 6000 \tag{9.5}$$

$$3x + y \leqslant 2400 \tag{9.6}$$

$$x + 2y \leqslant 2000 \tag{9.7}$$

$$x \geqslant 0 \tag{9.8}$$

$$y \geqslant 0 \tag{9.9}$$

This is a typical linear programming problem.

METHOD OF SOLUTION

The most general method of solving linear programming problems is by using an algebraic algorithm called the *simplex method*. This will solve problems with any number of variables (for instance, problems with any number of products to be manufactured), and is suitable for use on a computer. However, this method is beyond the scope of this book.

Problems with only two variables, such as the one described above, can be solved by using graphical methods. Three-variable problems can also be solved this way, but are difficult because of the resulting need for three-dimensional graphs.

First, consider the representation of one of the constraints in detail, for example

$$x + 2y \leqslant 2000$$

This, of course, includes the line

$$x + 2y = 2000$$

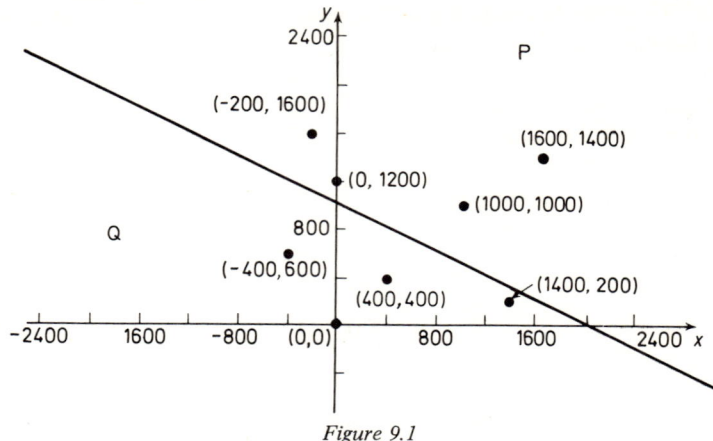

Figure 9.1

which is shown in Figure 9.1. This line divides the (x, y) plane into two sections, P and Q. Sample points lying in the section P are $(-200, 1600)$, $(0, 1200)$, $(1000, 1000)$, and $(1600, 1400)$. The value of $x + 2y$ for each of these points is

$$x + 2y = -200 + 3200 = 3000$$
$$x + 2y = 0 + 2400 = 2400$$
$$x + 2y = 1000 + 2000 = 3000$$
$$x + 2y = 1600 + 2800 = 4400$$

It can be seen that, for each of these points, $x + 2y$ is greater than 2000, i.e.

$$x + 2y > 2000$$

In fact, for all points in P, we would find that $x + 2y > 2000$. Similarly, for all points in the other section, Q,

$$x + 2y < 2000$$

This can also be checked by trying a few sample points in section Q, for example $(0, 0)$, $(-400, 600)$, $(400, 400)$, and $(1400, 200)$, i.e.

$$x + 2y = 0 + 0 = 0$$
$$x + 2y = -400 + 1200 = 800$$
$$x + 2y = 400 + 800 = 1200$$
$$x + 2y = 1400 + 400 = 1800$$

all of which are less than 2000. Therefore the points represented by the constraint

$$x + 2y \leqslant 2000$$

are the points in section Q together with the points on the line
$x + 2y = 2000$. If the area *not* represented by the constraint
$x + 2y \leqslant 2000$ is shaded, we obtain the diagram shown in Figure 9.2.

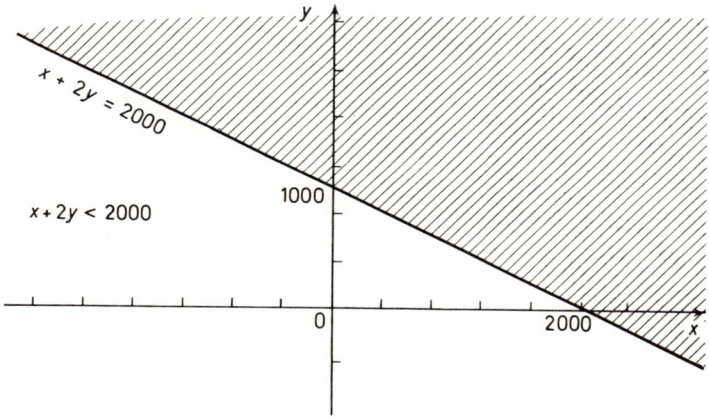

Figure 9.2

Repeating this process for all the other constraints represented by the
inequalities 9.2–9.6, we obtain the five diagrams shown in Figure 9.3.
However, the solution to the problem must simultaneously satisfy every
one of these constraints. If therefore all of the constraints are drawn on
the same pair of axes, as in Figure 9.4, then the area left *unshaded* will
indicate the points satisfying every constraint. Any pair of values of x
and y that satisfies all the constraints is a possible solution of the
problem. Such a solution is called a *feasible solution*, and the region of
feasible solutions (the unshaded area on the graph) is called the *region
of feasibility*.

We now have a set of feasible solutions to the problem, but so far
no attempt has been made to optimise. We must now find the feasible
solution that gives the greatest profit, i.e. that gives the greatest value
of $3x + 2y$, and must also find this greatest profit. We do not yet know

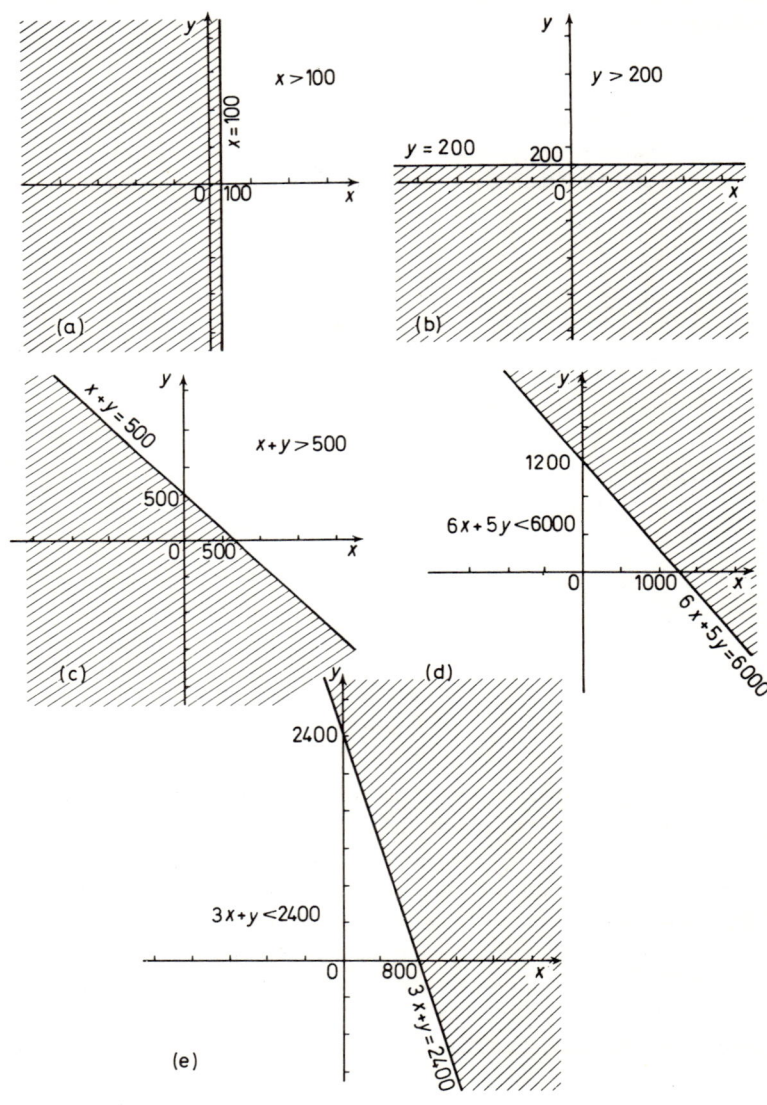

Figure 9.3

this greatest profit, but consider, for instance, a profit of £100. The values of x and y giving a profit of £100 will lie on the line

$$3x + 2y = 100$$

Similarly, those values giving a profit of £200 lie on

$$3x + 2y = 200$$

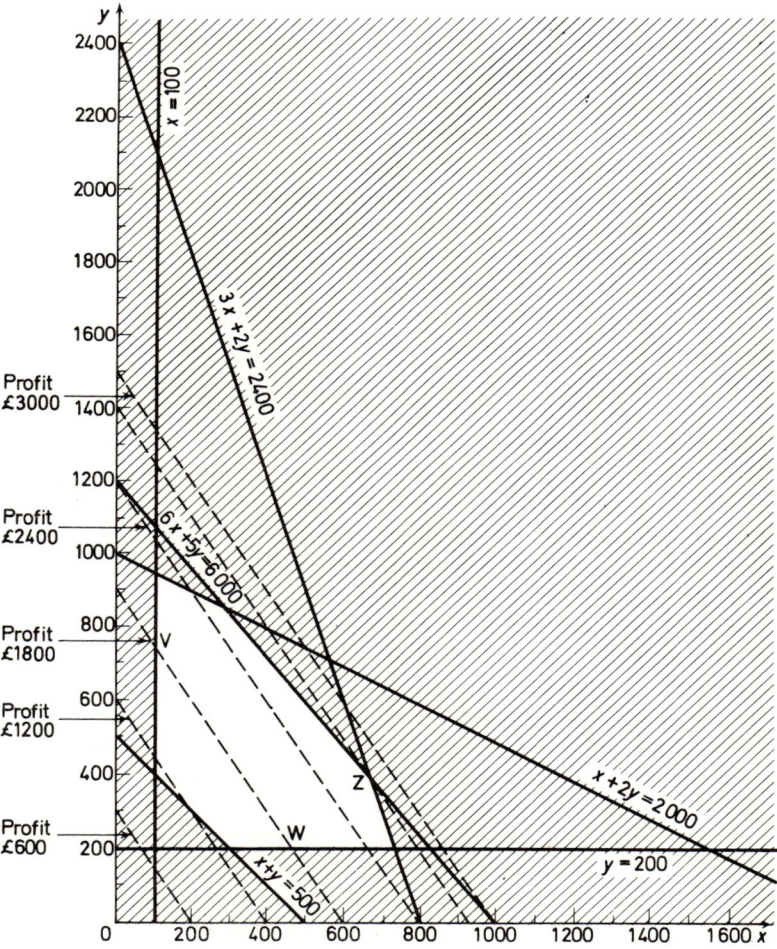

Figure 9.4

a profit of £600 on

$$3x + 2y = 600$$

and so on. If these lines are drawn (Figure 9.4), it can be seen that they are all parallel. In fact, the whole (x, y) plane will be covered by parallel profit lines, each one representing a different profit level. There could be a line for every possible profit, although obviously every profit line has not been drawn in. Note that, along any one line, the values of x and y produce the same profit, and that profit increases as we move out from the origin.

If we consider the £1800 profit line, for example, then all the points between V and W are feasible values of x and y that will produce a profit of £1800. In order to optimise profit, we look for values of x and y, within the region of feasibility, that lie on the highest possible profit line. It can be seen that the required point is Z, at which (by reading from the axes)

$$x = 667 \quad \text{and} \quad y = 400$$

giving a profit of

$$3(667) + 2(400) = 2000 + 800 = 2800 \text{ approx.}$$

This point Z is the only one within the region of feasibility that lies on the £2800 profit line. At any profit higher than £2800 there would be no points on the profit line which lay within the region of feasibility. The solution to the problem is therefore that the company should produce 667 X's and 400 Y's, which will give a profit of £2800.

Notes

The optimal solution to this problem is found at a 'corner' of the region of feasibility, and this is no coincidence. Such a 'corner' is called an *extreme point* of the region of feasibility, and the solution to a linear programming problem is always found at an extreme point.

In a two-variable problem an extreme point lies at the intersection of two constraint-lines (in a three-variable problem an extreme point will be at the intersection of three constraints, and so on). However, the intersection of two constraint lines is not necessarily an extreme point. For example, the intersection of the constraint $3x + y = 2400$ and $x + 2y = 2000$ does not lie within the region of feasibility.

The optimal solution to a linear programming problem will be at a *unique* extreme point unless the objective function lines are *parallel* to a constraint line. Then, all the points on this constraint line between, and including, two extreme points are optimal solutions to the problem

The fact that an extreme point lies at the intersection of two constraint lines means that at the optimal solution only two constraints are critical. In the present example, the two are $6x + 5y = 6000$ and $3x + y = 2400$. This implies that all the time on the machines is used and all of raw material A is used. The other constraints are not critical, and so not all of raw material B is used up — in fact $667 + 2(400) = 667 + 800 = 1467$ lb are used. Similarly, more than the minimum quantities demanded are manufactured, i.e. the total is more than 500 (total $= 667 + 400 = 1067$) and more than 100 X's and 200 Y's are made.

The Simplex method mentioned earlier finds an extreme point and then 'walks' round the boundary of the region of feasibility from extreme point to extreme point in a systematic way until it arrives at the one optimising the objective function.

INDEX